The Migrant Maternal
"Birthing" New Lives Abroad

Funded by the Government of Canada
Financé par la gouvernement du Canada

Demeter Press
140 Holland Street West
P. O. Box 13022
Bradford, ON L3Z 2Y5
Tel: (905) 775-9089
Email: info@demeterpress.org
Website: www.demeterpress.org

Demeter Press logo based on the sculpture "Demeter" by Maria-Luise Bodirsky
<www.keramik-atelier.bodirsky.de>

MIX
Paper from
responsible sources
FSC® C004071

Printed and Bound in Canada

Front cover artwork: Kazimiera Pałka "Gdie jest twój skarb, tam twoje serce," 2016, acrylic paint on paper, 21 x 14.5 cm.

Library and Archives Canada Cataloguing in Publication

The migrant maternal : 'birthing' new lives abroad / edited by Anna Kuroczycka Schultes and Helen Vallianatos.

Includes bibliographical references.
ISBN 978-1-77258-080-8 (hardback)

1. Motherhood--Social aspects. 2. Mothers--Social conditions. 3. Women refugees--Social conditions. 4. Women immigrants--Social conditions. 5. Mother and child. I. Vallianatos, Helen, author, editor II. Schultes, Anna Kuroczycka, 1984-, author, editor

HQ759.M52 2016   306.874'3089   C2016-905194-3

The Migrant Maternal
"Birthing" New Lives Abroad

EDITED BY

Anna Kuroczycka Schultes
and Helen Vallianatos

DEMETER PRESS

Anna:
To my daughter Adriana, who has honoured me with the gift of motherhood, my husband Scott for sharing this amazing journey of parenting with me, and my parents for their unwavering love and support.

Helen:
To all of those from whom I learned what motherhood means, particularly my son Jacob, who brought me the joys of motherhood, and my husband Rob, without whose support mothering would be so much more challenging.

Table of Contents

Acknowledgements

We both wish to acknowledge the work of the contributors to this volume, the constructive advice by the anonymous reviewers that strengthened our collective work, and, most importantly, all the mothers who informed this work—both real and imagined.

Introduction

The Migrant Maternal

ANNA KUROCZYCKA SCHULTES AND HELEN VALLIANATOS

T HE MANY CONFLICTS AROUND THE WORLD in the past two
years, including the military conflicts in the Middle East, have
caused a tremendous shift in migration patterns. The United Nations High Commissioner for Refugees (UNHCR) estimated that
in mid-2014 an average of thirteen million refugees were await-
ing repatriation, local integration, or resettlement. In 2015, that
number escalated dramatically, with various sources estimating
it at circa fifteen million (Ruffer). In his book *The Figure of the
Migrant*, Thomas Nail calls the twenty-first century the "century
of the migrant" (1). Worldwide, one in seven people is considered
to be a regional or international migrant (Nail 1), whereas one
in 122 people is a refugee, an internally displaced person, or an
asylum seeker (Vick 40).

At the start of this book, we, the editors, feel that it is important
to delineate the differences between who ought to be referred to
as a "migrant" versus a "refugee," especially in the light of the
barrage of media coverage and personal opinions expressed on
social networks that frequently conflate the two terms. The 1951
Refugee Convention indicates that a refugee is someone who

> As a result of events occurring before 1 January 1951
> and owing to a well-founded fear of being persecuted for
> reasons of race, religion, nationality, membership of a
> particular social group or political opinion, is outside the
> country of his nationality, and is unable to, or owing to
> such fear, is unwilling to avail himself of the protection of

1

that country; or who, not having a nationality and being outside the country of his former habitual residence as a result of such events, is unable or, owing to such fear, is unwilling to return to it. (UNHCR 14)

This definition, however, is problematic in the context of the current refugee crisis. Whereas the 1951 definition focuses on a very specific group of people—those escaping Europe after World War II—today's refugees are oftentimes stateless and have no government to turn to in order to seek protection or even apply for a passport, such as Haitians in the Dominican Republic, who have never been to Haiti but are not recognized by the Dominican state (Ruffer). The UNHCR has, thus, expanded this definition to include those who are fleeing "generalized violence" or have no national protection:

Migrants, especially economic migrants, choose to move in order to improve the future prospects of themselves and their families. Refugees have to move if they are to save their lives or preserve their freedom. They have no protection from their own state—indeed it is often their own government that is threatening to persecute them. If other countries do not let them in, and do not help them once they are in, then they may be condemning them to death—or to an intolerable life in the shadows, without sustenance and without rights. ("Refugees")

Whereas many European countries, most notably Germany, have embraced the broader understanding of who may be considered a refugee in global political discourse, the United States has not and is resettling less than 1 percent of the world's refugees. Therefore, in part as a result of the semantic discrepancies, 80 percent of global refugees live in the least developed nations of the Global South (Ruffer).

MOTHER MIGRANTS

Prior to the mass exodus of people escaping the ongoing conflict in Syria, which has resulted in the largest wave of refugees since World War II, it was estimated that women constituted 49.6 percent of the economic migrants worldwide (Pearce et al. 2). It is critical, therefore, for scholars to give adequate attention to the phenomenon that we discuss in this book, one which some have referred to as the "feminization of migration" (Chang; Parreñas; Yinger). The average migrating woman is twenty-nine years old and comes from a country where female identity centres on motherhood (Hochschild). These women usually take on "pink collar" positions—such as babysitters, cosmetologists, maids, domestic servants, receptionists, and waitresses—that typically bring in less income than the more respected blue or white collar jobs (see also Nichols, this volume).

Oftentimes, however, the children that these women leave behind or as we illustrate in this collection, the children they take with them or bear in the host country complicate the migration process. As Janet Salaff and Arent Greve point out, "transnational migration affects women and men in gender specific ways, [as it assigns a much greater responsibility to women who] undertake the meshing of work and family systems" (160). Being a migrant mother, therefore, demands a flexibility that extends beyond the everyday "manual, physical, emotional, and psychological work of mothering [to] one that must take into account multiple time zones, competing schedules, and the uneven distribution of technology and resources" (Bryan 35). Women who migrate with their children are perceived as "good mothers" but oftentimes face great challenges in trying to care and provide for their children. Transnational mothering, on the other hand, is problematic and women who migrate alone for the betterment of their children are labelled as "bad mothers."

The act of mothering in contemporary society extends borders in both a physical and ideological way. Migrant mothers may be torn between performing motherhood in a way that resembles how they were raised or in the Western (European and American) ideal of intensive mothering, which assumes that children are social capital to be "invested in" (Vandenbeld Giles 9). As Faye Ginsburg and Rayna Rapp state in the introduction to their volume *Conceiving the New World Order: The Global Politics of Reproduction,* "questions of culture, politics, and biology are impossible to disentangle around the topic of reproduction, as they often involve transnational processes that link local and global interests" (2). These global "links" have created "care chains" (Hochschild 186) and have produced multiple narratives of affective work, as documented by Rhacel Salazar Parreñas, Pei-Chia Lan, and Shellee Colen, among others, who, respectively, describe the situation of Filipina, Indonesian, and West Indian migrant women domestic workers. Time and again, women leave their own families behind to be taken care of by relatives, a phenomenon known as the "care crisis," which has most famously been documented in the case of Filipino children, 30 percent of whom have one parent who works abroad (Hochschild). Some migrant women who leave their children in their homelands pursue employment as childcare workers in other countries, thereby transposing their sense of moral obligation to mother onto other people's children.

The migration process always involves a sense of loss: "the removal of territorial ownership or access, the loss of the political right to vote or to receive social welfare, the loss of legal status to work or drive, or the financial loss associated with transportation or change in residence" (Nail 2). Migrant mothers who reproduce their families in a foreign context face additional challenges; they often have to negotiate their sense of belonging in their host country, especially their "ability to adapt familiar mothering practices to new cultural and physical contexts" (Kačkutė, this volume). Shellee Colen has deemed the act of performing mothering duties differentially, based on one's upbringing, as "stratified reproduction." In "'Like a Mother to Them': Stratified Reproduction and West Indian Childcare Workers and Employers in New York," Colen describes this phenomenon as one where "physical and social reproductive tasks are accomplished differentially according to inequalities that are based on hierarchies of class, race, ethnicity, gender, place in a global economy, and migration status and that are structured by social, economic, and political forces" (380). Sociologist Annette Lareau further distinguishes between parenting styles based on class. "Concerted cultivation," the parenting style most commonly practised by the middle class, is based on engaging with children by reading or playing with them or by taking them to sports, music, or drama activities; it is an ideology that Lareau found manifests itself in parents who want to nurture their children's growth. Middle-class parents are "increasingly determined to make sure that their children are not excluded from any opportunity that might eventually contribute to their advancement" (Lareau 5) and strive to instill in their children the necessity of questioning adults and addressing them as relative equals. On the contrary, working-class parents are not concerned with soliciting the opinions of children, as they "see a clear boundary between adults and children [and] … tell their children what to do rather than persuading them with reasoning" (Lareau 3). This parenting style, referred to as the "accomplishment of natural growth," allows working-class and poor children greater control of their free time. It presumes that children essentially need someone only to watch over them and not be actively involved in their upbringing. They are free to engage with friends and relatives in the neighbourhood, instead of with extracurricular activities organized by their parents.

As the chapters in this volume show, for migrant mothers, these distinctions become highly problematic as a result of the struggles caused by the migration and translocation process. Migration—a process frequently associated with a drop in class status (Gans)—may force some mothers who believe in concerted cultivation practices to raise their children more in accordance with the accomplishment of natural growth, as financial, social, and cultural barriers, among others, may prevent them from enrolling their children in extracurricular activities, for example. As a result, immigrant mothers may also become increasingly isolated and feel that they do not "fit in" with the mainstream culture of the host country.

In this edited collection, we explore how and why immigrant and refugee mothers' experiences differ because of the challenges posed by the migration process, but also what commonalities underline immigrant and refugee mothers' lived experiences. The contributors use diverse theoretical lenses, which are at times informed by their own migrant trajectories as well (see Figure 1). This book adds to the field of women's studies the much needed discussion of how immigrant and refugee mothers' lives are dependent on cultural, environmental, and socioeconomic circumstances, and investi-

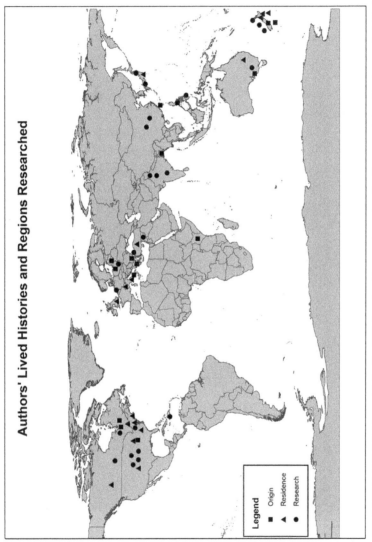

Figure 1: This map illustrates our contributors' lived histories: where they were born, where they live now, and where they have conducted their research for purposes of this volume. Point locations are representative, not exact. Map credit: Thomas J. Simon, owner of Synthos LLC, tom@tomjsimon.com

gates how refugee mothers' issues differ from those of immigrant mothers. The collection offers multiple perspectives on migrant mothering by including ethnographic and theoretical submissions along with mothers' personal narratives and literary analysis. We felt that it was important to include feminist ethnography, which privileges the importance of individual experience, in order to "interrogate and challenge the wide-reaching effects of neoliberal policies and practices" (Vandenbeld Giles x), which are often the causes of migration.[1]

We have chosen to divide the volume into two sections: 1.) Mothering in a Foreign Land I: "Birthing" New Families Abroad and 2.) Mothering in a Foreign Land II: Generational Dynamics in Settlement and Mothers' Responsibilities. The main difference between these two parts is the focus of the authors' exploration. In the first section, the focus is on mothers' roles in the family institution and the pressures and responsibilities that they face in creating and reproducing families physically and socially. The second section, however, shifts its attention to children and highlights mothers' continued roles in the development of their children abroad, along with the gendered and generational dynamics in settlement and mothers' responsibilities.

Both sections focus on "mothering" rather than "motherhood." Although these two terms are often used interchangeably in public discourse, our aim is to distinguish between "motherhood" as an identity and "mothering," which by centring on "beliefs, practices, and engagement," is constantly in flux (Walks 19). It is "mothering," therefore, that is key to the experiences of immigrant women, who need to continuously adapt their ways to the situation of migration.

MOTHERING IN A FOREIGN LAND I: "BIRTHING" NEW FAMILIES ABROAD

The chapters in this section focus on three main issues: the birthing experience abroad, mothers' refugee experiences, and migration as a site of "intense negotiations" (Kačkutė, this volume), which pertains to such things as how to style your child's hair, what to feed your family for dinner, or how to manage financial challenges and situations of unemployment.

Sara Bonfanti and Theano Lianidou discuss the reproductive challenges that women face in circumstances of migration. Bonfanti's study analyzes how procreation and infertility is thought of and practised within Punjabi communities in northern Italy. She discerns that *Punjabiyat* influences, shapes, and constrains local reproductive experiences through intersecting forms of power and resistance, despite the distance between Italy and South Asia. Bonfanti also introduces the idea of "gift babies" among Punjabi women as a culturally acceptable means of dealing with their infertile bodies. Although reproductive technologies are perceived as farfetched and classed in India, fostering a family member's child, or in essence receiving that child as a gift, places emphasis on familial piety and selfless giving.

In her compelling narrative centred on her own traumatic child delivery in Amsterdam, Theano Lianidou explores the notion that potential ethnic biases are a contributing factor to substandard perinatal care for immigrants in the Netherlands. After synthesizing the literature, Lianidou identifies language barriers, mothers' lack of health literacy, impaired general health, single motherhood, and delayed or irregular prenatal care visits as documented factors that lead to substandard care among the immigrant population. In the absence of these causes in her own personal experience, however, Lianidou calls for further exploration of ethnic biases as they pertain to perinatal care.

Both authors in their chapters tackle the issues of discrimination and ethnic bias being present in their respective locales, and report that gynecologists and obstetricians lament a lack of sound family planning among migrant women in general. More specifically, as these chapters show, this bias is encountered by the Indian community in Italy (Bonfanti) and among Turkish, Moroccan, Surinamese, and Indonesian women in the Netherlands (Lianidou).

Helene Connor, Irene Ayallo, and Sue Elliott introduce a group of African immigrant and refugee mothers living in Auckland, New Zealand, whereas Nurcan Ozgur Baklacioglu provides a glimpse into the distressing lives of Syrian mothers in Istanbul. Both chapters underscore the main challenges caused by the mothers' stateless status: lack of health care, social isolation, and the way in which single and divorced or widowed mothers are stigmatized in their respective communities. These chapters highlight the immediacy of these women's situations and how migrant mothers are placed in the most precarious of positions through illegalization, criminalization, marginalization, and victimization during their transits and stays in the destination country.

The final set of chapters in this section focuses on the challenging negotiations that women engage in with themselves and their children when living in situations of migration. Leslie Nichols examines the experiences of unemployed immigrant mothers in Toronto. She has found that situations of employment precarity place mothers at greater risk of negative health outcomes, especially anxiety and depression, as they try to figure out how to provide their children with a nutrient-rich diet on a resource-poor budget. Financial insecurity, a biproduct of the immigrant settlement period, is further exacerbated by the necessity to provide care and nurturance to growing children.

Egle Kačkutės chapter explores immigrant and refugee mothers who mother primarily in their own native language rather than in English by focusing on two multilingual pieces: the play *Mother Tongue* (1996) by Chinese Canadian playwright Betty Quan and the novel *Chorus of Mushrooms* (1994) by Japanese Canadian author Hiromi Goto. Kačkutė uses migration theorist Irene Gedalof's ideas to explain how migrant women's subject position as mothers helps them negotiate and create a sense of belonging for themselves in their host country. She identifies these "homing" practices as "the embodied work of mothering, such as childbirth and childcare, and the work of reproducing cultures and structures of belonging, such as the passing on of culturally specific histories and traditions regarding food, dress, family and other inter-personal relationships" (Gedalof 82).

The reproductive sphere in the context of migration is, thus, far from reiterative of the home culture women left behind. Helen Vallianatos's chapter explains how food beliefs and practices shifted after migration among a group of South Asian migrants to an urban area in Western Canada. By discussing habitual acts that are performed in new, nonhabitual environments, Vallianatos elaborates on Gedalof's notion of "repetition," which "undoes, or that recollects forward" (96). Vallianatos makes clear how food is a way for mothers to transmit their love and values to the next generation, which becomes especially important when it comes to being a member of a particular ethnocultural community. The act of children requesting the food of the host country while simultaneously rejecting traditional food may be perceived as a rejection of the family's cultural values.

MOTHERING IN A FOREIGN LAND II: GENERATIONAL DYNAMICS IN SETTLEMENT AND MOTHERS' RESPONSIBILITIES

The second part of the collection sheds light on the demands that accompany raising children in foreign contexts—namely, maintaining home language and culture among the next generation and mothers' attitudes towards local norms. Cirila Limpangog surveys the childcare expectations of professional Filipina women in Melbourne. She calls for the "care deficit"—the need for care which has outgrown the available amount of caregivers (Hochschild)—to finally be addressed, as women in circumstances of migration are likely to endure more guilt for not accomplishing their mothering duties well. With careers often delayed or reconfigured in the new setting, men's lack of care participation—what Limpangog deems the "care-share deficit"—needs to be remediated, especially since Filipino cultural norms demand that childcare may only be relegated to trusted kin.

Rehnuma Sazzad examines the pressure of isolation for newly immigrant women in her discussion of Jhumpa Lahiri's writings. For Sazzad, Lahiri's texts highlight "the question of whether diasporas provide enabling contexts in which previous gender norms can be challenged or whether they reproduce and possibly even harden existing gender ideologies and relations" (Al-Ali 119). In examining the Bengali mothers present in Lahiri's short stories, Sazzad underscores how diasporas can either harden or challenge gender ideologies.

In her chapter, Yu-Ling Hsiao focuses her attention on working-class Chinese women in the United States and how their limited understanding of the host culture's norms and practices affects their ability to educate their children, ultimately leading to a sense of guilt, isolation, and powerlessness. Mothers come up with parental strategies based on their (mis)interpretations of local community and school cultures, which can then result in more harm than good when it comes to their children's educational experiences.

Children's educational choices are further explored in Anna Kuroczycka Schultes's and Agata Strzelecka-Misonne's chapters. Both pieces examine Polish immigrant women raising children in the two largest centres of Polish migration in the United States: Chicago and New York City. Schultes's study examines the choices that mothers make in an attempt to raise bilingual and bicultural children. Her research reveals that mothers believe their native language to be inextricably intertwined with teaching children about Polish culture; it is also a means of passing cultural capital onto their children. She introduces the concept of "heritage language" in this chapter to refer to the language that is acquired first by children born to immigrant mothers but that may not end up being completely acquired because of a switch to another dominant language (in the case of Schultes's research participants, English) in the future (Kozminska 2).

Strzelecka-Misonne, on the other hand, produces a personal reflection on the importance of intercultural awareness when raising children abroad, which is grounded in her background as a cultural studies scholar. She claims that it is crucial for migrant mothers to "kindle" their children's interest and broaden their knowledge of the language and culture of the country of origin. Strzelecka-Misonne argues that an intercultural identity provides both children and adults a sense of safety in that they are able to interpret cultural codes and messages present in multiple environments.

The final two chapters deal with the way in which the migration experience may often cause women to be disobedient towards local norms and customs in order to do what they think is best for their families. Meredith Stephens recounts her cross-cultural experiences as an immigrant mother from Australia raising her two daughters on a sparsely populated island in Japan. She discusses her own internal conflict on whether to respect local assumptions about motherhood or to act in accordance with her own values, which reflect alternative expectations of motherhood and women's roles. Stephens admits that although at times, she conformed to what was expected of Japanese mothers, she also exploited stereotypes of the role of Western mothers in order to avoid fulfilling those expectations if they made her uncomfortable or interrupted with work duties.

Lastly, Justine Dymond conducts a literary analysis of the memoir *Brother, I'm Dying* by Edwidge Danticat, a Haitian-American writer who struggles with the significance of giving birth as a naturalized citizen while her uncle and many other migrants are being deported from the United States. Dymond argues that Danticat's experience of motherhood is inextricably bound up with her identity as an immigrant and simultaneously strengthens and fractures her sense of national belonging, which is further problematized by post-9/11 anti-immigrant rhetoric and stricter border control policies.

Although we have chosen to divide this collection into these two sections, we recognize multiple connections that can be drawn between chapters across sections as well. Bonfanti, Vallianatos and Sazzad consider the challenges that mothers in the Indian diaspora face in Italy, Canada, and the United States. Through their reproductive choices, and childrearing practices, the mothers in these chapters strive to maintain their connection to India. Kačkutė's and Dymond's chapters both provide examples of how women can better adapt to the "otherland" by projecting "homely features of the motherland onto it" (Draga Alexandru 125). The personal narratives of Lianidou, Strzelecka-Misonne, and Stephens raise awareness of the many decisions that mothers struggle with when raising children in a different sociocultural context and the challenges that they face, despite possessing the cultural and social capital that our authors did. When this capital is lacking, as the chapters by Hsiao and Nichols most notably underscore, mothers are left feeling isolated and powerless in their adopted communities.

In bringing to light the (her)stories of immigrant and refugee women, we hope to highlight how mothering practices are constantly in flux in foreign environments and get modified further depending on the situation of migration. As our contributors' chapters show, although these changes may be positive when they provide a platform for intercultural awareness and intercultural identity (Schultes; Strzelecka-Misonne; Stephens), they oftentimes place women who are already vulnerable by virtue of being in an unknown land in situations of even greater precarity (Lianidou; Hsiao; Ozgur; Connor, Ayallo, and Elliott).

NOTE

[1]A number of neoliberal policies (i.e., devaluing of local currency, the cutting of social services, and imposing wage freezes, implemented by the International Monetary Fund (IMF) and World Bank) act as "push" and "pull" factors in attracting migration out of one country and into another (Schultes 75).

WORKS CITED

Al-Ali, Nadje. "Diasporas and Gender." *Diasporas: Concepts, Intersections, Identities*, edited by Kim Knott and Seán McLoughlin, Zed Books, 2010, pp. 118-122.

Bryan, Catherine. "Multiplying Mothers: Migration and the Work of Mothering in Canada and the Philippines." *Mothering in the Age of Neoliberalism*, edited by Melinda Vandenbeld Giles, Demeter, 2014, pp. 35-49.

Chang, Grace. *Disposable Domestics: Immigrant Women Workers in the Global Economy.* Cambridge, MA: South End Press, 2000.

Colen, Shellee. "'Like a Mother to Them': Stratified Reproduction and West Indian Childcare Workers and Employers in New York City." *Feminist Anthropology: A Reader*, edited by Ellen Lewin, Blackwell Pub, 2006, pp. 380-396.

Colen, Shellee. "With Respect and Feelings: Voices of West Indian Child Care and Domestic Workers in New York City." *All American Women: Lines That Divide, Ties That Bind*, edited by Johnetta Cole, Free Press, 1986, pp. 46-70.

Draga Alexandru, Maria-Sabina. "Constructing the Female Self in Migrant Postcolonial Fiction." *Crossing Boundaries: Thinking through Literature*, edited by Julie Scanlon and Amy Waste, Sheffield Academic Press, 2001, pp. 121-129.

Gans, Herbert J. "First Generation Decline: Downward Mobility among Refugees and Immigrants." *Ethnic and Racial Studies*, vol. 32, no. 9, Oct. 2009, pp. 1658-1670.

Gedalof, Irene. "Birth, Belonging and Migrant Mothers: Narratives of Reproduction in Feminist Migration Studies." *Feminist Review*, vol. 93, no.1, Nov. 2009, pp. 81-100.

Ginsburg, Faye D., and Rayna R. Rapp. *Conceiving the New World Order: The Global Politics of Reproduction*. University of California Press, 1995.

Hochschild, Arlie Russell. "Love and Gold." *The Commercialization of Intimate Life: Notes from Home and Work*. University of California Press, 2003, pp. 185-97.

Kozminska, Kinga. "Language Contact in the Polish-American Community in Chicago." *International Journal of Bilingualism*, vol. 9, no. 3, June 2015, pp. 1-20. *Sage Journals*. Accessed July 28 2016.

Lan, Pei-Chia. *Global Cinderellas: Migrant Domestics and Newly Rich Employers in Taiwan*, Duke University Press, 2006.

Lareau, Annette. *Unequal Childhoods: Class, Race, and Family Life*, University of California Press, 2011.

Lipszyc, Cecilia. "The Feminization of Migration: Dreams and Realities of Immigrant Woman in Four Latin American Countries." Reclaiming the Streets. Uruguay, Montevideo. Apr. 2004, www.diba.cat/urbal12/PDFS/CeciliaLipszyc_en.pdf. Accessed 11 Nov. 2015.

Nail, Thomas. *The Figure of the Migrant*, Stanford University Press, 2015.

Parreñas, Rhacel Salazar. *Servants of Globalization: Women, Migration and Domestic Work*, Stanford University Press, 2001.

Parreñas, Rhacel Salazar "The Care Crisis: Children and Transnational Families in the New Global Economy," *Global Woman: Nannies, Maids, and Sex Workers in the New Economy*, edited by Barbara Ehrenreich and Arlie Russell Hochschild, Metropolitan Books, 2003, pp. 39-54.

Pearce, Susan C., Elizabeth J. Clifford, and Reena Tandon. *Immigration and Women: Understanding the American Experience*, New York University Press, 2011.

"Refugees." *UNHCR : The UN Refugee Agency*, UNHCR, www.unhcr.org/pages/49c3646c125.html. Accessed 28 July 2016.

Ruffer, Galya B. "Refugee Crises and Human Rights: Africa and the Middle East." The Newberry Consortium, 9 Feb. 2016, Newberry Library, Chicago. Guest Lecture.

Salaff, Janet W., and Arent Greve. "Can Women's Social Networks Migrate?" *Women's Studies International Forum*, vol. 27, no. 2, July 2004, pp. 149–62.

Schultes, Anna Kuroczycka. "'I'm Not a Maid!'—A Critical Look at Au Pairs vis-à-vis Migrant Domestic Workers." *Journal of Research on Women and Gender*, vol. 1, no. 1, Mar. 2010, pp. 75-97. *Texas State University*, digital.library.txstate.edu/bitstream/handle/10877/4431/Kuroczycka%20Schultes.pdf?sequence=1. Accessed 28 July 2016.

UNHCR. The UN Refugee Agency. *UNHCR News*. UNHCR Communications and Public Information Service, Dec. 2010. Web. 14 Aug. 2016.

Vandenbeld Giles, Melinda. "Introduction: An Alternative Mother-Centered Economic Paradigm," edited by, Melinda Vandenbeld Giles. *Mothering in the Age of Neoliberalism*, Demeter, 2014, pp. 1-30.

Vick, Karl. "The Great Migration." *Time*, Time Inc., 19 Oct. 2015, pp. 38-47.

Walks, Michelle. "Identifying an Anthropology of Mothering." *An Anthropology of Mothering*, edited by Michelle Walks and Naomi McPherson, Demeter, 2011, pp. 1-47.

Yinger, Nancy V. "The Feminization of Migration: Limits of the Data." *Population Reference Bureau*, Population Reference Bureau, Washington D.C., www.prb.org/Publications/Articles/2007/FeminizationofMigrationLimitsofData.aspx. Accessed 28 July 2016.t

I.

MOTHERING IN A FOREIGN LAND I

"Birthing" New Families Abroad

1.
Reproducing *Punjabiyat*

Family Rhetoric and Birth Control among Indian Migrant Women in Italy

SARA BONFANTI

"WHAT WOULD YOU SAY: are *we* still Indians among *you* Italians, or are we becoming some different *people*?" (emphasis added). With these words Asha,[1] my long-time Punjabi friend, teased me one Sunday afternoon, while she drank *chai* and chatted away in her master bedroom with a couple of other Punjabi friends. With our kids outside playing cricket, we sat on her double bed, grumbling over our respective husbands. Oddly enough, *karva chaut* had just concluded, a ritual fast that Hindu wives observe to guarantee longer and wealthier lives for their male partners. Our nattering was interrupted by a phone call: Akal rang to inform us she would not join that day, as she was assisting her neighbour, who had just had a "miscarriage."[2] I did not dare ask questions, as I knew two other Punjabi women who were then with us had recently gone through a similar experience; from these women, I learned that "abortion" and "miscarriage" lie on a slippery border between chosen and unintentional end of pregnancy.

As this ethnographic vignette suggests, the following chapter is based on the empirical data that I collected during eighteen months of multisite ethnographic fieldwork (Falzon) in northern Italy and northern India, mainly Lombardy and Punjab, respectively. I analyze and discuss procreation as it is thought of and practised within Punjabi communities, and focus on the reproductive experience of women and on how they manage their in/fertile bodies.

To contextualize my analysis, I first examine the macrosocial scenario of Punjabi social reproduction. On the one hand, the bio-politics of population control have been applied in the homeland since the Sixties in order to comply with the Indian government *diktat* on restricting birth rate (Mamdani). On the other, "family-engineered" transnational migration (which followed the script "male-first emigrant, household reunification or new formation in resettlement") has ensured continuity through dispersal of this Indian diaspora (Bertolani). Acknowledging the current economic crisis and stagnation in the agro-industrial districts across northern Italy, I consider whether the precariousness of the labour immigrants' life conditions may affect the desire for a family and the social imagery of childbirth. I will set the reproductive experiences of Indian migrant women not only in their Punjabi birth culture but also against the frame of Italian birth care, local medical institutions, and dominant discourses on female sexuality and procreation. I compare four individual cases to illustrate my analysis. Using reproduction as an entry point into the study of social life, the diasporic "family dramas" that I discuss prove how seemingly distant influences shape and constrain local reproductive experiences while intersecting forms of power and resistance.

REPRODUCING *PUNJABIYAT* HOME AND ABROAD

Few other transnational migrations match the Punjabi one in heterogeneity. "Unity in diversity," the Hindi national motto, may be the apt tag for Punjabi plurality. Punjabi-ness cuts across multiple axes of social differentiation, from faith to caste and class, and builds on painful collective memories of displacement—such as those following the postcolonial Partition in 1947 when British India split into independent India and Pakistan, or those of 1984, the infamous year of the Sikh genocide (Axel). The changing demography of contemporary Punjab grapples with a deep-seated culture of emigration (from refugees to labour movements) and with a sex ratio disproportion induced by a wide female feticide practice, which is sternly opposed but still in use. (The 1994 Prohibition of Sex Selection Act criminalizes the practice, for example.) Without elaborating on the dowry system, it is important to note that socioeconomic organization and property laws have encouraged the historical desire of having sons rather than daughters[3] in Indian households (Duvvury et al.; Talwar). Child gender preference has also intersected with population control since the 1960s, when India launched a sterilization program (Mamdani). Punjab's birthrate in the past decades has not contributed to the country's demographic overgrowth, as it has remained at replacement level, but has preserved the moral male gender as a family's first choice (India, "Governmental Census").

If reproductive discourses in Punjabi communities, home and abroad, seem entrenched in ideologically laden frames (Ayres), I tackle the meanings that procreation has for current Punjabi immigrant mothers in northern Italy, delve into personal female narratives, and explore the intersubjectivity with which these meanings are marked.

Kinship ties are decisive in scripting socially desired genealogies. For Punjabi expatriates, kinship is a matter of daily lived household relations and of virtually experienced transnational kin connections, though physical and emotional proximity or distance may not tally. Indian communities in Italy are slowly shifting from a first- to a second-generation migration (Bonfanti, "The Marriage Market"). The first-time migrants who have lived in the Po Plains since the late 1990s are approaching their forties and have young children, who were mostly born on Italian soil and have their citizenship issue pending (Galloni; Bertolani et al.; Colombo and Rebughini). Grandparents and collaterals—who are still in Punjab or have resettled elsewhere in Europe, North America, or the Arabic Gulf—are occasionally granted visas to travel and meet their kin, according to migratory laws. Regardless of their locality, these transmigrants daily connect daily through e-diaspora networks (Diminescu), which maintain extended families on a long-distance and translocal basis.

Meanwhile, the Punjabi family model underwent a process of "Sanskritization" in the homeland (Charsley): a "traditional" patrilocal joint household, with countless kids and three generations under one roof, was often replaced with a "modern" nuclear family standard, which mimicked the upper-class fashion (Shah). In my sample, I have found that the ideal middle-class family consists of (normatively heterosexual) parents and two children (three at most), preferably a son (or two sons) and a daughter. Today, this family pattern is the most sought after across the Indian diaspora (Thapan, *Living the Body*). In Italy, since a Punjabi male immigrant is often the only breadwinner and has to provide for his local household besides sending remittances back home, stringent economic reasons may shape this family choice. A small nuclear household is also preferred in cultural terms as it profiles better social status (Mishra) and mirrors what is perceived to be the typical Italian middle-class household composition.

FRIENDSHIP AND ENGAGEMENT IN THE ETHNOGRAPHIC ENCOUNTER

Asha's family, my first and foremost interlocutor, embodies that culturally desired family structure; she admitted to "having been *blessed* with the birth of two kids with the *appropriate* gender and age difference" (emphasis added).

In her circle of friends, Asha—who is thirty-eight, middle class, and a bhakti Hindu from the Kshatriya caste—stands as a reference model. Many Indian women ask her for help, although it would be hard to describe her as a well-integrated immigrant woman. Her husband, a welder on a permanent post, just gained Italian citizenship, and their kids perform well at school and mingle easily with their Italian peers. As for her, Asha holds a degree in political science, but she has never worked outside her home and despite having lived in Bergamo for fifteen years, she has not yet mastered Italian. Although she has so far invested her time and energy to running the house as a stay-at-home mom, she is critical in analyzing her own migratory route and those of her co-ethnics.

Showing awareness of ordinary ethnocentrism in any culture, comprising her own, Asha discussed her prototypical Indian family:

> I know it happened *by chance*, or it was *Lakshmi*'s[4] interception, my mother prayed for it every day. I never had to face the states my friends found themselves in…. I mean, I was privileged. Suraj [her husband] is a good man, a real *dulaa*,[5] but you never know, when something ruins the norm of life…. It's not your husband who forces you to do anything; it's a kind of social pressure. You have to behave properly because you're expected to. A woman

has to follow her *stri-dharma*[6] ... the way of the wife. (emphasis added)

As she is the Punjabi woman with whom I struck up a longer and deeper friendship, I admit that many of my arguments are sieved through our mutual dialogues and her own interpretation (Gallini and Satta). All the narrations that I collected are life stories, *her*-stories in fact, and were reported firsthand from Asha's best friends, since she acted as a gatekeeper in granting me access to discourses and experiences that are not easily verbalized by women themselves, let alone discussed in brief interviews with an ethnographer. Our informal talks—which took place mainly in English, partly in Punjabi and in Italian, and at times worked out as impromptu focus groups—put into perspective the subjectivity and agency of my informants. Although I tried not to typecast my research subjects as subaltern, their life circumstances and social situatedness as Indian migrant women in southern Europe interrogated civic stratification and gender subordination, and revealed the forms of engagement that take place during fieldwork (Merry and Low). As silence and secrets are always part of the research process (Ryan-Flood and Gill), ethical and affective dilemmas prompted me to exercise self-censorship in writing up and disseminating knowledge on sensitive material.

EMBODYING CULTURES: FAMILY PLANNING AMONG THE PUNJABIS

Given that I did previous research on the topic with other migrant women (Bonfanti, "Farsi madri"), I have long known how birth cultures shape reproductive behaviours and to what extent women may be "pregnant with social meanings". Peeping into the reproductive experiences of these Indian friends, however, made me partake in their adjustments to dissonant normative orders. Childbirth across cultures, localized motherhood, and the embodied condition of being in/fertile through the migration process between northern India and northern Italy upset any alleged naturalness of reproduction, which may be otherwise taken for granted (Ivry). In particular, fertility management and birth control pose a series of questions, as different interests and stakeholders converge on women's bodies and their (in)ability to bear children, to fulfill a gender role, and to nurture their offspring, according to precise cultural scripts.

The predominant Punjabi mindset on childbearing (an ideology in which I did not appreciate sensible differences between Sikhs or Hindus, higher and lower castes [Malhotra and Mir]) imposes a normative model of femininity and motherhood, which requires married women to be devoted to their husbands and to be fecund and caring mothers (Bhachu; Thapan, *Living the Body*). Although this tenet may apply cross-culturally worldwide, it is oversimplified. Nowadays many women question and contest it in India and across its diaspora, from highly educated mothers to second-generation immigrant girls (Sangah and Gonsalves). However, most Punjabi women feel to be constrained between contradicting sexual and reproductive discourses over their life course. As young women, they are supposed to remain virgins until marriage and then bear children as soon as possible after the wedding. (Many young brides are referred to medical "sex specialists" if they do not conceive within a year.)[7] Though highly valued, female fertility must be limited to a set extent (giving birth to two children only, ideally, a son and a daughter), and women are eventually asked to prevent further undesired pregnancies through a variety of contraceptive methods, including abortion as a last resort.

Birth control is essentially a female affair; it rests in the hands of women, even though access to contraceptives may still be out of their grasp (Williamson et al.). This does not mean that men are unware of or uncaring about the reproductive process. On the contrary, they may be knowledgeable about the physiology of childbirth and, thus, perform their sexual activities according to their beliefs and their willingness (or unwillingness) to procreate. (This may include petty practices such as counting their partner's menstrual cycle, buying condoms, or drinking *neem* tree juice, known as an Ayurveda remedy for male contraception). Still, in most Punjabi households, women take full responsibility for childbearing and only through women did I gain enough ethnographic intimacy to explore the issue.

IN/FERTILITY AS LIVED EXPERIENCE IN
MIGRANT WOMEN'S NARRATIVES

Fertility is a complex social matter that exceeds the narrowness of demographic rate or biomedical description. It is a sensitive cultural artifact, which is bodily experienced, politically situated and emotionally infused (MacCormack; Greenhalgh). I now discuss fertility management as it was experienced by Asha and her friends while I acknowledge the serendipity and singularity of my sample: a bunch of Punjabi close girlfriends, with similar migratory paths, who constitute a minority within a minority, since all but one of them happen to be Hindu among a majority Sikh community (Jayaram). In my presence, her friends never singled out Akal, the only woman in the cluster who follows Sikhism. On the contrary, they showed mutual respect for one another's religious beliefs (not clear of the occasional witticism), sometimes even visiting one another's temples (Hindu *mandirs* and Sikh *gurdwaras*). Although not statistically significant, these women's narratives document the gendered complexity of the Indian diaspora and provide a pane through which sexuality, reproduction, and body politics are acted out transnationally (Thapan, *Living the Body*) between Italy and Punjab.

Notwithstanding their religious differences, Asha and Akal agreed that "Hindus and Sikhs are like 'nail and flesh,' *bhai bhai*, proper brothers." All these Indian women were married, in their late thirties, educated but unemployed and belonged to middle-class and mid-high caste backgrounds. Recounting their own in/fertility experiences, my informants eagerly discussed contraceptive choices and abortions within their immigrant community. Yet I could only elicit them to comment on the Punjabi skewed sex ratio and the appalling number of (female) orphans, as if these facts pertained to a rural Punjab increasingly modernized and urbanized, where these women traced "their roots but had since moved forward" (Akal).

5.1 Akal's Story: Transnational Kinship and the "Gift" Child
Whereas in northern Indian culture abandoning a newborn is despicable and deemed an act of material and moral deprivation, giving up a child for fostering is a moral choice envisaged

in many Punjabi families and recommended by Sikh and Hindu ethics. Adoption, though, is neither socially blind nor wide open; rather, close family relatives may take an interest in raising a kin newborn as theirs (Bharadwaj). Twenty years back, Asha's parents themselves, after giving birth to three daughters, adopted a baby boy, born in Canada to a sibling, who already claimed to have "enough" children.[8]

In the transnational Indian Diasporic context (Jain), a sister-in-law may be recruited from afar to *produce* a baby for a childless couple of relatives. Akal was diagnosed as unable to conceive after double checkups in India and in Italy (and despite her own personal efforts for getting pregnant, including bathing in *neem* leaves and vowing in *gurdwaras,* Sikh temples). She, thus, pleaded her husband's elder sister to "make a baby for her"[9] and flew over to Punjab the day after the baby girl was born to raise her as her lawful daughter. Akal and her husband are delightfully proud of their little girl, who is just three, and being quite wealthy, they annually organize a grand birthday party for her among the Indian community in Bergamo, inviting dozens of people to celebrate their very "home-made" offspring. On one single occasion, Akal resented that she felt "ever more indebted" to her in-laws because her only descendent is, in biological terms, merely her husband's brood. She confessed that she would have never had such a thought had she not been exposed, through her Italian medical doctors, to much data on assisted reproduction, which she sees as ordinary in Italy but only affordable to the wealthy in India (Unnithan). She was interested in new reproductive technologies (NRT), but she never dared to suggest this to her husband. Akal explained: "I was so frustrated, waited all my life to become *jacca* [pregnant] …Then my sister-in-law offered me such a gift…. This is the way we have always sorted it out, in Punjab … when a woman could not conceive, a female relative would do it for her!"

Despite Akal's emphasis on familial piety and selfless giving and receiving, arranged family fostering does not rest solely on mercy and kin affection. Spurred by parents' desire for economic well-being and the status of having a foreign connection, an increasing number of babies and children in Punjab are being adopted by their relatives abroad: legally foolproof,[10] adoption has emerged as a preferred route to circumvent stringent immigration laws and create ad hoc diaspora connections (Vertovec). Adoptive kinship, thus, proves full of contradictions, since the "gift" child may also be seen as a by-product of commodity thinking in a global market economy (Yngvesson).

Although Akal's experience as a mother-to-be involved coming to terms with her own infertile body and resorting to a traditional way to set up her family relying on her kinship network (being "gifted" with a baby daughter to adopt), many other Indian women may face the challenge of embodying *excessive* fertility, of bearing potentially more children than socially advisable.

5.2 Indian Immigrant Women and Birth Control: Anuradha's Story

From her own standpoint, Akal is slightly critical of deliberate abortions and advocates for alternative solutions; however, these practices occur in Indian migrant families, too. Although Sikh moral precepts are strict and generally condemn abortion as interfering with God's works (as stated in the *Sikh Reht Maryada*, the Sikh Code of Conduct), pragmatic considerations are taken into account also in Sikh families when children outnumber the ideal family size. Cultural preference for small families and sons over daughters overrules any theoretical religious ban, whether Hindu or Sikh. Voluntary interruption of pregnancy (VIP) requests are regularly filed by Punjabi women at the onset of an undesired pregnancy, as reported by Italian medical practitioners. The official figures available on migrant women's abortions in Italy (Italy, "Relazione del Ministero") do not separate data according to geographical origin, but they do indicate a steady rate of "foreign" women who interrupt their pregnancies, as compared to a fall in "native" rates.

Gynecologists and obstetricians alike lament a lack of sound family planning among migrant women in general and within the Indian community in particular. "Indians" is an encompassing identification most doctors adopt without being aware of national boundaries or ethnic and religious belongings; the term often entails all South Asians, including Bangladeshis and Pakistanis. Medical practitioners I interviewed a few years ago

(Bonfanti, "Farsi madri") held quite situated if not prejudicial views on migrant women, regarding them as a rather essentialized category. Many paternalistically depicted childbirth for immigrant women as an event more natural for them than for Italian women, or they denounced it as being such a trivial affair that abortion was mistaken for an ordinary contraceptive method (Tognetti; Lombardi).

Therefore, Punjabi women often face subtle discrimination when they enter a birth-care centre, hardly ever resisting some biases, which may result in "substandard perinatal healthcare" (see Lianidou, this volume). The infamous sex-selective feticide has since become the prime lens through which Italian doctors greet Punjabi women's requests in prenatal care; a media-fuelled social imagination has imbibed what doctors expect of Indian women (Stoetzler and Yuval-Davis). Although fetal sex is not easily detected before the fifth month of pregnancy, when VIP is no longer admitted, one gynecologist told me that he would refrain from confirming the sex of the baby to Indian couples during an ultrasound scan, as they could "act wickedly failing to recognize the sacred in a not-yet-born life." This remark not only displays a patent racism but also highlights the (chiefly Catholic) moral values assigned to childbearing and the stigma put on women who request their pregnancy to be interrupted. Considering the figure of local practitioners who claim conscience objection (Italy, "Relazione del Ministero"), it is no wonder that Anuradha, Asha's former neighbour and best friend, who once completed the protocol for a VIP, was put on a waiting list and admitted to treatment only five weeks after uneasily filing the request. That was a sorrowful deferral for a woman who did not feel her family choice matched her personal desires.

Since she already had two sons, Anuradha knew her husband, Naveen, would urge her not to go on with the pregnancy. In fact, he argued that it was a time of hardships and a larger family would not be sustainable. Naveen's words took me aback, since I considered him the best-integrated and most well-off Indian I knew in the area, who spoke a near-native Italian and worked as an interpreter in the local court besides having a high-skilled administrative job. Anuradha cried her eyes out at the time and explained that "as a mother, she felt, knew and swore" that the baby she expected was going to be a girl and could fulfill her most inner wish: having a young female ally in her own home. The midwife she had consulted suggested her to apply for *Nasko*, a funding project financed by the Lombardy Region since 2010, which could grant her with three thousand euros for a newborn. Although this program is designed and implemented through the local CAVs (Catholic-oriented, pro-life family-planning centres), Anuradha replied that the point was not that they could not provide for another child, but that they did not want to. Although it was not her own wish, Anuradha would not oppose her husband or deceive her *stri-dharma* because this unplanned pregnancy would disrupt two normative social orders: one relating to ideal family size and the other concerning the hierarchy of intimate gender relations. Yet that experience gave Anuradha the chance to impose her views on contraception; she started to take "the pill" while negotiating this choice with an initially reluctant husband.

I know no Indian woman on oral contraceptives other than Anuradha. Many disregard this method as not a viable alternative for them; they either question its safety or see it as something that their husbands could use to accuse them of being unfaithful. This plain consideration reveals that women's fertile bodies are in first instance sexual bodies and that female self-control over childbirth is subtly linked to male (hetero)control over women's desire and pleasure (MacCormack).

Apart from withdrawal and periodical abstinence, condoms are the preferred daily method of birth control among Indian migrant couples and to prevent sexually transmitted infections (STIs). Asha herself was following the advice from her gynecologist, and she joked about the "little helpers" her husband would wear during their "nightshifts." However, recently she has started to fret over it and has considered turning to an IUD (coil) implantation, a technique not common in northern India but, according to her doctor, used by generations of Italian women with success. Since condom misuse may rarely end up in unwanted pregnancies, this is a dread that Asha fears after what happened to Majeeda, her sister-in-law.

5.3 Majeeda's Story: "Clandestine" Abortions and Medical Censures

Majeeda's experience with reproductive health care sounds like the ultimate outcome of several bad practices. Once, during sexual intercourse, the condom slipped off. Knowing very little about the day-after pill, she eventually found out that she was pregnant and talked over the matter with her husband. Commenting on their alleged low income and newly set mortgage, he put off the possibility of a third child, since their family was "perfect as it was," comprising of a little girl of four and a baby boy who was just a toddler. Recalling the troubles that Anuradha had gone through, Majeeda did not trust the local family counselling available, whose personnel she had previously found unwelcoming and rude, even when she attended their facilities as an expecting mother. Cultural and language barriers do hamper therapeutic relations (Balsamo; Rizzi and Iossa Fasano): the communication flow is restricted, some information gets lost, and misunderstandings may rise on each side—patients and practitioners (see Lianidou, this volume).

Following the advice from her sister, Majeeda entrusted her husband, Gurinder, who was going back to Punjab at Christmas for visiting and minor dealings, to bring her a chemical abortive pill, which is sold over the counter all across India (Williamson et al.). By the time he got back, she was already twelve weeks pregnant, but she took the medication anyway and waited for the pains to come in. After two nights of intense bleeding, Asha called me over to drive Majeeda to the hospital. She had to undergo a surgical abortion and remained under scrutiny for five days. Both recounted how upon discharge, the doctors were harsh; they reproached Majeeda for risking her life, attempting a "clandestine abortion," and circumventing the laws surrounding the trafficking of illegal pharmaceuticals. Lastly, they charged her for exploiting the national healthcare system.

Majeeda's account of the episode bore the trauma lived, the way she felt objectified, marginalized, and excluded. It was striking to note the absence of her husband in her narration, who had played a major role in the experience. She said that she felt "completely out of tune" after being verbally insulted by the local doctors. Instead of recovering her wellbeing, the condemning gaze of public health personnel worsened her perception of not being able to conform to family plans, community expectations, and society's requests. Her troubled experience has since made her perceive with distress her unruly body and any sexual approach from her husband so that she intends to undergo a "tubectomy," a lifelong means of contraception.

Female sterilization is relatively common in India, and it is estimated that in some areas up to 80 percent of women turn to tubectomy after their second delivery, a surgery for which health workers have to reach a certain annual quota (Williamson et al.). Nonetheless, its incidence is lower across the diaspora, where the improved life conditions are said to have set women free from the "all or nothing" options of childbearing (Thapan, *Living the Body*). In Majeeda's case, the failed encounter with the Italian health care system made her turn to this permanent method of contraception and moved her away from other provisional techniques of spacing or preventing births. Even though tubectomies are carried out in Italian hospitals, Majeeda, because of bureaucracy and her own distrust of the system, has planned a temporary return to Punjab to have her surgery done in Jalandhar with the aid of her mother-in-law.

CONCLUSIONS

South Asian migrant women engage in a polarized arena for reproductive choices and fertility management (Sangah and Gonsalves). The cases reported unveil how Punjabi immigrant mothers navigate between a longstanding Indian family model, which demands women produce the right heirs in number and gender, and Italian public opinion, which is framed on a dominant biomedical discourse that allows for abortions but covers them with moral shame. Indian immigrant women have to take extra care of their bodies, particularly their reproductive potential, whereas their male partners and extended families have the last say. Besides living with insecurity and uncertainty, excluded or discriminated against in the healthcare system and hardly accessing the treatments they considered most effective, these migrant women are trying to take control and partake in the decision-making process of childbearing. Religious beliefs and material (dis)possessions were taken into account, but they did not define fertility management, which is rather a privileged ground for reproducing cultural norms through intersubjective performances that traverse unequal gender relations and mandatory household formation. These women's personal experiences may be seen as "social dramas" (Turner), in which their embodied (in)/fertility threatens to breach cultural norms around childbearing. As a result, normative practices are called upon to restore normality while enacting symbolic and structural violence (Krais). The cases discussed prove how seemingly distant influences—Italian and Punjabi, recent and established, familial and governmental—shape and constrain local reproductive experiences, and intersect transnational forms of power and resistance (Rapp and Ginsburg).

Though limited, the accounts presented here seemed relevant to me because of the confidence that I gained with my research participants and the close bonds these women had established among one another, rebuilding in diaspora a female net of otherwise lost gendered intimacies (Thapan, "Pathways of Integration"). This degree of confidence ensured some much-needed communication by word of mouth and engendered an informal repertoire of reproductive behaviours and emotions, likely shared with new generations. As far as procreation is concerned, Indian first-generation migrant women seem to reproduce a patriarchal system, which they rarely contest in public and only at times challenge in private. Some reshuffling in gender relations may surface among second generation Punjabi young women. This youth is coming of age (Bonfanti, "The Marriage Market") and crosses cultural borders every day, at once within their community and the host society, which has since become a new homeland in a scape of diasporic connections. However, the role of the first-migrant generation remains decisive in opening up, albeit with tensions and conflicts, possibilities and change (Sandu).

That Sunday afternoon, described at the start of this chapter, Deepti, Asha's eight year-old daughter, ran in and threw herself on her mother's bed, interrupting our talk. We shushed and turned to a different topic, since she had not yet reached the age to be disclosed all the secrets that her mom and "aunties" were sharing. Shifting the attention from "motherhood" as an institution enforced on women to "mothering" as a relationship of any woman to her children (O'Reilly), Asha guided me to widen the research on South Asian diaspora mothers well beyond medical anthropology to consider first-person accounts more than anecdotal evidence (Sangah and Gonsalves). Gently combing Deepti's glossy hair, Asha acutely observed, "I'll soon have to teach my daughter what it takes to live in a girl's body. I just want her future as a woman to be her choice ... whether she will be a doctor or a cashier, a spinster or a wife and mother.... Whether she will see herself as an Indian or an Italian, I want it to be her choice." To me, that sounded like a feminist mother's stance (Phadke).

In this chapter, I have advanced feminist reflections, aims, methods, and analysis, which follow the admonishments of Ryan-Flood and Gill: "Feminist research is informed by a history of breaking silences, of demanding that women's voices be heard, recorded and included in wider intellectual genealogies and *his*tories" (1). In these narratives, Punjabi migrant women recognize their relative power in embodying (in)fertility and their partial resistance to taming it, under the supervision of men, families, healthcare institutions, and governments. Their steps toward social recognition and gender equality also pass through the acknowledgment of their desires and agency in fertility management and eventual childbearing, in being fully included as autonomous agents in reproducing their kin genealogies and making their community stories.

NOTES

[1] In order to protect the privacy of my interlocutors, I have used pseudonyms throughout the text.

[2] "Spontaneous miscarriage" was an emotionally softened term with which my Indian women interlocutors referred to an intentional end of pregnancy. Talking about the clinical experience of abortion in Italy, they often used the acronym IVG "*interruzione volontaria di gravidanza*," which they read in their medical papers (standing

for VIP, voluntary interruption of pregnancy).

[3]The widespread preference for male rather than female heirs in India should not suggest that daughters are systematically mistreated or neglected. In my ethnographic experience with Punjabi immigrants in Italy, I did not witness any abuse, although I reported some gender-based discrimination in accessing higher education. Sons were often encouraged to pursue third level study while daughters were assumed to be soon married off.

[4]*Lakshmi* is the Hindu goddess of wealth and prosperity; she is the wife and active energy of Lord Vishnu.

[5]*Dulaa* is a colloquial form to denote a man who is respectable, sensible and good at heart.

[6]*Stri-dharma*, "the path of the wife," stands for the "code of conduct" that an Indian wife is asked to abide by in order to comply with her womanly duties in the family and the society at large.

[7]That is what I witnessed while doing fieldwork in Punjab. In one of my host-families' homes, a fretting mother-in-law forcefully took her son's young bride to see a gynecologist because she was still "barren" a year after the wedding.

[8]Asha's adopted brother retained Canadian nationality. Actually, when he grew up, his biological parents tried to persuade him to move back there, but he refused. As Asha said with mellow words, "nature melts in front of daily *mata pyaar*," 'mother's love' (my trans.). The family bond with foster parents proved stronger than biological ascendency.

[9]Akal's sister-in-law was not a "surrogate" mother (MacCormack 105-29). She conceived the baby with her husband, after they had convened to help his expat brother's desires for a family that apparently his wife could not fulfil. I actually did not enquire if this adoption implicated any financial transaction, although the flows of remittances between the expats and their kin who remain in the homeland may suggest so.

[10]The biological parents of Akal's adopted baby relinquished all their parental rights. If they change their minds later, they may file a lawsuit to get their baby back (provided they can pay for a skillful attorney). Akal noticed that such a behaviour would disrupt the extended family's harmony; thus, it would be strongly discouraged by all other relatives.

WORKS CITED

Axel, Brian Keith. *The Nation's Tortured Body: Violence, Representation and Creation of a Sikh Diaspora*. Duke University Press, 2001.

Ayres, Alyssa. "Language, the Nation, and Symbolic Capital: The Case of Punjab." *The Journal of Asian Studies*, vol. 67, no. 3, 2008, pp. 917–946.

Bharadwaj, Adhitya. "Why Adoption Is Not an Option in India: The Visibility of Infertility, the Secrecy of Donor Insemination and Other Cultural Complexities." *Social Science and Medicine*, vol. 56, no. 2, 2003, pp. 1876-1880.

Balsamo, Franca. *Famiglie di migranti: trasformazione dei ruoli e mediazione culturale* [*Families of Migrants: Transformation of Roles and Cultural Mediation*]. Carocci, 2003.

Bertolani, Barbara. "Transnational Sikh Marriages in Italy." *Sikhs across Borders: Transnational Practices of European Sikhs*, edited by Kristine Myrvold and Knut Jacobsen, Bloomsbury, 2012, pp. 68-83.

Bertolani, Barbara, et al. "Mirror Games: A Fresco of Sikh Settlements among Italian Local Societies." *Sikhs in Europe: Migration, Identities and Representation*, edited by Kristine Myrvold and Knut Jacobsen, Ashgate, 2011, pp. 133-161.

Bhachu, Parminder. *Dangerous Design: Asian Women Fashion the Diaspora Economics*. Routledge, 2004.

Bonfanti, Sara. "Farsi madri. L'accompagnamento alla nascita in una prospettiva interculturale" ["Becoming Mothers. Motherhood Training in an Intercultural Perspective"]. *Quaderni di Donna&Ricerca*, vol. 27, 2012,

Bonfanti, Sara. "The Marriage Market among Indian Migrant Families in Italy: Designs, Resistances and Gateways." *Human Affairs*, vol. 25, no. 1, 2015, pp. 16-28.

Charsley, Simon. "Sanskritization: The Career of an Anthropological Theory." *Contributions to Indian Sociology*, vol. 32, no. 1, 1998, pp. 527-549.

Colombo, Enzo, and Paola Rebughini. *Children of Immigrants in a Globalized World: A Generational Experience*. Palgrave Macmillan, 2012.

Diminescu, Dana. "Le passage par l'écran: ou l'émergence de nouvelles frontiers". *Actes du colloque Les frontières de l'Europe.* Edited by Bucuresti Universitatii, 2007, pp. 263-274.

Duvvury, Nata, et al. *Connecting Right to Reality: A Progressive Framework of Core Legal Protections for Women's Property Rights.* International Center for Research on Women. 2008. Print.

Falzon, Marcus Anthony. *Multi-sited Ethnography: Theory, Praxis and Locality in Contemporary Research.* Ashgate, 2009.

Gallini, Clara, and Gino Satta. *Incontri etnografici: processi cognitivi e relazionali nella ricerca sul campo* [*Ethnographic Encounters: Cognitive and Relational Processes within the Fieldwork*]. Meltemi, 2007.

Galloni, Francesca. *Giovani indiani a Cremona* [*Indian Youth in Cremona*]. CISU, 2009. Greenhalgh, Susan, editor. *Situating Fertility: Anthropological and Demographic Inquiry.* Cambridge University Press, 1995.

Ivry, Tsipy. *Embodying Culture. Pregnancy in Japan and Israel.* Routledge, 2010.

India. Governmental Census of India 2011." *Census India,* 2011, www.censusindia.gov.in/2011-common/census_2011. htmlhttp://censusindia.gov.in/2011-prov-results/data_files/india/ Final_PPT_2011_chapter3.pdf. Accessed 12 Aug. 2016.

Italy. "Relazione del Ministero sull'Attuazione della Legge." *Salute* 2011, www.salute.gov.it/imgs/C_17_pubblicazioni_2226_allegato.pdf. Accessed. 10 Jan. 2015.

Jain, Ravindra K. *Nation, Diaspora, Trans-Nation: Reflections from India.* Routledge, 2010.

Jayaram, Narayana. *Diversities in the Indian Diaspora: Nature, Implications, Responses.* Oxford University Press, 2011.

Krais, Beate. "Gender and Symbolic Violence: Female Oppression in the Light of Pierre Bourdieu's Theory of Social Practice." *Bourdieu: Critical Perspectives,* edited by Craig Calhoun, University of Chicago Press, 1993, pp. 156-178.

Lombardi, Lia. *Società, culture e differenze di genere. Percorsi migratori e stati di salute* [Society, Culture, and Gender Differences. Migration Routes and Health States]. Franco Angeli, 2006.

MacCormack, Carol P., editor. *Ethnography of Fertility and Birth.* Waveland Press, 1994.

Malhotra, Anshu and Farina Mir, editors, *Punjab Reconsidered: History, Culture and Practice*. Oxford University Press, 2012.

Mamdani, Mahmood. "The Myth of Population Control: Family, Caste and Class in an Indian Village." Monthly Review Press, 1972.

Merry, Engle, and Setha Low. "Engaged Anthropology: Diversity and Dilemmas." *Current Anthropology*, vol. 51, no. S2, 2010, pp. 1-24.

Mishra, Vijay. "The Diasporic Imaginary: Theorizing the Indian Diaspora." *Textual Practice*, vol. 10, no. 3, 1996, pp. 421-447.

O'Reilly, Andrea. *From Motherhood to Mothering. The Legacy of Adrienne Rich's* Of Woman Born. State University of New York Press, 2004.

Phadke, Shilpa. "Feminist Motherhood? Some Reflections on Sexuality and Risk from Urban India." Special Issue, Unfamiliar Ground: Security, Socialisation and Affect in Indian Families, *Journal of South Asian Studies*, vol.36, no.1, 2013, pp. 92-106.

Rapp, Rayna, and Faye Ginsburg, editors. *Conceiving the New World Order: the Global Politics of Reproduction*. University of California Press, 1995.

Rizzi, Renato, and Augusto Iossa Fasano, editors. *Ospitare e curare: dialogo interculturale ed esperienze cliniche con gli immigrati* [*Hosting and Caring: Intercultural Dialogue and Clinical Experiences with Immigrants*]. Franco Angeli, 2004.

Ryan-Flood, Roisin, and Rosalind Gill, editors. *Secrecy and Silence in the Research Process: Feminist Reflections*. Routledge, 2010.

Sandu, Adriana. "Transnational Homemaking Practices: Identity, Belonging and Informal Learning." *Journal of Contemporary European Studies*, vol. 21, no. 4, 2013, pp. 496-512.

Sangah, Janjit K., and Tahira Gonsalves, editors. *South Asian Motherhood: Negotiating Culture, Family and Selfhood*. Demeter Press, 2013.

Shah, Arvind M. *The Family in India: Critical Essays*. Orient Longman, 1999.

Stoetzler, Martin, and Nira Yuval-Davis. "Standpoint Theory, Situated Knowledge and the Situated Imagination." *Feminist Theory*, vol. 3. no., 3, 2002, pp. 315-333.

Thapan, Meenakshi, editor. *Living the Body: Embodiment, Wom-*

anhood and Identity in Contemporary India. Sage, 2009.

Thapan, Meenakshi. "Pathways of Integration: Individual and collective Strategies in Northern Italy." *CARIM-India Research Report 2013/28*. European University Press, 2013.

Tognetti Bordogna, Mara, editor. *I colori del welfare; i servizi alla persona di fronte all'utenza che cambia* [*The Colours of Welfare: Personal Services in the Light of New Users*]. Franco Angeli, 2005.

Turner, Victor. *The Anthropology of Performance*. Paj Books, 1985.

Talwar, Veena Oldenburg. *Dowry Murder. The Imperial Origins of a Cultural Crime*. Oxford University Press, 2002.

Unnithan, Maya. "Infertility and Assisted Reproductive Technologies (ARTs) in a Globalising India: Ethics, Medicalization and Agency." *Asian Bioethics Review*, vol. 2, no. 1, 2010, pp. 3-18.

Vertovec, Steven. *The Hindu Diaspora: Comparative Patterns*. Routledge, 2000.

Williamson, Lisa, et al. "Limits to Modern Contraceptive Use among Young Women in Developing Countries: A Systematic Review of Qualitative Research." *Reproductive Health*, vol. 6, no. 3, 2009. doi: 10.1186/1742-4755-6-3. Accessed 22 Aug. 2016.

Yngvesson, Barbara. "Placing the 'Gift Child' in Transnational Adoption." *Law and Society Review*, vol. 36, no. 2, 2002, pp. 227-256.

2.

From Mama Africa to *Papatūānuku*:[1]

The Experiences of a Group of African Immigrant and Refugee-Background Mothers Living in Auckland, Aotearoa-New Zealand

HELENE CONNOR, IRENE AYALLO, AND SUE ELLIOTT

Guri aan hooyo lahayni waa lama degaan—
"A home without a mother is like a desert" (RIMA)

THIS CHAPTER IS BASED ON RESEARCH with a group of ten African mothers living in Auckland, Aotearoa-New Zealand. There is a relatively small population (approximately eighteen thousand) of people from Africa living in Aotearoa-New Zealand, and the majority live in Auckland, the largest urban area in the country (NZ, Statistics NZ, and "2013 Census"). The project explored ways in which both immigrant and refugee-background[2] mothers perceived New Zealand's cultural and social contexts of motherhood. Commentary on themes from the interviews, along with an indigenous perspective, is also provided. The rationale for this comparison is twofold. Helene Connor, the lead author of this chapter, is of Māori descent with *whakapapa* (genealogy) affiliations to *Te Atiawa iwi* (tribe) and *Ngati Rahiri hapu* (sub-tribe), and she brought a Māori lens to the research. Secondly, when analyzing the themes that emerged from the interviews, the authors were struck by the similarities between the values and beliefs of the mothers interviewed and Māori culture. These similarities provided a counter-narrative to the predominant hegemonic institutional norms prevailing in New Zealand society, which are derived from a British colonial heritage and, subsequently, European epistemologies.

"Aotearoa," means "the land of the long white cloud" and is the Māori name for New Zealand, which is situated in the South Pacific

Ocean and is made up of two main islands: the North Island or *Te-ika-a-Maui*, which means "the fish of Maui"; and the South Island or *Te-Wai-Pounamu*, which means "the waters of Greenstone." The country's total landmass of around 268,680 square kilometres makes it slightly larger than the United Kingdom. Aotearoa-New Zealand is one of the more recently settled major landmasses, and the first people to arrive there may have originated from Eastern Polynesia and arrived in a series of migrations sometime between seven hundred and two thousand years ago. Over time, these settlers developed into a distinct culture, divided into *iwi* tribes and *hapu* subtribes, which is now known as Māori (King).

Aotearoa-New Zealand has a population of just over 4.6 million. Most of the country's population is of European descent, with approximately 74 percent identifying as European. The indigenous Māori is the largest non-European ethnic group, accounting for 14.9 percent of the population, whereas Asian ethnic groups make up 11.8 percent of the population and 7.4 percent of people are of Pacific Island decent.[3] Africans make up less than 1 percent of the population (NZ, Statistics NZ, "2013 Census"). Before the late 1990s, immigrants from Africa tended to be white South Africans. In the 2013 census, approximately eighteen thousand people identified as African, although the majority of African migrants continue to be white South African (Lucas).

AFRICAN SETTLEMENT IN AOTEAROA-NEW ZEALAND— SKILLED MIGRANTS AND REFUGEES

In its guide to understanding how migrants and refugees enter New Zealand, Immigration New Zealand notes several distinctions between the two groups, which are in line with international understanding. In summary, the key differences are that migrants choose to leave their homeland and settle in a country of their choice, whereas refugees do not choose to leave their homeland. They flee in response to a crisis.

Aotearoa-New Zealand's formal refugee resettlement program began in 1944 when eight hundred Polish people (including 734 orphaned Polish children) were given sanctuary during World War II and then permanent settlement due to the political situation in Poland after 1945 (Beaglehole). Nowadays, refugees come to New Zealand in three ways. The way that the country currently accepts refuges is through an annual quota system of 750 refugees referred to Immigration New Zealand by UNHCR. Included in this number are up to seventy-five places for women at risk. All refugees complete a six-week orientation program at the Mangere Refugee Resettlement Centre before being resettled. The orientation program includes information about New Zealand life, laws, and expectations, and access to English-language classes. All new arrivals are also screened for any special needs that they may have in relation to education, social support, physical and mental healthcare, and the like (Marlow and Elliott).

In addition to the quota of refugees, New Zealand also considers applications from asylum seekers who claim refugee status on arrival or after a period of time in the country (NZ, Ministry of Business, Innovation and Employment, *Immigration New Zealand*). Up to three hundred people from a refugee background or refugee-like situations are accepted each year under the Refugee Family Support Category, the main vehicle for refugee family reunification ("Refugee Family Support Category). These groups, however, do not receive the same entitlements as those arriving as part of the annual quota.

The majority of African refugees are from Eritrea, Ethiopia, Somalia, Sudan, Burundi, the Democratic Republic of Congo, and Congo-Brazzaville (Yusuf). Until the 1990s, the bulk of African skilled migrants came to New Zealand from South Africa. According to Statistics New Zealand, eighteen thousand people identified themselves as belonging to an African ethnic group in the 2013 census, although there are no statistics distinguishing their status as either skilled migrants or refugees ("2013 Census").

DEMOGRAPHIC BACKGROUND OF THE MOTHERS

The women interviewed for this study came to New Zealand as refugees under the New Zealand quota system, asylum seekers, partners of skilled migrants, or skilled migrants themselves. The countries that they came from include the following: Eritrea, Ethiopia, Burundi, the Democratic Republic of the Congo, Rwanda,

Uganda, and Zimbabwe. The women were all aged between twenty and forty-five years. All of the women had at least one biological child, and some also had adopted or fostered children or stepchildren; moreover, a few of the women were carers for their nieces or nephews. The children ranged in age from two to eighteen. Most of the women were in either full-time or part-time employment and worked in a range of occupations, including social workers, community-development workers, nurses, caregivers, and early childhood workers. Several of the women were also studying towards a tertiary qualification. There was a mix of married women; women living with partners; separated, divorced, or widowed women; and women raising children on their own. No names are used in this chapter, as the African community is relatively small, and even pseudonyms could identify the women.

Informed consent was gained prior to conducting the interviews. The consent forms for the participants had information such as the opportunity for the interviewees to ask questions, and they also alerted the women to the need for interviewers to take notes during the interview and to audiotape and transcribe the interviews. The participants were assured of their confidentiality by only being identified as "Participant A," "Participant B," and so forth.

THEMES THAT EMERGED FROM THE INTERVIEWS

The main themes and subthemes, together with supporting quotations from the mothers, identify common issues relevant to being both women and mothers. Main themes included "birthing new lives," need for social support, mothers caring for their children, and the value of motherhood.

"Birthing" New Lives

All of the women interviewed talked about birthing new lives both metaphorically and literally. Leaving Mama Africa for the unknown of *Papatūānuku* involved not only crossing international borders but also crossing emotional and cultural boundaries, in which new identities had to be forged within an unfamiliar society and unfamiliar communities. In her 2006 research on migrant mothers, Ruth DeSouza contends that migration can frequently be a traumatic life event and becoming a mother in an unfamiliar country can add to feelings of dislocation and displacement ("Pregnant with Possibility"). Migrant mothers, she argues, are more at risk of experiencing depression or other mental health issues. Several of the women in this study articulated these experiences as "feeling sad or lonely." Loneliness comes, in part, from lack of familial support in New Zealand. Issa Yusuf, discussing this phenomenon regarding Somalian refugees, states: "Many refugees from Somalia are widowed women who face the burden of caring for a large family without the support of the traditional extended family. In other cases, families may face adjustment issues associated with the changing gender and intergenerational roles" (24).

The lack of extended family support also affected many of the women in this study, as articulated by Participant F:

> Having my daughter was really hard. I had to stay in the hospital for a month. I was so scared I was going to lose my daughter and then when I had her, I couldn't trust anyone even to take care of her. Back then, the hospital system wasn't as good as today. They were unfriendly, the midwife and everyone. Back home you go back to your mum's home, even if you're married then your mother will look after you for forty days. At home, everyone's responsible.

This mother decided to return to Africa after the birth of her second child so that she could enjoy the support of her extended family: "After I had my son, I said to myself, 'I have to go back to Africa, I can't stay here.' I didn't want to come back in New Zealand until my son was big enough. I had the whole other family there like aunts and uncles; so it was really very good."

Similarly, another refugee mother, Participant H, also commented on the challenges of not having extended family support: "In Africa, the kids belong to everybody—anyone can look after the child. But in New Zealand, the child is only yours. It is challenging when you are new to New Zealand and do not know much about this culture."

In her discussion on the lack of extended family support for African mothers in New Zealand, Adesayo Adelowo argues that since there are no isolated parents or families in Africa, it is very stressful for most African women in New Zealand, especially if they are first generation migrants, to learn how to juggle work and family commitments without the support they are used to (102). These experiences of mothering were similar to those within traditional Māori society, which was also carried out within the context of the wider *whanau*, (family) with children being raised by multiple "parents," including biological parents, grandparents, uncles, aunts, cousins, and siblings (Connor, "Māori Mothering"). Although our participants' reflections on the role of family as a social support network is echoed within traditional Māori values, it contrasts with their perceptions and experiences of hegemonic New Zealand practices.

With limited extended family support, many of the women returning to work or study often had to find childcare for their children, as Participant F explained.

> I used to work a part time job in the mental health area, then I decided to retrain. My daughter was in school, and I put my sons in daycare. One thing as an African I found out [is] if you take your kids to daycare then everyone thinks you're an evil mother in terms of culture. It was like, "Why are you leaving your children in the daycare and going to work, and study?" I was strong enough to think what they think was wrong because if I stay home, I get depressed; if I stay home, I don't have a better life.

The cost of childcare can pose a barrier to employment or further study, particularly for solo mothers. In addition, many migrant and refugee women prefer members of their own families and communities to care of their children rather than strangers (DeSouza, "Doing it for Ourselves").

In addition to the lack of support from extended family, the women also discussed some cultural differences they faced after birth, including attitudes to sleeping arrangements and feeding. Several mothers discussed how difficult it was for them not to sleep with their baby on the same bed. Their views were best summarized by Participant A:

Something I will never understand is the "sleeping arrangement." This is because the closeness I have with my children cannot allow me to put them in a cot or in a separate room. I will never do that. I have had three daughters and none of them has had an "incident" sleeping with me in my bed. When I was in hospital to deliver my second baby ... she cried every time they put her in the hospital cot ... but when the nurse brings her to my bed she stops crying. The nurse growled at me when I told her in Africa, we don't let our babies sleep on their own.... She told me that I had to adapt.

Discouraging mothers from sleeping with babies is evident in the discourses of "safe sleep" put out by the New Zealand government to try and prevent sudden unexplained deaths in infants (NZ, Ministry of Health, "Safe Sleep"). Nevertheless, some mothering groups in New Zealand, such as the La Leche League, the breastfeeding mothers network, do support babies sleeping in bed with their parents and breastfeeding in bed in order to assist mothers in the continuation of breastfeeding on demand and maintaining breast milk supply.

There were also differences in how the women fed their children. Most women discussed the cultural importance of breastfeeding their children and cooking food for their family (including young children), as opposed to feeding babies dry food from the supermarket shelves. As Participant F related: "I breastfed for two years. Every mother in Ethiopia knows this. They believe strongly you leave a baby close to your heart to build the relationship." Participant G shared a similar sentiment: "I have to give my children cooked food. I can't finish the whole day without cooking. I have to stand at the pot. I mean at the stove and cook for the kids. That's part of being a mother. Sometimes, it's hard like maybe you are so tired and have a headache. Because they are yours they are still going to wait for a cooked dinner."

Adelowo discusses the importance of food to most African cultures (100). Traditionally, women have to have food ready in the pot or ready to be cooked for guests at all times. Welcoming visitors into one's home by serving them food and water without expecting anything in return is an acceptable practice among Africans. This aspect of African culture is very similar to Māori culture. Providing food and hospitality for guests is known as *manaakitanga* and is a cultural practice in which respect and generosity are shown for others. Newborn Māori infants were also fed from the breast soon after birth and were generally breastfed until the child was two years old (Connor, "Māori Mothering"). These similarities can help forge new friendships between African and Māori mothers and help African mothers feel at home.

Importance of Social Support

Several of the mothers in this study spoke about how they had been able to overcome the challenges that they faced during and after birth. The majority emphasized the need of forming new connections and social bonds, in the absence of extended family. In place of support from extended family members, most of the women have been able to form close friendships and networks. Participant G, for example, arrived in New Zealand on her own. After being housed with a family for several months, she found accommodation in a hostel and stayed there for approximately nine months, during which time her daughter was born. She met two Somalian women at the hostel and has remained close to these women, whom she considers to be like sisters.

The networks and connections have been particularly important for several of the women in this study who were solo mothers, which is an issue for many mothers in the African communities (Yusuf). Several also had friends who were raising children on their own; Participant G felt that a stigma exists around solo motherhood: "There is a stigma about being a single mum—she's on benefit,[4] she will take your husband. You know, this kind of stigma so it separates people."

Some of the women had also noticed that their unmarried friends in their thirties were being stigmatized.

She's thirty and she has never married, what's wrong with her?" So there's [sic] different stigmas in the community. There's also divorce; the marriage doesn't last and no love just because a person was pressured to marry to meet cultural expectations. I have seen also those woman that are struggling because here our community is so small there is not enough guys! They're all women. (Participant G)

The stigma towards solo mothers is also discussed by Nurcan Ozgur Baklacioglu, in her article in this volume, where she explores the plight of Syrian refugee mothers in Istanbul.

Many of the women have also found support in their spiritual and religious network, and many discussed the importance of spirituality and religion in their lives and how they were supported by their churches and mosques. Participant G spoke about her church in the following way: "I had a good church—they supported me all along and would take turns to take my son out so I can have time to lie down." Similiarly, Participant H spoke about the values taught at school and in church:

> I'm Christian; I've been taking my children since they were young to church. My daughter goes to a Catholic school, actually all three of them, apart from my son, they go to a Catholic school. What we talk at home, about respect, it's reinforced at church and school, loving one another, all that. I found that values I instilled at home are also at church and school.

Participant A spoke about the joy that African women experience while attending church: "I go to church and meet other women. We sing African songs.... We laugh, we cry ... with women from all over Africa.... [It] makes me feel connected.... They lift me up."

Mothers Caring for Themselves and their Children

Generally, the mothers in this study were determined to care for themselves and their children. The majority of the women had tertiary qualifications or aspired to achieve quality education for themselves—and in some cases their spouses—and for their children. Finding good education for their children was also one of the motivating factors for migration for many of the skilled migrants in the study. Similar findings were also evident in research carried out by Adelowo. She argues that the majority of African communities hold education in high esteem, and the women in her study considered education a tool to improve their future.

The mothers valued the New Zealand education system, as responsibility for education is shared between the family and the school. Participant G said that she liked how the schools "value parents [and] their comment is very good" compared to back home where "teachers have power over the children; they don't communicate." Participant H liked how in New Zealand "parents have a greater relationship with school ... [they] feel like [they] are part of that community [and] can go and talk to the teacher."

However, when mothers have limited English, the communication between school and home is hindered, which marginalizes the women. As Participant A explained, "Communication with the school and teachers is hard if you cannot speak English. There is no interpreter, the teachers just talk, and all you do is say yes, yes to everything because you do not understand. In most cases my husband would go because he could speak English."

Semahar Gebremariam argues that schools can play a significant role in supporting refugee families through facilitating connections between refugee-background families and the wider community. In her study on Ethiopian refugee-background families, she finds that the parents sought out support with the community to help select schools and find ways to participate in their children's education. Despite their best intentions though, the parents often faced a number of barriers, including English proficiency, limited educational background, financial hardship, and availability of time, especially for solo mothers.

The mothers in this study were determined to preserve their cultural identity while integrating into New Zealand society. For instance, although all the mothers spoke English (described as "African English"), they were also fluent in their mother tongue. However, several mothers commented that their "African English" accents limited their interactions with non-Africans and their accents could be barriers to employment. Adelowo also notes that when Africans in her study spoke "African English," they were ignored and corrected rather than listened to (31).

Fluency in one's own language is essential for cultural identity, and loss of language has been identified as a stressor that could affect immigrants' mental health (Adelowo). Certainly, many of the mothers in our study were concerned about maintaining their mother tongue, not only for themselves but for their children. Participant H elaborated on this concern: "Language is one thing that I think as mother, I'm failing my children a bit because I'm not talking to them in my mother tongue or making an effort for them to learn and that would have been different if I was back home because it's the language that would be around, they would be immersed in it" (Participant H). Similarly, *te reo Māori* (the Māori language) is also central to Māori culture and identity. It forms part of the cultural identity and heritage of Aotearoa-New Zealand and was made an official language of New Zealand in 1987.

All the mothers in our study wanted their children (and families) to be healthy. Traditional African perspectives on health include mental, physical, spiritual, and emotional stability for one's self, family, and community (Tuwe). This perspective is similar to Māori perspectives on health, which also include *taha tinana*, the physical dimension; *taha hinengaro*, the mind; *taha wairua*, the spiritual dimension; and *taha whanau*, the family (NZ, Ministry of Health NZ, "Māori Health Models").

Overall, the mothers found the New Zealand health system to be excellent, although they appeared more impressed with the medical aspects of care than a sense of being cared for within the system. Participant E related how "Health practices in New Zealand are favourable to children and pregnant mums." She further said that she has "high-risk pregnancies and ... receive[s] high quality care for no payment, whereas ... in Zimbabwe that kind of care would have cost ... quite a lot of money."

Exposure to racism was a deep concern for many of the mothers, regarding their children's wellbeing. Participant G talked about the racism her son experienced at school: "He's very sensitive with these race issues. I took him out of a school because he was experiencing racism. He was being called 'Black Obama,' all of those names and he was just five. The boy did not want to go to school at the age of five. He said, "Mum let's move this house; I don't want this school." Another mother, Participant B, also had a similar experience:

There are times people make negative comments [being racist] to the kids—and this really hurts me as mother. You are always on a rollercoaster assuring the children that they are okay as they are. I teach my kids to be strong—but there are times when I have had to go and talk to the teacher [report bullying]. Fortunately, the school my kids go to responds really fast.

Schools can also perpetuate stereotypes, as Participant F shared:

My thirteen-year-old son is learning about the whole refugee thing and he came home and he was like, "Mum guess what?" and I was like, "What?" He was like, "Guess what my teacher said that since I am a refugee I should know more about this and that." And then I'm like, "You're not a refugee. Your mum was a refugee because she came here as a refugee but you are not, you were born here." And he was like, "So I'm not a refugee?" and I was like, "Do you even know what a refugee is?" So I had to explain that and then I did call the school and asked them why, was it because of his skin colour.

Participant F also told the story about when her son first went to intermediate school and they put him into an English for Speakers of Other Languages (ESOL) class. "It was like, okay why do you need to be in ESOL if actually English is your first language because we mostly speak English at home and we don't speak any other language. When I went to ask them it was like, 'Because he's African and straight up we assumed that he needed that.'"

In her 2012 study of resettlement experiences of refugee women in New Zealand, Ruth DeSouza highlights how many of the women and their families have been subjected to a range of racism, including institutional and interpersonal. Children often experienced verbal forms of racism, such as being taunted for the ways that they looked, for the clothes they wore, and for the way they spoke.

Almost all of the women Adelowo interviewed for her study identified racism as one of the stressors that they had experienced since they migrated to New Zealand (111). The women in her study spoke extensively of experiencing interpersonal and insti-tutional racism in the form of verbal abuse, discrimination, and marginalization in different settings.

Several of the mothers in our study also talked about how they dealt with racism. Learning to "brush it off" or "ignore it" was a common strategy. Participant C also talked about openly con-fronting racism: "Me [sic] and my son have experienced racism. Some parents at play group don't want my son to play with their children. I told them off."

CONCLUSION

Although the mothers spoke about some of the challenges of being migrant mothers, including the loss of support from the extended family, most of the mothers still valued being a mother. Indeed, the theme of motherhood within the narratives was clearly imbued with a sense of both cultural and personal significance. Participant B explained the feeling in the following way:

> What I like about being a mother is being with my kids, talking to them, playing with them. It is just amazing. It is amazing because without kids for me and being a foreign country.... I would be traumatised. I would be thinking so much about home—so the kids keep me occupied and focused on the future. I thank God for them and for me.

Integration from Mama Africa into the land of *Papatūānuku* involved a number of opportunities as well as challenges for the mothers interviewed for this research project. Many of their expe-riences were similar to those of Māori mothers (Connor, "Land"). This similarity provides a potential social bridge for migrant mothers adapting to a new social landscape and is an opportunity for program and policy developers to foster immigrant mothers' settlement and support their children in developing an Afro-Kiwi[5] identity.

The mothers in this study also discussed the need for community activities and networks and their need to preserve their cultural identities while, at the same time, learning about New Zealand and becoming more familiar with New Zealand culture and society. This is a fundamental aspect of resettlement, in which cultural practices and settlement experiences are shared with members of similar ethnic groups, who assist integration through increased health and wellbeing and employment opportunities (Elliott and Yusuf).

Both Māori and African women's maternal bodies have been subjected to racializing and sexualizing discourses. Experiences of racism towards the women and their children at both an institutional and individual level were a pervasive theme throughout this research. In common with Māori women, African women showed ways in which they contest Western maternal discourses and strive to maintain a degree of control over their maternities, particularly with regard to sleeping with infants, feeding their children, retaining respect for elders, re-establishing kin-type relationship with friends in lieu of extended family, and honouring the value of spirituality. An alignment with Mama Africa and *Papatūānuku* can be viewed not only as an affirmation of African birthing practices and mothering ideologies but also as a critique of Western ones.

These sisters are doing it for themselves.

He aroha whaerere, he potiki piri poho—
"A mother's love is the greatest treasure"

Acknowledgements: We would like to thank the ten mothers who graciously gave of their time to be interviewed for this project. Their stories of courage, survival, perseverance, and determination were both inspirational and powerful.

NOTES

[1]*Papatūānuku* is the earth mother of the indigenous Māori people of Aotearoa-New Zealand.
[2]The term "refugee background" is used because refugees coming to New Zealand under the government humanitarian program are given permanent residence on arrival and are, therefore, no longer refugees and have the same rights and responsibilities as other New Zealanders.
[3]These percentages come to more than 100 percent because people

can identify with more than one ethnic group (NZ, NZ Statistics, "2013 Census").

[4]The term "benefit" refers to the New Zealand government's Sole Parent Support Benefit program, which helps single parents and caregivers of dependent children get ready for future work and helps supports them to find part-time work and provides financial help through a weekly payment (NZ, Ministry of Social Development, "Sole Parent Support").

[5]The term "Kiwi" is a colloquial term for New Zealander.

WORKS CITED

Adelowo, Adesayo. *The Adjustment of African Women living in New Zealand: A Narrative Study*. Dissertation, Auckland University of Technology, 2012. *Research Gateway*, aut.researchgateway.ac.nz/bitstream/handle/10292/4601/AdelowoA. pdf?sequence=3&isAllowed=y. Accessed 9 Aug. 2016.

Beaglehole, Ann. "Refugees." *Te Ara: The Encyclopedia of New Zealand*, Government of New Zealand, 13 July 2012, www.teara.govt.nz/en/refugees. Accessed 9 Aug. 2016.

Connor, Helene. "Land, Notions of 'Home' and Cultural Space: The Location and Articulation of Power and Gender in Māori Society." *Gender and Power in the Pacific: Women's Strategies in a World of Change*, edited by Katarina Ferro and Margit Wolfsberger, Transaction Publishers, 2003, pp.159-184.

Connor, Helene. "Māori Mothering: Repression, Resistance and Renaissance." *Indigenous Mothering, Family and Community: International Perspectives*, edited by Dawn Memee Lavell-Harvard and Kim Anderson, Demeter Press, 2015, pp. 231-250.

DeSouza, Ruth. "Pregnant with Possibility: Migrant Motherhood in New Zealand." Reproduction, Childbearing, and Motherhood," edited by Pranee Liamputtong, Nova Science Publishers, Inc., 2007, www.academia.edu/1847279/Pregnant_with_possibility_Migrant_motherhood_in_New_Zealand. Accessed 31 Aug. 2015.

DeSouza, Ruth. *Doing it for Ourselves and Our Children: Refugee Women on Their Own in New Zealand*, Auckland University of Technology, 2012.

Elliott, Susan, and Issa Yusuf. "'Yes, We Can; But Together': Social Capital and Refugee Resettlement." *Kōtuitui: New Zealand Journal of Social Sciences Online*, vol. 9, no. 2, 2014, pp. 101-110. *Research Bank*, unitec.researchbank.ac.nz/bitstream/handle/10652/3329/Social%20capital%20presentation.pdf?sequence=1. Accessed 9 Aug. 2016.

Gebremariam, Semahar. *Parental Participation in Primary Schools: A Case Study of Former Ethiopian Refugee Parents in Auckland 2015*. Dissertation, University of Auckland. 2015.

La Leche League New Zealand. La Leche League New Zealand Inc, 2016, www.lalecheleague.org.nz/. Accessed 9 Aug. 2016.

Lucas, David. "Africans in New Zealand." *ARAS*, Vol. 29, No. 1&2, 2008), pp. 113-118.

Research on Islam and Muslims in Africa (RIMA). "Somali Proverbs," *Muslims in Africa*, WordPress, 2013, https://muslimsinafrica.wordpress.com/2013/06/26/somali-proverbs/. Accessed 15 Aug. 2016.

Marlow, Jay, and Elliott, Susan. "Global Trends and Refugee Settlement in New Zealand." *Kōtuitui: New Zealand Journal of Social Sciences Online*, vol. 9, no. 2, 2014, pp. 43-49. *Taylor and Francis Online*, doi: 10.1080/1177083X.2014.953186

New Zealand, Ministry of Business, Innovation, and Employment. *Immigration New Zealand*. Government of New Zealand, 2016, www.immigration.govt.nz/new-zealand-visas. Accessed 9 Aug. 2016.

New Zealand, Ministry of Business, Innovation, and Employment. "Refugee Family Support Resident Visa." *Immigration New Zealand*. Immigration New Zealand, 2016, www.immigration.govt.nz/new-zealand-visas/apply-for-a-visa/about-visa/refugee-family-support-resident-visa. Accessed 9 Aug. 2016.

New Zealand, Ministry of Social Development, "Sole Parent Support." *Work and Income*. Government of New Zealand, 2016, www.workandincome.govt.nz/products/a-z-benefits/sole-parent-support.html. Accessed 9 Aug. 2016.

New Zealand, Ministry of Health, "Māori Health Models—Te Whare Tapa Whā." *Ministry of Health*, Government of New Zealand, 2016, www.health.govt.nz/our-work/populations/maori-health/maori-health-models/maori-health-models-te-whare-tapa-wha. Accessed 9 Aug. 2016.

New Zealand, Ministry of Health, "Safe Sleep." *Ministry of Health*, Government of New Zealand, 2016, www.health.govt.nz/your-health/pregnancy-and-kids/first-year/helpful-advice-during-first-year/safe-sleep. Accessed 9 Aug. 2016.

New Zealand, Statistics NZ, "2013 Census Quick Stats about Culture and Identity." *Statistics New Zealand*. Government of New Zealand, 2016, www.stats.govt.nz/Census/2013-census/profile-and-summary-reports/quickstats-culture-identity/middle-east-latin-african.aspx. Accessed 9 Aug. 2016.

Tuwe, Kudakwashe. *The Challenges of Health Promotion within African Communities in New Zealand*. MPhil, Auckland University of Technology, 2012.

Yusuf Issa. *The Somali Diaspora: The integration and Re-establishment of the Community of Somali Refugees in Aotearoa/New Zealand*. MSocP Thesis, Unitec Institute of Technology, Auckland, 2015.

3.

Mother Tongue as the Language of Mothering and Homing Practice in Betty Quan's *Mother Tongue* and Hiromi Goto's *Chorus of Mushrooms*

Survival Strategies and Identity Construction of Migrant and Refugee Mothers

EGLĖ KAČKUTĖ

LANGUAGE OF MOTHERING AND IDENTITY CONSTRUCTION

"I AM MY LANGUAGE. I speak Chinese. Your voices. Your words. You drown me out" (Quan 14)—says the mother to her children in Betty Quan's play *Mother Tongue*. This quote underlines the crucial aspect of mothering in exile: the language of mothering is a site in which cultural and ethnic identity, sense of self, and maternal subjectivity intersect and are negotiated.[1] This chapter explores the language of mothering through two fictional accounts of immigrant mothering, both of which underscore the tension between mothering practices and linguistic difference. It aims to address this tension by suggesting that in the context of migration, the language of mothering can be conceptualized as a mothering and homing practice that functions as a structuring, creative force, which produces and shapes both migrant mothers' and their children's subjectivities. The chapter will consider two pieces of fiction: the play *Mother Tongue* (1996) by Chinese Canadian playwright Betty Quan and the novel *Chorus of Mushrooms* (1994) by Japanese Canadian author Hiromi Goto. Both of these texts feature immigrant and refugee mothers who mother primarily in their own mother tongue rather than English or French, the languages of the host country, Canada.

Both Quan and Goto are award-winning authors. Quan writes for stage, radio, and television as well as for children, whereas Goto is primarily a novelist, who also writes for young adults. They both make extensive use of Chinese and Japanese folklore respectively in their work and explore issues of identity, racism, belonging, cultural difference, and the generation gap. Goto was born in Japan and immigrated to Canada with her family as a young child. She is fully bilingual and uses Japanese to speak to her sisters and bilingual friends (Grant). Quan is a first-generation Chinese Canadian who spoke Cantonese at home as a child, but with assimilation, she lost much of the vocabulary and uses "Chinglish"[2] to communicate with her mother. The play was inspired by Quan's school friend, whose Chinese mother was a widow with no other immediate family members in Vancouver. Quan's play is, therefore, partly based on firsthand observations of the difficult experience of immigrant mothering.[3] Goto's novel draws on her experience of growing up on a mushroom farm with her immigrant parents and the character of the grandmother, *Obāchan*, who is loosely based on her own monolingual Japanese grandmother.

In recent decades, mothering in Asian Canadian and American women's writing has often been read through the paradigm of "woman speech" (Collins 69), which has been interpreted as a source of power and maternal agency in the face of North American "discourses and practices of domination" (Lee-Loy 318). For example, Wendy Ho conceptualizes the "talk story"[4] as a means through which racialized mothers equip their daughters with survival strategies to construct and establish a specific ethnic identity for both mothers and daughters (Ho), whereas the lack of the "talk story," that is "silence as the act of mothering" (Lee-Loy 320), is associated with the inability to do so. I argue that the actual language of mothering in this case the mother tongue of the immigrant mother can also be read as a mothering practice and a productive, positive force as well as a source of maternal and cultural agency.

Both literary texts chosen for the analysis are arguably multilingual. Written in English for the most part, they also borrow from other languages—Cantonese and American Sign Language (ASL) in *Mother Tongue* and Japanese in *Chorus of Mushrooms*—and use them as important structural and artistic devices. *Mother Tongue* features three main characters with different linguistic identities. The mother mainly uses Cantonese and some broken English. Her son Steve speaks ASL, and her daughter Mimi is fluent in all three languages, which forces her into the role of a communication facilitator between her mother and her younger brother. The relatively equal weight in languages used in the play is a metaphor for an immigrant family in which all three members enjoy different linguistic and cultural identities, and reflects the equally shared perspective among the three characters. The printed text of the play is written entirely in English with linguistic difference marked in parenthesis before each phrase as (C) for Cantonese, (E) for English and (ASL) for American Sign Language, thus, indicating that it too is granted the status of a language in the play (Samuels).[5] In contrast, *Chorus of Mushrooms* features phrases in Japanese without the English translation and sometimes even Japanese characters without Romanization. Like the stage productions of *Mother Tongue*, such an artistic device makes readers feel like members of minority language community, who experience varying degrees of confusion in their everyday lives, and makes the reader identify with the immigrant mothers portrayed in the play and the novel in question.[6]

Both immigrant mother characters, who constitute the focus of this discussion, left their homelands out of necessity and struggle to feel at home in Canada, but they are not drawn towards what they left behind either. The mother in *Mother Tongue* left China for political reasons at the age of eighteen and is disenchanted with her new life in Canada: "I left China for Canada. Alone. We were rich. Capitalists. (E) But the war had brought the Japanese, followed by Mao's government.... Over twenty years gone and I sometimes wonder why I ever came at all" (Quan 25). She is a widow of a Chinese man with whom she had two children: an elder daughter, Mimi, an aspiring architect, and a teenaged son, Steve, who lost his hearing because of an ear infection at the age of eleven. She speaks Chinese to her children and feels unable to learn either of their languages.

The *Chorus of Mushrooms* features two mother figures: the grandmother, or *Obāchan*, who is called Naoe; and her own daughter Keiko (Kay in English), the mother of Naoe's granddaughter Murasaki (Muriel in English), who is the main character and narrator in the novel. Interestingly, Naoe, who is also one of the narrators, is a second-time immigrant. She followed her husband to China as a young woman and a new mother but later joined Keiko's family in Nanton, a small town in Alberta, as a divorced woman and a mother dependant on an adult daughter. In China, she was a powerless and voiceless wife of a man who would build bridges used to exploit the country during Japan's occupation of China. She "never learnt to speak Mandarin or Cantonese or any other dialect" (Goto 53), although a Chinese servant boy looked after her young daughter Keiko for her. At the time when the novel is set, she is an independently minded and self-conscious woman, who enjoys a strong sense of identity in terms of gender, ethnicity, nationality, age, and motherhood. Nevertheless, she remains strangely isolated by the "noisy silence" (Goto 56) of her native Japanese, which nobody from her immediate environment seems to understand.

The novel opens with the image of Naoe sitting on an uncomfortable wooden chair in the hallway, obstructing the entrance to the house and speaking Japanese so loudly that she silences all other conversation in the house: "Obāchan, please! I wish you would stop that. Is it too much to ask for some peace and quiet?" (Goto 16) – implores her daughter Keiko. Keiko, who insists on being called Kay, came to Canada deliberately and set up a mushroom farm with her Japanese-born husband Shinji. She would tenaciously not speak a word of Japanese, and it is unclear whether she has made a conscious and wilful choice, or like her husband, who following their joint decision to "put Japan behind us and fit more smoothly with the crowd" (Goto 211), suffers from an inability to do so. Keiko is not granted a narrative voice in the book and is only heard through direct speech in dialogue with either her mother Naoe or her daughter Murasaki, which gives her an authentic and autonomous voice and perspective that the reader is discouraged to identify with. This suggests Keiko's independence and a distance from Naoe and Murasaki, but at the same time implies her lack of control over her own identity. Indeed, when Naoe runs away without an explanation and disappears, Keiko falls into a debilitating depression, takes to her bed, and becomes dependent on her daughter, who nurses her back to physical and emotional health. Anne-Marie Lee-Loy reads Keiko's silence vis-à-vis her daughter as an act of mothering that ensures the daughter's survival by preventing her from standing out in the culture that she lives, but concludes that this mothering strategy fails to provide the daughter with an authentic sense of ethnic identity (319). Consequently, Keiko's identity comes across as complex and multiple. Her silence in her native Japanese seems to be both an expression of a lack of identity and a source of agency. In a newspaper article, "The Multicultural Voices of Alberta," featured in the novel she highlights her deliberate decision to move to Canada and to adopt the host culture as her own. Keiko runs a successful business, creates jobs, and actually supports her mother Naoe on the road trip that she embarks on after leaving her daughter's house. Naoe uses Keiko's credit card, which she steels on her departure to pay for her meals in Asian restaurants and the hotel bills. The credit card receipts that Keiko regularly receives and pays let her know that her mother is alive and, as she remarks to Murasaki, eats well (Goto 204). Such an impersonal, an estranged, and a silent form of daughterly care is an interesting metaphor for mother-daughter relationships in migration, which occur across an insurmountable cultural distance. As conventional expressions of love between a mother and adult daughter—such as conversations, meals, shared household activities, common interests, or hobbies—are inaccessible to Naoe and Keiko due to their enormous cultural and linguistic differences, Keiko resorts to following her mother's news through reading the credit card receipts, which contain information on her mother's whereabouts and diet. Financing her trip is also Keiko's only way of looking after her old mother: she can provide her with only comfortable accommodation, a clean bed, and regular meals.

LANGUAGE OF MOTHERING AS MOTHERING AND HOMING PRACTICE

Lee-Loy interprets Naoe's refusal to speak anything but Japanese as her bid "to protect and fortify Muriel's ethnic identity, and in doing so, to provide Muriel with the confidence needed to define and claim space for herself as a Japanese Canadian" (321). I take this idea further and demonstrate that the mother tongue as the language of mothering in diaspora can function as a productive mothering and homing practice, which helps immigrant mothers create a lasting bond with their children, establish both their and their children's identities as positively different, and provide both immigrant mothers and their children with a sense of ethnic, cultural, and maternal identity.

My theoretical framework combines feminist migration theories and theories of maternal subjectivity. Migration theorist Irene Gedalof claims that migrant mothers often negotiate and create a sense of belonging in their host country through their subject position as mothers, especially their ability to adapt familiar mothering practices to new cultural and physical contexts. She describes migrant mothers' homing practices as follows: "the embodied work of mothering, such as childbirth and childcare, and the work of reproducing cultures and structures of belonging, such as the passing on of culturally specific histories and traditions regarding food, dress, family and other inter-personal relationships" (Gedalof 82). She notes that in migration theory such homing practices have traditionally been "conceptualized in the history of Western thought as being linked to sameness, being, 'mere' repetition" (82). Conversely, she argues that such homing practices are dynamic, transformative, and productive, which is to say they help construct new identity. Her point of contention is that the reproductive sphere in the context of migration is far from being repetitive: immigrant mothers do not simply reproduce the identity they left behind. On the contrary, she believes that mothering in migration is a site of intense negotiation of difference, which consists of a constant reformulation of identity. Therefore, Gedalof sees embodied mothering practices—such as dressing, styling one's and one's children's hair, furnishing and adorning one's house, or cooking—as performative manifestations of cultural identity that are gradually reshaped and given a new meaning by repetitively adapting those practices to a foreign environment, each time modifying them further. Drawing on feminist interpretations of the domestic sphere, Gedalof advances the notion of "repetition that undoes, or that recollects forwards" (Gedalof 96). "Repetition that undoes" suggests performing habitual daily acts in a new nonhabitual environment, with different tools and modified devices, whereas "remembering forwards" entails training children to perform certain elements of immigrant mothers' birth culture so that they can be practised as their own. As Gedalof remarks: "It is marking time through the 'same' family and cultural rituals taking place in a different context that requires endless subtle re-inventions and adaptations to a different range of possible private and public spaces, appropriate dress and adornment, food and drink, etc." (96). Such mothering practices create identities that are familiar but also new and original. They are transformative and innovative because they take place in an unnatural environment. I suggest that the idea of a repetitive mothering practice that "undoes" and "remembers forward" can be extended to thinking about the language of mothering and, more specifically, the native languages of the immigrant mothers featured in the chosen texts. Like other culturally specific mothering practices, such as cooking or dressing, language also requires "endless subtle re-inventions and adaptations" and, as such, can be considered to be an embodied mothering practice that produces and shapes identity.

Philosopher Alison Stone proposes a psychoanalytical theory of maternal subjectivity. She develops a useful concept of maternal space as relational and characterized by a dynamic connectedness as well as distinctiveness of the mother and child. Stone describes it as follows: "A mobile, temporal space, it takes concrete embodied shape over time as the mother and child's patterns of coming and going, thus, intrinsically embodying the significance of their particular modes of being-together" (Stone 76).

The maternal space is largely based on Julia Kristeva's notion of the "semiotic *chora*," which is a womblike mother-child corporeal space defined by prelinguistic production of meaning and socialization that initiates the child into the world of codes and denotations (Kristeva 22-30). Despite it being relational, the space is called maternal, as it is dominated and regulated by the mother. Stone observes: "the mother figures twice over within the *chora*: once as the emerging other with whom the child is entwined, second as the overall corporeal context of their entwinement" (Stone 65). Being herself a subject in the process of becoming and the background of her own and her child's becoming, the mother provides the stability necessary for the child's development, symbolized by her nurturing body, and creates conditions for the change necessary for her own and her child's identity formation.

Significantly, Stone situates the nurturing and structuring *chora* outside of the mother's body, between the mother and child, which makes it not just the mother's zone but a shared one.[7] This way, the maternal space that is dominated and regulated by the mother is no longer suffocated by maternal authority and, as a result, does not necessitate the child's leaving it completely. Maternal space is corporeal, but it also performs a social function and is situated between the mother and child. As such, it displays nurturing and fostering qualities without the mother's uninterrupted presence in it and can serve as a mother's substitute or extension of sorts. Stone writes: "The child comes to accept the mother's difference insofar as potential space establishes a field of secure and ongoing connection with the mother" (71). Thus, the maternal space, the uninterrupted connectedness to the mother, continues to provide security, nurturance, and structure, even if the actual mother temporarily extracts herself from the physical proximity to the baby. This structure also suggests that it is not only the child that receives the nurturing necessary for growth and development, but the mother receives it, too, as "containing, supporting, nurturing is then received by the mother as much as given by her" (Stone 76).

This theory can be productively applied to immigrant mothering, as an immigrant mother raises her children in a cultural and linguistic context that she herself does not easily navigate; the mother, therefore, needs to be "mothered" or supported in some way by her own children, who quickly develop a higher degree of belonging in the host culture because of schooling and socialization. Furthermore, the mother tongue of the immigrant mother and her language of mothering can be conceived as the maternal space: the overall context of the mother-child connectedness, in which both mother and child function as culturally different to the point of being alien. Stone suggests that the principal aspect of the maternal that accompanies human beings throughout their life is language. "Our speaking lives," Stone claims, "are organised by fantasy patterns and relational structures first laid down in childhood" (79). If linguistic maternal presence has such a lasting impact on an individual life, then the language of mothering also shapes that individual in many important ways and provides the mother with the possibility of an enduring and a meaningful relationship with her offspring, even if her children develop a linguistically and culturally different identity over the years.

MOTHER TONGUE AND MATERNAL AGENCY

The mother in *Mother Tongue* and the grandmother in *The Chorus of Mushrooms* insist on speaking only their own mother tongue to their children and in the case of *Obāchan*, to the granddaughter as well. For *Obāchan*, who can but will not speak English, it is, firstly, an act of defiance vis-à-vis her daughter Keiko and, secondly, as Lee-Loy suggests, an act of mothering in relation to her granddaughter Murasaki. Naoe believes that Keiko "has forsaken identity. Forsaken!" (Goto 24) and has failed to teach her daughter Murasaki Japanese. Nevertheless, Naoe says, "She calls me Obāchan and smiles… she can read the lines on my brow, the creases beside my mouth" (Goto 26), which suggests a deep connection between the grandmother and granddaughter.

The mother's initial attachment to her native Cantonese in *Mother Tongue* is a reaction to the threat of losing her identity in the process of migration; it is a mechanism of self-preservation. She says: "I am my language. I speak Chinese. Your voices. Your words. You drown me out" (Quan 14). It is as if the foreign languages her children speak to her have the power to obliterate her own existence.

Both Naoe and the mother feel physically close to their children but are unable to connect on a symbolic, deeper level, their linguistic difference being responsible for their alienation. Naoe says that Keiko is

> A child from my heart, a child from my body, but not from my mouth. The language she forms on her tongue is there for the wrong reasons. You cannot move to a foreign land and call that place home because you parrot the words around you. Find home inside yourself first, I say. Let your home words grow out from the inside, not the outside in. *Che!* (Goto 56)

"Home," here, is an essentialist concept, as it is contained inside of one's body; it is also inseparable from the native language, which, too, belongs in the realm of the body. Home can and should be found or identified inside the psycho-physical space in order to be further developed into a sustained cultural identity of which language is an integral part. Home has to be grown, as it is created through daily, embodied practices because the "inside" here refers to the maternal body, which has the capacity to grow, nurture, and birth an autonomous being out of the familiar inside. For Naoe, home is not a ready-made edifice one can move into and appropriate by mimicking the identity markers of the local population. It is, rather, a new identity that can and should be gradually and patiently constructed through familiar practices, such as performing native cultural rituals, cooking and eating familiar foods and using the native rather than adoptive language whilst progressively integrating aspects of the adopted culture, including learning the language of the host country. For example, Naoe picks up English just by listening to it for twenty years. Creating this sort of home is a productive mothering practice that has the power to offer both mother and grandmother as well as daughter and granddaughter a sense of identity, which would be anchored in their embodied relationship with the maternal culture, in this case Japanese. This mothering practice also permits an embodied relationship with the culture they both live in, as that grows on them imperceptibly from the outside.

Similarly, the mother in *Mother Tongue*, despite having mothered two children in Canada, deplores her loneliness in the country and the disconnection that she suffers from her children:

> My husband dead and me alone. None of my own family to comfort me. No. There are my children. But I often feel as if I bore strangers whose souls have been stolen by invisible spirits. I wonder, when I am dead, if my children will remember to honour me on *Chingming*. Will they follow tradition? (Quan 25)

Despite their physical similarity to their mother, the children lack something essential (she calls it souls) that would make them recognizable to her. Her children cannot reproduce the Chinese cultural rituals or speak Chinese and to her these are the main markers of her identity that make her who she is.

In both texts, the characters' fidelity to their respective native languages is reminiscent of Gedalof's theory of homing practices in migration, as it is tightly knit with the repetitive work of reproducing cultures and relational structures by passing on culturally specific stories, cooking traditions, dressing habits, behavioural and relational conventions. The mother in *Mother Tongue* is, for example, concerned with teaching her daughter to perform the ritual of burning spirit money and making offerings of oranges to the spirits on the occasion of the traditional Chinese festival of *Chingming*, the tomb-sweeping day associated with Chinese ancestral veneration. She also tells her children the popular Chinese mythical tale of *jingwei,* a metaphorical story of migration and identity transformation. Furthermore, the family is portrayed in the play as having traditional Chinese food for dinner. The *Chorus of Mushrooms*, similarly, is also full of traditional tales that Murasaki inherits from *Obāchan*, but she readjusts them to suit her own purposes of identity construction. Naoe, Keiko, and Murasaki all engage in the traditionally Japanese cultural practice of ear cleaning, which is the ultimate expression of intimacy in Japanese culture and becomes a metaphor for otherwise incommunicable mother-daughter affection and love in migration. Japanese food plays a particularly significant role in the *Chorus of Mushrooms* as Keiko, who, according to Naoe, "has forsaken" her identity by "convert[ing] from rice and *daikon* to wieners and beans" (Goto 24). In other words, she has adopted Canadian culinary culture, whereas Naoe, who would not eat at the family dinner table, sticks to dried salted squid and rice crisps. Most significantly, food in the novel is semantically linked with language, the native language of origin, which is imagined as a nourishing source of sustenance ensuring the survival of identity in the process of migration. As Naoe's granddaughter, Murasaki, explains: "I was always hungry for words, even when I was very little. Dad, the man without opinion, and Mom hiding behind an adopted language.... Obāchan took another route, something more harmonious. Showed me that words take form and live and breathe among us. Language is a living beast" (Goto 104). Keiko's daughter, Murasaki, is shown here unable to become an independent person because she was raised with her mother's adopted cuisine and language. She needs her grandmother's constant and unintelligible, but vitally charged flow of Japanese coming from the "inside," from the productive maternal body and thus itself alive and nourishing as well as nurturing. *Obāchan*'s native language in this passage, and indeed in the entire novel, is an important source of life and agency. After Naoe's departure, Murasaki nurses her mother back to health by feeding her Japanese food of the same name as their family name, *Tonkatsu*. Towards the end of the novel, Keiko, who refuses to understand or speak Japanese, says: "At least she's eating well, *Mattaku*! But I still hope you can do better than one postcard!" (Goto 204).[8] All of this goes to show that the mother's native language, along with other modes of "reproducing cultures and structures of belonging" (Gedalof 82), is an important parameter that helps to sustain the mother's identity and to structure the children's identity, at least to a degree.

According to Gedalof's theory, repetitive mothering practices set around food, cultural rituals, and, as I argue, language is a dynamic process that "requires endless subtle re-inventions and adaptations" (Gedalof 96). For Gedalof, this is the repetition that recollects forward and births something that is both new and familiar. Thus, the embodied and repetitive homing practices that the mother engages with in the *Mother Tongue*, including the repetitive use of Cantonese, can be seen as producing identities— her own and her children's—that are familiarly Chinese but Canadian enough to be new and autonomous. In one of the scenes, the mother attracts the daughter's attention to her ritualistic activity to remind her of its significance and symbolism:

> MOTHER: (C) The incense is very fragrant, isn't it?
> MIMI: Moon festival?
> MOTHER: *Chingming*. (C) Have you forgotten already?
> MIMI: No, I remember. I just get all of them confused, that's all. (Quan 30)

The short exchange and the two different languages used in the dialogue—Cantonese by the mother and English by the daughter—

demonstrate that Mimi is already initiated into Chinese culture enough to recognize what the mother is doing and clearly fluent enough in Chinese to understand what is being said.[9] In another scene featuring a trilingual conversation between three family members, language is also represented as a dynamic element that is transformed and adjusted according to the speakers' needs, as they participate in the creation of a new but familiar identity that "remembers forwards."

> MIMI: Mother, remember when you would tell us stories?
> MOTHER: (C) I remember.
> MIMI: We were young.
> MOTHER: (*E then repeat in C.*) Before all the trouble.
> (*STEVE's inner voice is not heard by the others.*)
> STEVE: I remember your voice, Mother. This is the sign for Mother.
> (*MIMI looks at STEVE and sees the meaning of his signing.*)
> (*He signs as he speaks it.*) ....
> MOTHER: (C) What? What? I don't understand. Mimi? ....
> MIMI: Steve says the same thing: tell us a story. Like you used to.
> MOTHER: (C) I know a good one. A favourite. (E) My father used to tell it to me when I was a little girl. You'll remember this one, Mimi.... (C) a long time ago—
> MIMI: (ASL) Long-time-ago.
> MOTHER: (C) What does that mean?
> MIMI: A long time ago.
> STEVE: (ASL) Long-time-ago. Story. Yes. Understand.
> (*MOTHER begins the motion of the hand sign, but stops and stares ahead.*) (Quan 19-20)

Mimi addresses her Chinese-speaking mother in her own native language, English. The mother replies in Cantonese, which suggests a degree of the mother's linguistic hybridity. She understands what the daughter said but choses to answer in her own language, which emphasizes her respect for her daughter's linguistic identity but also highlights her own difference. Mimi continues to speak English, which signals her linguistic competence in Cantonese as well as in English. The mother replies in both English and Cantonese, repeating the same phrase twice, which suggests that both mother and daughter share some degree of communicational linguistic competence while both enjoy different linguistic and cultural identities. In other words, both mother and daughter experience some cultural, linguistic, and emotional connectedness but recognize each other's otherness and alterity at the same time.

The Chinese story that the mother was raised with and is now telling her own children in a mix of Chinese and English is a form of remembering forward. It is a story of a little girl who turns into a bird as a result of drowning in the sea, which is a metaphor for identity transformation through migration and forever tries to fill the sea with stones and sticks, which is a metaphor for trying to bridge the cultural gap between pre- and postmigration identity. As such, the story provides the children with the knowledge of their own cultural provenance, but through the pertinence of its message to their own and their mother's lives, it also affords them with the sustenance and cultural capital needed to construct a new identity of a second-generation Chinese person. When the third character, Steve joins the conversation, he immediately evokes the corporeal experience of his mother's voice. The mother's language is imprinted in his body as a memory trace, which he can now use to reconnect with her through ASL, a language foreign to her that can be made familiar through their embodied linguistic bond. Interestingly, in this scene, the mother makes a feeble and almost automatic attempt at repeating the hand sign made by her son, but she stops as if she is short of physical or mental strength. However, at the end of the play, the mother clearly decides to attempt to enter into a corporeal linguistic relationship with Steve: "Her hand holds out the orange.... (MOTHER reaches out again, this time using her other hand to force STEVE to face her)" (Quan 46). By doing so, she engages "in a process of seeing-listening," which defines communication with a deaf mute (Samuels 20).

Such a mother-child relationship based on an embodied linguistic association between the mother and child recalls Stone's theory of maternal subjectivity and the nurturing relational maternal space, which "suggests a mother who is not the mere background to her child's speech and imaginings but who actively co-speaks and co-imagines with her child and does so from their bodily related-ness" (Stone 68). Seen through this lens, the trilingual conversation and the mother's repetition of the same phrases in two languages seems to be an expression of such a space in which both mother and her children participate in mutual negotiations of their linguis-tic and cultural identities. They engage in endless repetitions and innovations, as Gedalof would have it, in order to develop their respective identities that would be shared to a degree and would be respectful of each other's linguistic and cultural difference.

Embodied linguistic mother-child relations and the maternal space as theorized by Stone are also explored in *Chorus of Mushrooms*. Naoe's granddaughter Murasaki grows up speaking English, as such was her parents' design. However, thanks to Naoe's bid to speak exclusively Japanese, Murasaki learns to speak it as a young adult: "Obāchan away when my words are born so I'm responsi-ble for the things I utter" (Goto 104). When *Obāchan* disappears and Keiko falls into emotional and physical disarray, Murasaki is the only one responsible for sustaining her own and her mother's lives. She effectively mothers her own mother with the telepathic help from *Obāchan*, with whom she has mental conversations in Japanese and gets useful advice as to how to go about looking after her ill mother. The advice includes feeding her Japanese food and talking to her in English and when she is well enough, asking her to clean Murasaki's ears, a symbolic act of giving Keiko a possibility to mother her own daughter with a meaningful embodied cultural practice, which brings out the long-forgotten mother tongue in her. Murasaki's learning to speak Japanese coincides with *Obāchan's* departure. Thus, Naoe's connectedness with her own daughter and granddaughter as well as the nurturing and structuring quality of the Japanese, which continues to provide sustenance even in her absence, can be read as maternal space—the space in which the mother receives the nurturing as much as she provides it (Stone 76).

In conclusion, mothering with and through linguistic difference is an enormous challenge for all immigrant and refugee mothers who have left their homelands and cultures out of necessity and have often arrived in culturally and linguistically unrecognizable environments. Exercising their native languages with their chil-dren as well as engaging with culturally familiar practices in their mothering is not only a survival strategy safeguarding their sense of identity, but also a necessary structuring and nurturing force that produces their new migrant identities, which they develop together with their children. Therefore, mothering in the mother's native tongue, as opposed to the language of the host country, should be read not as maternal silence and disengagement but rather as the source of maternal agency and power. By building a lasting embodied linguistic relationship with her children, the mother opens up to being "mothered" into the host language and culture by her children without suffering a devastating sense of self loss.

NOTES

[1] Cirila P. Limpanong makes a similar point about the intersection of gender and cultural mothering roles that are experienced as proper ways of being in her chapter in this volume.

[2] The nickname for the fusion of English and Chinese.

[3] Personal email correspondence with Betty Quan between May and June 2015.

[4] "Talk story is a Hawaiian expression describing casual everyday storytelling particularly concerned with the sharing of life stories. Subsequent to Maxine Hong Kingston's use of the term in *The Woman Warrior* talk story has become a popular means of describing mother/daughter storytelling in Asian American literature" (Lee-Loy 330).

[5] Stage productions of the play have been made problematic by its multilingual character, and the play has even been judged "unperformable except to a uniquely trilingual audience" (Samuels 19). Conversely, Samuels argues that the play opens up "new hybrid realms of performance and communication" (30).

[6] Goto writes:

> I also integrate Japanese words for my Japanese Canadian characters who are bilingual.... Much of it remains untranslated in my texts because, although books often make transparent the translation for narrative purposes, language in everyday life doesn't work that way. We don't live with universal translators. If you don't know the word, meaning is not always accessible. What then? You ask someone or

you look it up. Or you don't bother and you never know. I'm not interested in writing novels that ultimately narrow down into a "We're actually all alike" kind of mentality. Very real differences exist across all spectrums of human interaction. I'm interested in making language "real," not smoothing over the difficult terrain. (qtd. in Grant)

[7]Stone uses Donald W. Winnicott's concept of potential space, which "mediates between a mother and child who are becoming differentiated" to introduce that move (Stone 69).

[8]The Japanese word *mattaku* means "honestly."

[9]The fact that the elder daughter Mimi speaks Chinese and Steve does not, as well as the fact that only Mimi is invited to partake in the Chinese traditions, signals an interruption in the process of the dynamic and embodied transmission of the mother's native language and culture to the children. There is evidence in the text to suggest that both pre- and post-migration trauma, ensuing from the circumstances of the mother's departure from China and the early loss of her husband, is directly responsible for this interruption.

WORKS CITED

Collins, Patricia Hill. "Shifting the Centre: Race, Class, and Feminist Theorizing about Motherhood." *Representations of Motherhood*, edited by Donna Bassin et al., New Yale University Press, 1994, pp. 56-74.

Gedalof, Irene. "Birth, Belonging and Migrant Mothers: Narratives of Reproduction in Feminist Migration Studies." *Feminist Review*, vol. 93, no. 1, 2009, pp. 81-100.

Goto, Hiromi. *Chorus of Mushrooms.* 1994, NeWest Press, 2014.

Grant, Gavin J. "Interview with Hiromi Goto." *Indie Bound*, American Booksellers Association, 2015, www.indiebound.org/author-interviews/gotohiromi. Accessed 9 Jan. 2015.

Ho, Wendy. *In Her Mother's House: The Politics of Asian American Mother-Daughter Writing.* AltaMira Press, 1999.

Kristeva, Julia. *Revolution in Poetic Language.* Columbia University Press, 1984.

Lee-Loy, Anne-Marie. "Asian American Mothering in the Absence of Talk Story: *Obasan* and *Chorus of Mushrooms*." *Textual Moth-*

ers. *Maternal Texts*, edited by Elizabeth Podnieks and Andrea O'Reilly, Wilfrid Laurier University Press, 2010, pp. 317-331.

Quan, Betty. *Mother Tongue*. Scirocco Drama, 1996.

Quan, Betty. "Email Correspondence." Received by Eglė Kačkutė, May-June 2015.

Samuels, Ellen. "'Speaking as a Deaf Person Would': Translating Unperformability in Betty Quan's Mother Tongue." *Amerasia Journal*, vol. 39, no.1, 2013, pp. 19-32.

Stone, Alison. *Feminism, Psychoanalysis, and Maternal Subjectivity.* Routledge, 2012.

4.
Perinatal Care for Immigrants in the Netherlands

A Personal Account

THEANO LIANIDOU

TRANSNATIONAL WOMEN WHO MIGRATE, temporarily or permanently, from one country to another are at risk of suboptimal perinatal health outcomes in comparison to native women. Reports in Europe have indicated different health outcomes between immigrant and native mothers, both for mothers and babies (Machado et al.). As an example, Essén et al. have demonstrated that in Sweden the rate of perinatal deaths among East African women was significantly higher than that among native Swedish women. Furthermore, in Belgium, a cohort study from 2010 of all babies born between 1998 and 2006 whose mothers were living in Brussels indicated inequalities in perinatal mortality in groups of immigrants as compared to Belgians (Racape et al.). Studies in the Netherlands point in the same direction for non-Western ethnic groups.

This chapter focuses on the Netherlands, where I gave birth to my son in April 2002. My narrative, as a Mediterranean transnational woman receiving perinatal care in Amsterdam, constitutes a subjective personal account, and gives insight into causes for disparities in perinatal health outcomes between immigrants and the native population in the Netherlands.

Overall, the maternal mortality,[1] maternal morbidity, and neonatal mortality ratios among transnational women in the Netherlands are significantly higher than those of the native population (Van Roosmalen et al.; Zwart et al., "Ethnic"; Zwart et al., "Severe"; Ravelli et al.; Van Enk et al.). Transnational women of non-Western origin—mainly from Turkey, Morocco, Surinam, and Indonesia—constitute 16 percent of the total pregnant women in the Netherlands (Ravelli et al.).

A FEW WORDS ABOUT THE DUTCH HEALTHCARE SYSTEM

Prenatal and perinatal care in the Netherlands is provided primarily by midwives. If the midwife judges that there is a medical need, she refers her patient to a specialist (Troe et al.). In general, because the Dutch gatekeeper system gives the general practitioner (GP) or the midwife a central place in healthcare, there is very little flexibility for the patient (Lamkaddem et al.).

In the case of an expectant mother, flexibility could mean being able to choose between home and hospital birth and having that choice respected. In general, home versus hospital birth is highly controversial. For example, on the one hand, reports tend to agree that home birth results in fewer medical interventions, including episiotomy, epidural analgesia, electronic fetal heart monitoring, operative vaginal delivery, and Caesarean delivery (Wax et al.). On the other hand, Joseph Wax and colleagues, after conducting a meta-analysis of peer-reviewed publications from developed Western countries in 2010, concluded that "less medical intervention during planned home birth is associated with a tripling of the neonatal mortality rate" (243.e1).

Based on her interviews of middle-class white women who had opted for private prenatal or perinatal care, Robbie Davis-Floyd has challenged the "technocratic model" of the U.S., which because of unnecessary intervention and medicalization, may compromise the birth experience of the woman. At the same time, in her conclusion to Birth as a Rite of Passage, she states that "a woman's ultimate perception of her birth experience as positive or negative, empowering or victimizing, all depend to the degree to which her experience confirms or undermines the belief system in which she enters the hospital" (306).

In the Netherlands, the home birth rate is 33 percent (McIntyre), in contrast to 0.9 percent in Australia (McIntyre) and 0.6 percent in the U.S (Committee on Obstetric Practice), which suggests that the Dutch are more comfortable with home birth than populations of other countries. However, although home birth may be part of the Dutch belief system, it may be in contradiction to the values and beliefs of transnational women residing in the Netherlands. Nevertheless, because of the control over the situation that the midwife has, a migrant woman opposing home birth can deliver in a hospital only if the midwife arrives at the woman's home in time and decides to refer the woman to a hospital, also in time. If the midwife does not recognize and respect the cultural differences, according to Davis-Floyd, the birthing experience may be a negative one for the transnational woman.

Home versus hospital birth is not the only potential tension between the values of transnational mothers and those of the host country's healthcare system. Sara Bonfanti, in her chapter in this volume, provides other examples of conflict between the values of Indian migrant mothers and those of the Italian medical system.

COMPARISON OF PERINATAL OUTCOMES BETWEEN IMMIGRANT AND NATIVE MOTHERS

A number of studies[2] confirm a significant discrepancy in perinatal health outcomes in the Netherlands between native Dutch and non-Western immigrant mothers, with variances reported in maternal mortality, maternal morbidity, and neonatal mortality. Reports indicate that the risk of maternal mortality for immigrants is three times greater than for native Dutch women (Zwart et al., "Ethnic"). According to the LEMMoN Study, the risk of severe maternal morbidity among non-Western immigrant women is 1.3 fold that of the native Dutch or others of Western origin (Zwart et al., "Severe"). In addition, the risk of fetal and neonatal mortality in the Netherlands is significantly higher among Turkish, Moroccan, and other non-Western populations, as compared to the native Dutch population (Ravelli et al.). Infant mortality is 6.4 per thousand live-born children among non-Western immigrants, compared to 4.9 for the native Dutch and for other people of Western origin (Statistics Netherlands, Department of the Ministry of Economic Affairs). In the post-neonatal period, Turkish and Moroccan infants have more than a twofold risk of dying compared to the native population (Troe et al.).

It should be noted that although different non-Western ethnic groups do not have the same health outcomes, they all fare worse than the native population. Discrepancies between minority ethnic groups and the native population exist also when risk factors associated with specific ethnic minorities are taken into account. For example, Ravelli et al. reported that stillbirth and early neonatal mortality rates varied among Turkish, Moroccan, African, and South Asian infants; however, in all these cases, these rates were higher when compared to those reported for the Dutch. Pre-existent medical conditions, maternal age, and other risk factors could not explain the differences. In fact, the researchers concluded that "the ethnic differences in mortality became even more visible in women without these risk factors" (Ravelli et al. 701).

SUBSTANDARD CARE

Substandard healthcare is one of the main factors responsible for perinatal death or morbidity. Overall, substandard care is primarily associated with, on the side of healthcare providers, delayed referral, delayed diagnosis, and delayed therapy, and with, on the side of the patient, refusal to act on advice (Schutte et al., "Rise").

Substandard care is found to be present more frequently in the case of immigrants. Research on maternal mortality in the Netherlands has indicated that substandard healthcare was present in 62 percent of the native deaths and in 76 percent of immigrant deaths (Van Roosmale et al.). Furthermore, a study by Schutte et al. found that the percentages of delay in diagnosis and in no or inadequate therapy were significantly higher for immigrants than for Dutch natives (Schutte et al. "Rise"). In addition, a study on indirect maternal mortality (i.e., maternal death due to pre-existing disease or disease that developed during pregnancy, not due to direct obstetric causes but aggravated by the pregnancy) showed similar trends: substandard care was found to be present in 53 percent of the non-native maternal deaths versus 26 percent in the native Dutch group (Schutte et al., "Indirect").

The discrepancies mentioned above could be understated because underreporting has been identified (Schutte et al., "Rise"; Zwart et al., "Severe"; Zwart et al., "Underreporting"), and there is lack of data for those who do not find their way into the healthcare system (Ingleby). Particularly for undocumented immigrants, the risks of adverse perinatal outcomes and suboptimal healthcare are even greater than those of documented ethnic minorities (De Jonge et al.). Undocumented immigrants have no legal right to healthcare services unless they can pay for them. There are two exceptions: when care is needed to protect public health and when care is medically necessary, although the second exception is not clearly defined (Grit et al.). A 2010 study by researchers at the Radboud University Nijmegen Medical Centre indicated that 69 percent of undocumented female immigrants in the Netherlands reported obstacles in accessing healthcare facilities (Schoevers et al.).

CAUSES OF MORE FREQUENT SUBSTANDARD CARE FOR IMMIGRANTS

According to studies primarily based on data from healthcare providers, often cross-checked with registries, language barriers (Van Roosmalen et al.), the mother's lack of health literacy (Jonkers et al.), the mother's impaired general health (Schutte et al., "Indirect"), single motherhood (Troe et al.) and delayed or irregular prenatal care visits (Ravelli et al.; Posthumus et al.) have all been documented as substandard care factors.

One needs to keep in mind that the causes of substandard healthcare to immigrant mothers are complex and, sometimes, the data are contradicting. For example, low socioeconomic status as a factor explaining the discrepancy in certain studies has been contradicted by further analysis (Van Enk et al.; Ravelli et al.; Jonkers et al.). Studies that indicate discrepancies in health outcomes between native and immigrant mothers, typically based on data from hospitals crossed-checked with registries, do not provide an explanation for such variances. Schutte et al., in an attempt to explain the higher risk of women from Surinam and the Dutch Antilles, state that these women "might be in poorer general health" (Schutte, et al., "Indirect" 766). Van Roosmalen et al., for another example, have speculated that language barriers and social factors could explain increased frequency of substandard care in immigrant deaths, and have urged for more detailed studies.

MOTHERS' LIVED EXPERIENCES

Unlike the studies mentioned above, which are primarily based on data from hospitals and registries, qualitative research provides greater insight on the experiences of immigrant mothers. An example is a study conducted by Marina Jonkers et al., which consisted of in-depth interviews with forty immigrant women who had suffered severe maternal morbidity. In that study, there are reports of healthcare providers underestimating complaints and not providing enough information about the diagnosis and treatment. In one case, a well-educated Japanese expatriate complained to her obstetrician more than once about headaches and unusual weight gain. In addition, she experienced higher than usual blood pressure and fluid retention. She was health literate enough to understand the risks and ask whether a Caesarean section should be planned. The doctor told her that everything was normal and planned a vaginal delivery. At thirty-weeks of gestation, she was hospitalized with preeclampsia, and a hysterectomy was performed at the end of a series of complications, after which she remained in intensive care for three weeks. In another case, a second-generation Moroccan immigrant at thirty-six weeks of gestation had to deliver at home without skilled attendance, despite having phoned the midwife several times because she felt contractions. The midwife interpreted the complaints as Braxton Hicks contractions, uterine contractions that can occur before labour, and visited the mother at home only after the baby was delivered (Jonkers et al).

Interestingly, in the discussion section of the article by Jonkers et al., the poor doctor-patient interaction is primarily explained as caused by the low health literacy of immigrants, who also "talk less and show more agreement with native Dutch GPs than native Dutch women" (Jonkers 151). This explanation contradicts some of the cases Jonkers et al. report, such as the ones mentioned above. Based on the examples reported, it is clear that the behaviour of the Dutch healthcare providers towards immigrant women should also be questioned.

International entities have expressed concerns about ethnic discrimination in the Netherlands, either in regards to perinatal care specifically or to health services in general. For example, the organization Humanity in Action has reported cases of immigrant women feeling that they were not taken seriously by healthcare providers in the Netherlands (Jelia and Kembabazi). The committee for the Convention on the Elimination of all Forms of Discrimination Against Women (CEDAW) Committee has said that "black, Muslim and migrant women in the Netherlands suffered from numerous forms of discrimination," including in the area of health services (CEDAW). In addition, a study by Jeanine Suurmond et al., not specific to perinatal care but healthcare in general, has indicated that immigrants feel excluded from optimal care partly because of prejudice and discrimination from healthcare providers.

MY EXPERIENCE AS A TRANSNATIONAL WOMAN RECEIVING PERINATAL CARE IN THE NETHERLANDS

My personal experience with the Dutch healthcare system adds to the examples summarized in the preceding section. Although Greeks are generally considered Westerners in literature, people from Mediterranean countries have different facial characteristics from those of Northern Europeans and have been considered historically inferior to Northern Europeans (Gans; Cruz-Janzen). In my case, I am a Greek with a typical Mediterranean appearance, dark hair and brown eyes. One could easily think that I am Turkish, the nationality of origin of many immigrants in the Netherlands. Between 2001 and 2004, I was an expatriate in Amsterdam, which is where I gave birth to my son in April 2002.

My pregnancy was uneventful. All prenatal care was provided by a midwives' practice. I had not missed a single visit, when, at some point during my pregnancy, the midwives' practice informed me that I could not see a doctor or visit a hospital without a referral from a midwife. During more than one visit, I expressed a very strong wish to give birth in a hospital and explained that the home-birth option was frightening to me. The midwife assured me that my wish to deliver in a hospital would be respected, and I believed her.

On the due date, rupture of the membranes occurred early in the morning. I called the midwife, who told me to stay home and call her again when I felt pain. In the afternoon, I started worrying about the risk of infection because of the many hours since the rupture of the membranes. In addition, after about ten hours since my first call to the midwife, I stopped feeling the baby. I called the midwife again, voiced my concerns, and she agreed to refer me to a hospital close to my home. At the hospital, I explained my worry for possible infection, but I was told to return home and wait. Pain started in the evening, and I called the midwife twice. She came but refused to allow me to go to the hospital because in her first visit, she could "see that the pain was not strong enough" and in her second visit, the dilation was not at the point at which she would agree to refer me to a hospital. At midnight, seventeen hours after the rupture of the membranes, I called the midwife again. By then, I had acute pain and high fever, a result of a severe infection, and the midwife was finally convinced to call the hospital. My husband, who was with me, was given the address of the hospital, which was not in the area that we were residing. We were asked to take a taxi there, and we did.

At the hospital, I was attended to by a nurse. Although I continued to have fever, I was not given antibiotics to protect the baby from my infection. Other nurses came and at some point, they all seemed to be convinced that the baby could not be delivered without assistance. At around 4:00 a.m., about twenty-one hours after the rupture of the membranes, the nurse decided to call a doctor for an assisted birth— a vacuum extraction. The baby was delivered about an hour later seriously affected by my infection, with an Apgar score of five. He was immediately taken to a separate room for cardiopulmonary resuscitation (CPR). Then, I held him for a few minutes before he was taken to intensive care. The doctor left, and later the nurse left after informing me that a student would perform the stitching, which was badly performed and was later corrected.

I was taken to a room of eight women. They were, I believe, all of Turkish or Moroccan origin, which was surprising in a country where non-Western immigrant pregnant women were only 16 percent of all pregnant women, particularly if one assumes that, similarly to my case, the hospital selection was not based on the area of residence of the mother. Although my newborn son was in intensive care, I was refused any contact with a pediatrician, despite my numerous requests. Within the first forty-eight hours after my son was born, I was informed by the nurses that he needed to be x-rayed, and he was. Nobody explained to me why and in my understanding, there was no value from the x-ray to the diagnosis, which was an infection. However, there was no pediatrician I could talk to about the infant's health, and the nurses were not forthcoming at all with information. Both my husband and I were basically told to "just trust the hospital." I stayed in the hospital for eight days, and my son stayed for ten days.

During a visit from my midwives' practice at home a few weeks after the delivery, I complained to the midwife about the unnecessary risks that my son and I were exposed to because of (1) the delay in admission to the hospital; (2) the omission to administer antibiotics to protect the baby from my infection, which was indicated by my high fever; and (3) the delay of the arrival of an obstetrician, which prolonged the time in distress for the baby. The reply was that many things went wrong, and I could sue the hospital if I wanted to. Of course, as I could not even find my way around the Dutch healthcare system to give birth safely, I did not even attempt to navigate the Dutch judicial system. Instead, I decided to find a pediatrician in Belgium and drive two hours there with the baby for both regular checkups and ad-hoc issues. Because of the inflexible gatekeeper healthcare system in the Netherlands, the only alternative is cross-border care (Brouwer et al.). By contrast, in Belgium, my family had direct and immediate access to a pediatrician, who was referred by Belgian friends. That doctor seemed to care about our son; she listened to our concerns, and she did not hesitate to refer us to other specialized care when needed. However, it should be noted that cross-border care is not accessible to all immigrant women because of the costs associated with it, such as travel and out-of-pocket payments to doctors.

During my stay in Amsterdam, I became aware of similar stories of expatriates who also had difficulties accessing decent healthcare. These are not published cases but my own recollections. A six-month pregnant woman who tried to use the ER was sent home after she was abruptly told that the fetus had died. She was shocked, but the only communication that she received was to call later for an appointment for induction in a few days. In another case, a couple had nobody skilled to attend the birth of their son, despite all the assurances from the midwife that birth would take place in the hospital. Even after the couple made several phone calls, the midwife arrived well after the delivery had taken place at home. In both examples above, the individuals were well-educated expatriates, and, therefore, language barriers, socioeconomic factors, and health illiteracy are not reasonable explanations for the substandard care that they received. In comparison, I never heard any stories about substandard perinatal care received by Dutch women, including by women who had chosen home birth.

MY STORY IN CONTEXT

Compared to the literature, my own situation contradicted all the reasons why immigrants receive substandard perinatal care in the Netherlands, except one: ethnic biases from the side of the healthcare providers. Contrary to findings that suggest poor general health, missed prenatal appointment, low socioeconomic status, single motherhood, low health literacy, and language barriers explain the substandard healthcare that immigrants receive in comparison to the native Dutch, in my case, none of these issues applied. My health overall, including throughout the pregnancy, was good. I had been very diligent about prenatal care. I had sought prenatal care before the twelfth week of my pregnancy and had never missed an appointment with the midwife. In addition, there was no advice that the midwife provided that I did not follow. My socioeconomic status was not low. I was an expatriate with a bachelor's and a master's degree and a career with international companies. Single motherhood did not apply. I was married and living with my husband. In addition, my health literacy was high. I had done enough research and read enough books to know about the risk of infection due to the rupture of the membranes, a risk that my midwife refused to acknowledge even after I raised the issue several times.

Moreover, I did not encounter any language barriers. I was fluent in English and all the healthcare providers I interacted with were fluent in English as well. In fact, most Dutch seemed to be multilingual. During my three-year stay in Amsterdam, I do not recall ever having any issue communicating in English.

As a result of the aforementioned evidence, it is clear that despite my good health, education, health literacy, and ability to community in English, the perinatal care that my son and I received was substandard. First, the midwife refused to acknowledge or respect the fact that I had a different belief system to the Dutch one and as a result, I was not comfortable with home birth. Dismissing my wish for hospital birth was unacceptable given the numerous times I had requested hospital birth during my pregnancy and the reassurances I had received from her that my wish would be respected. Second, the midwife and the nurses at the hospitals ignored my concerns about a possible infection, my pain, and the actual sign of infection (fever). As a result, the health of my son was jeopardized. Furthermore, although I was residing in the centre of Amsterdam, I was sent to a hospital in the far western part of Amsterdam, Slotervaart, and placed in a room with a vastly disproportionate representation of immigrants. This may have been a coincidence, but it may also have been because of my Mediterranean appearance. Moreover, in the course of our hospitalization, the behaviour of the nurses had been harsh and patronizing.[4]

Someone not familiar with the Dutch system could question why I did not act according to my belief system (i.e., go to the hospital even without a referral). This was a possibility that I had explored both with my GP and my midwives' practice, but I was told that no hospital would admit me without a referral from my midwife. There is research indicating that although Turkish and Moroccan people use GP services more than the native Dutch, they use specialized services less than the native population (Stronks et al.). The study suggests that the limited access of ethnic groups to specialized services could be because of language barriers and cultural issues. However, ethnic biases on the part of the GPs, which result in fewer referrals to specialized services for immigrants than for the native Dutch, could also be an explanation.

CONCLUSION

In the absence of any other cause for substandard care in the literature that fits my situation, ethnic biases should be considered a reasonable explanation for the substandard perinatal care that I received. In fact, the general sentiment in the Netherlands between 2001 and 2004, the period that I lived there was characterized by anti-immigrant feelings (Ingleby; Grit et al.).

One of the reasons that ethnic biases are not sufficiently explored in the literature could be that minority research in the Netherlands is characterized by denial of racism and "problematization of ethnic minorities" (Essed and Nimako 297). Perhaps due to the fact that research on ethnic minorities is funded directly or indirectly by the Dutch government, racism research is delegitimized (Essed and Nimako). However, as Lamkaddem et al. point out, any "country with large immigrant populations should take the effects of racial discrimination into account when assessing the equity in access to public services like healthcare" (477).

In order to assess the role that ethnic biases play, studies need to consider data not only from healthcare providers and registries but also from mothers. There is increasing awareness that in assessing healthcare in general, the experience of the patient also needs to be taken into account because the "objective" outcomes are not enough (Van den Berg et al.). Particularly when it comes to peri-natal care received by immigrants, the experience of mothers with the healthcare system should be recorded and assessed without a "blame the victim" mindset.

Finally, as David Ingleby suggests, in order to get multicultural healthcare off the ground, decisive government intervention is imperative.[3] Specifically, in regards to perinatal care, once data, including mothers' perspectives, are assessed objectively and take ethnic biases into consideration, appropriate policies should be developed and implemented aiming to make access to proper perinatal care equitable and to eliminate the discrepancies of health outcomes between immigrant and Dutch mothers in the Netherlands.

NOTES

[1] The overall maternal mortality ratio in the Netherlands in 2002, the year of the personal experience I describe, was higher than that

of other European countries. Specifically, maternal mortality in the Netherlands was 13 deaths per 100,000 live births. This ratio was lower in other European countries, including Germany (8), Belgium (8), Austria (8), Norway (6), Italy (5), and Sweden (5). However, the latest World Bank data indicate a different situation. In 2015, the maternal mortality ratio in the Netherlands was 7 per 100,000 live births, similar to that of other European countries, including Germany (7), Belgium (7), Norway (5), Austria (4), Italy (4), and Sweden (4) ("World Bank Open Data").

[2]This chapter covers only studies available in English. Research available only in Dutch is not covered.

[3]The Dutch government may be taking some action, perhaps taking ethnic biases into consideration, but this information has not been made available to me. My request for information about policies to address the relatively higher mortality and morbidity rates of immigrant mothers to the Ministry of Health, Welfare, and Sport of the Netherlands—through their public website on February 19 and by mail on March 2, 2015—was acknowledged, but I still have not received a response.

[4]Bonfanti, in this volume, discusses the paternalistic and potentially harmful views of medical practitioners on migrant women in Italy.

WORKS CITED

Brouwer, Werner, et al. "Should I stay or should I go? Waiting lists and cross-border care in the Netherlands." *Health Policy*, vol. 63, no. 3, 2002, pp. 289-298.

Committee on Obstetric Practice. "Planned Home Birth." Committee Opinion. 2011 - Reaffirmed 2015.

Cruz-Janzen, Marta I. "Lives on the Crossfire: The Struggle of Multiethnic and Multiracial Latinos for Identity in a Dichotomous and Racialized World." *Race, Gender & Class*, vol. 9, no. 2, 2002, pp. 47-62.

Davis-Floyd, R. E. *Birth as an American Rite of Passage.* University of California Press, 1992.

De Jonge, Ank, et al. "Limited Midwifery Care for Undocumented Women in the Netherlands." *Journal of Psychosomatic Obstetrics & Gynecology*, vol. 32, no. 4, 2011, pp. 182-188.

Essed, Philomena, and Kwame Nimako. "Designs and (Co)Incidents: Cultures of Scholarship and Public Policy on Immigrants/Minorities in the Netherlands." *International Journal of Comparative Sociology*, vol. 47, no. 3-4, 2006, pp. 281-312.

Essén, Birgitta, et al. "Are Some Perinatal Deaths in Immigrant Groups Linked to Sub-Optimal Perinatal Care Services? Perinatal audit of infants to women from Africa's Horn delivered in Sweden 1990-96." *BJOG: An International Journal of Obstetrics and Gynaecology*, vol. 109, no. 6, 2002, pp. 677-682.

Gans, Herbert J. "Race as Class." *American Sociological Association*, vol. 4, no. 4, 2005, pp. 17-21.

Grit, Kor, et al. "Access to Health Care for Undocumented Migrants: A Comparative Policy Analysis of England and the Netherlands." *Journal of Health Politics, Policy and Law*, vol. 37, no. 1, 2012, pp. 37-67.

Ingleby, David. "Getting Multicultural Health Care off the Ground: Britain and The Netherlands Compared." *International Journal of Migration, Health, and Social Care*, vol. 2, no. 3-4, 2006, pp. 4-15.

Jelia, Hosay, and Allana Kembabazi. "Knowledgebase: Maternal Health Care in the Netherlands: A Right for Some." Humanity in Action, Humanity in Action Inc., 17 July 2015, www.humanityinaction.org/knowledgebase/431-maternal-health-care-in-the-netherlands-a-right-for-some. Accessed 10 Aug. 2016.

Jonkers, Marina, et al. "Severe Maternal Morbidity among Immigrant Women in the Netherlands: Patients' Perspectives." *Reproductive Health Matters*, vol. 19, no. 37, 2011, pp. 144-153.

Lamkaddem, Majda, et al. "Perceived Discrimination Outside Health Care Settings and Health Care Utilization of Turkish and Moroccan GP patients in the Netherlands." *European Journal of Public Health*, vol. 22, no. 4, 2012, pp. 473-478.

Machado, M.C., et al. *Maternal and Child Healthcare for Immigrant Populations*. International Organization for Migration (IOM), 2009.

McIntyre, Meredith J. "Safety on Non-medically Led Primary Maternity Care Models: A Critical Review of the International Literature." *Australian Health Review*, vol. 36, no. 2, 2012, pp. 140-147.

Posthumus, Anke G., et al. "The Association of Ethnic Minority Density and Late Entry into Antenatal Care in the Netherlands." *PLoS ONE*, vol. 10, no. 4, 2015, pp. 1-12.

Racape, Judith, et al. "High Perinatal Mortality Rate among Immigrants in Brussels." *European Journal of Public Health*, vol. 20, no. 5, 2010, pp. 36-542.

Ravelli, A.C.J., et al. "Ethnic differences in Stillbirth and Early Neonatal Mortality in the Netherlands." *Journal of Epidemiology and Community Health*, vol. 65, no. 8, 2011, pp. 696-701.

Schoevers, Marianne A., et al. "Health Care Utilisation and Problems in Accessing Health Care of Female Undocumented Immigrants in the Netherlands." *International Journal of Public Health*, vol. 55, no. 5, 2010, pp. 421-428.

Schutte, Joke M., et al. "Indirect Maternal Mortality increases in the Netherlands." *Acta obstetricia et gynecologica Scandinavica*, vol. 89, no. 6, 2010, pp. 762-768.

Schutte, Joke M., et al."Rise in maternal mortality in the Netherlands." *BJOG: An International Journal of Obstetrics and Gynaecology*, vol. 117, no 4, 2010, pp. 399-406.

Netherlands. Statistics Netherlands, Department of the Ministry of Economic Affairs. "Higher Infant Mortality among Immigrants." Statistics Netherlands, Government of Netherlands, 20 Mar. 2002, www.cbs.nl/engb/news/2002/.../eb78e3ef8fe04b-d391544ad4e15eb15b.ashx. Accessed 10 Aug. 2016.

Stronks, K., et al. "Immigrants in the Netherlands: Equal Access for Equal Needs?" *Journal of Epidemiology and Community Health*, vol. 55, no. 10, 2001, pp. 701-707.

Suurmond, Jeanine, et al. "Negative Health Care Experiences of Immigrant Patients: A Qualitative Study." *BMC Health Services Research*, vol. 11, no. 1, 2011, pp. 113-117.

Troe, Ernst-Jan W. M., et al. "Ethnic differences in total and cause-specific infant mortality in the Netherlands." *Paediatric and Perinatal Epidemiology*, vol. 20, no. 3, 2006, pp. 140-147.

United Nations. Convention on the Elimination of all Forms of Discrimination Against Women (CEDAW). "Consideration of Reports Submitted by State Parties under Article 18 of the Convention: Fifth Periodic Report of the Netherlands." Office of the United Nations High Commissioner for Human Rights,

United Nations, 3 Mar. 2010, http://www2.ohchr.org/english/bodies/cedaw/docs/CEDAW.C.SR.916.pdf. Accessed 10 Aug. 2016.

Van den Berg, Michael J., et al. "The Dutch Health Care Performance Report: Seven Years of Health Care Performance Assessment in the Netherlands." *Health research policy and systems / BioMed Central*, vol. 12, no. 1, 2014, pp. 1-7.

Van Enk, Adam, et al. "Perinatal Death in Ethnic Minorities in the Netherlands." *Journal of Epidemiology and Community Health*, vol. 111, no. 8, 1998, pp. 735-739.

Van Roosmalen, Jos, et al. "Substandard Care in Immigrant Versus Indigenous Maternal Deaths in The Netherlands." *BJOG: An International Journal of Obstetrics and Gynaecology*, vol. 109, no. 2, 2002, pp. 212-213.

Wax, Joseph R., et al. "Maternal and Newborn Outcomes in Planned Home Birth Vs Planned Hospital Births: A Metaanalysis." *American Journal of Obstetrics and Gynecology*, vol. 203, no. 3, 2010, pp. 243.e1-243.e8.

World Bank. "World Bank Open Data." The World Bank, 2015, data.worldbank.org/. Accessed 10 Aug. 2016.

Zwart, Joost J., et al. "Ethnic Disparity in Severe Acute Maternal Morbidity: A Nationwide Cohort Study in the Netherlands." *European Journal of Public Health*, vol. 21, no. 2, 2011, pp. 229-234.

Zwart, Joost J., et al. "Severe Maternal Morbidity during Pregnancy, Delivery and Puerperium in the Netherlands: A Nationwide Population Based Study of 371,000 Pregnancies." *BJOG: An International Journal of Obstetrics and Gynaecology*, vol. 115, no. 7, 2008, pp. 842-850.

Zwart Joost J., et al. "Underreporting of Major Obstetric Haemorrhage in the Netherlands." *Transfusion Medicine*, vol. 20, no. 2, 2010, pp. 118-122.

5.
Motherhood and Unemployment

Immigrant Women's Experiences in Toronto

LESLIE NICHOLS

WHEN WORKERS LOSE THEIR JOBS in Canada, they expect to be able to access unemployed workers' support because they have paid into the federal employment insurance (EI) program while employed. Many workers, however, have not been able to access these benefits since the policy changed from unemployment insurance (UI) to EI in 1996. This change produced stricter rules and regulations, notably in relation to the number of hours required to obtain support (MacDonald, "Income Security for Women"; "Women and EI in Canada"). This policy change, however, does not affect all workers in Canada to the same degree. Those most affected by the changes are workers from lower socioeconomic levels—notably women, because of their traditional role as mothers (McGregor; Nichols, "Analyzing Policy Frames," "Women in Neoliberal Canada"; Silver et al., "Job Restructuring and Worker Displacement," "The Excluded, the Vulnerable, and the Reintegrated"). The demands of motherhood make it more complicated for women to access the labour market and retain attachment to it (Townson and Hayes).

The effects of increasingly underfunded and deregulated childcare programs in Canada have yet to be fully assessed, but it is likely that such programs will increase the inequalities already found in the labour market (Mikkonen and Raphael). One potential effect is that women will be rendered permanent losers in the workforce because of their conventional connection to childrearing. As Krahn et al. argue, having a past employment record of marginal jobs can create barriers to accessing the better jobs with benefits because of the common belief that workers with such records have unstable work habits. These barriers imply that to address the needs of their growing families, women need to take on precarious employment, with the potential threat of having to remain permanently in the secondary labour market.

In 2013, I conducted a study in Toronto of the lived experiences of unemployed women with diverse backgrounds. These women had intersecting identities, which included being a single parent, lacking a partner's income, having previous precarious employment, having a partner who was precariously employed, being the mother of one child, being the mother of multiple children, and caring for parents. I approached the interviews in this study using intersectionality theory, as this approach helps provide "a clearer picture of the way the intersections of identity impact individuals' access to social policies, and, indeed, to full social citizenship" (Nichols, "Analyzing Policy Frames" 234–235). Intersectionality theory allows for a fuller understanding of individuals' lives, including the options that they have and the decisions they make (Manual). Fifteen participants were interviewed to probe the socioeconomic and psychosocial impacts of being unemployed, notably financial implications and health. Six participants in the study were immigrants to Canada. Although all women in the study faced challenges, this chapter focuses on the experiences of the unemployed immigrant mothers.

WOMEN'S EMPLOYMENT

Despite gender roles and the household division of labour, more women are working in Canada today, although many work in nonstandard, contracted, and precarious employment. In December 2013, 58.3 percent of Canadian women and 67.6 percent of Canadian men were employed (Canada, Statistics Canada, "Table"), whereas in 1976, 41.9 percent of Canadian women and 72.7 percent of Canadian men were employed (Ferraro). Regardless of this increase in women's employment, few Canadian women today are able to access unemployment supports if they become jobless as a result of of labour market participation barriers.

Historically, primary and secondary labour markets have structured the labour supply on the basis of social differences, such as race and gender (Gordon et al.). The primary sector, which is characterized by white male privilege, features better working conditions, better jobs, higher income, more secure employment, and more possibilities for promotion than the secondary sector (Krahn et al.; Peck; Reich et al.). Women have been generally employed in the secondary labour market because of their presumed domestic duties (Peck), whereas men have had more access to the primary labour market.

Dominant social policy paradigms, which suggest that men are the breadwinners and women are the caregivers, are reinforced in labour markets and influence the types of jobs that women hold (Peck). Women, for example, primarily occupy care-related jobs, such as teaching or childcare, which have been traditionally perceived as feminine (Gordon et al.; Kershaw). Labour markets, therefore, are socially constructed and segmented in such a way that women are slotted into insecure jobs in the secondary sector that are characterized by low wages and high insecurity (Krahn et al.). Peck argues that women will remain in the insecure secondary labour market until both "real and perceived" assumptions about the division of labour within the family are overturned (67). If the government can help change who is responsible for social reproduction (i.e., the tasks required to regenerate and maintain the working population [Benzanson]), then the division of labour within the family may become more equitable—providing universal childcare is one example. Such a change could recast the characteristics of the primary labour sector and its accessibility, at least in theory.

Not every mother enters the labour market willingly. Some women are forced to work when a lack of resources prevents them from choosing to be stay-at-home mothers. Others, particularly those in the middle and upper classes, have abilities or resources that enable them to choose how they participate in the labour market (Little). To address this social inequity, it is paramount that mothers have access to adequate childcare, so that *if* they choose to work, they will be on an equal footing with men (Little).

CHANGES FROM UNEMPLOYMENT INSURANCE TO
EMPLOYMENT INSURANCE

Unemployment Insurance (UI) was introduced in the early 1940s to address the large-scale unemployment that developed as a result of the Great Depression. The program was designed to provide financial assistance to unemployed workers (Lin). Initial eligibility was based on the number of weeks worked during the previous fifty-two weeks, depending on the region in which the claimant lived. With UI, claimants in different regions were required to have worked twelve to twenty weeks, with a minimum of fifteen hours per week, and the amount of benefits was based on the total work hours and the total earnings during the previous year (Townson and Hayes).

In1996, when unemployed worker support changed from UI to EI, the most significant changes to the policy were an increase in the total number of hours that a claimant had to work and a decrease in the EI benefit payouts. For EI, an unemployed worker now needs to have documentation for 180 days of paid labour during the previous two years with at least a thirty-five-hour work week (Townson and Hayes). Thus, workers must prove that they have double the previously required number of hours to be EI claimants. In addition, the average UI claimant received 595 dollars per week in 1995 and when inflation is taken into account, the same claimant received 514 dollars in 2014 (Battle et al.; Canada, "Amount of Weekly Benefits"). These changes have had a significant effect on unemployed workers. For example, only 39 percent of unemployed workers were approved for benefits in 2009, compared to 83 percent in 1990 (Mendelson et al.).

EI policy does not take into account the range of reasons why someone may not be attached to the labour market (Cooke and Gazo). As a result, women are significantly affected when they leave the labour market temporarily to raise children (Cooke and Gazo; Townson and Hayes). Along with other Canadian workers, mothers are viewed as re-entrants or new entrants to the labour market when they have temporarily left the labour market. This rule means that they are not credited with any previous work but must, nevertheless, satisfy the requirement of having worked 910 hours during the past fifty-two weeks in order to obtain benefits (Townson and Hayes). This requirement limits a worker's ability to obtain EI benefits, even if the benefits are needed to reattach to the labour market (Bezanson and Murray).

IMMIGRANT SETTLEMENT EXPERIENCE

The immigrant settlement experience in Canada has been affected in regards changes to social programs as a result of neoliberal policy paradigm changes, including a retrenchment of social supports as a means to reduce public expenditure. Despite this, in Canada in 2011, 20.6 percent of the population was foreign born, which was the largest proportion among the Group of Eight (G8) countries. Tyyskä has summarized that (1) financial complications are usual for years after migration; (2) those who migrated to Canada prior to the 1990s are better off than more recently arrived immigrants; (3) immigrants with comparable academic degrees do not do as well as their Canadian-born counterparts, particularly if race is also factored in; (4) the reason immigrants have not been doing as well as prior to 1990s is generally associated with their racialized status; and (5) the tough financial situation that many immigrants face influences their ability to achieve affordable housing, causes low levels of home ownership, and reduces their access to health-care, education, and retraining (Tyyskä).

Although the majority of immigrants face difficulties in the settlement process, there are significant gender differences among immigrants. In Canada, immigrant men are more often represented as the principal applicant in the economic class, as a direct result of their traditional breadwinner role; in 2012, 51.5 percent of men entered in the economic class, whereas 57.6 percent of women entered in the family class (Citizenship and Immigration Canada). Since women are not usually the primary applicants in the economic class, they are not seen as providing significant economic contributions (Gabriel 164, 172; Thobani 39-40; Arat-Koç 36).

IMMIGRANT WOMEN IN CANADA

In Canada, the unemployment rates are high for immigrant women. In 2009, immigrant women had an unemployment rate of 7.0 percent (Nichols and Tyyskä). There is also a notable gendered division of labour between immigrant men and women in Canada. Immigrant women often occupy caring and service sector jobs; most men occupy manual labour positions. Also, some evidence suggests that immigrant women in Canada find employment faster than men because they are willing to take survival jobs (Nichols and Tyyskä. This gendered division of work is notable in their wages. In 2010, the median income for recently arrived immigrant women in Canada was 15,590 dollars (Canada, Statistics Canada, "Table").

Integration, both economically and culturally, is directly connected to the way that women are located within immigration policy (Gabriel; Arat-Koç). Canadian immigration policies favour those who have money, investments, or human capital potential, as evidenced by the point system introduced in 1967 (Gabriel 162, 164, 171; Man 135). Primary applicants who are considered the labour market participants receive benefits when they migrate to Canada. For instance, Canadian language programs were originally only for primary applicants (Arat-Koç 39). Such policies ignore immigrants who come to Canada through the family class, who are often women and who still contribute to the labour market (Thobani 39, 40). Even with changes to official language programs, these programs are not gender neutral because there is limited eligibility for those who have been in Canada for less than one year, and childcare centres for children six months to six years old are available at only a few locations.

RESULTS FROM THE STUDY

The study resulted in many findings related to the experience of motherhood for immigrant women in Toronto. There were two main findings. First, the neoliberal policy paradigm has eroded the state infrastructure. There is now a paucity of support for unemployed women workers, as these women not only face poor EI support but also have inadequate support related to health care, childcare, retraining, and the labour market. Accordingly, many of these women face inadequate living conditions unless they have a domestic partner on whom they can rely. Second, I found that personal health is negatively affected when women are unemployed or precariously employed. Women must cope with the insecurity surrounding their inability to plan for the future, with having to live on a limited income, and with not having adequate healthcare benefits. Neoliberal market policies clearly place these women in jeopardy, especially those who are mothers and those with specific intersecting identities.

SOCIAL ASSISTANCE PROGRAMS

Four mothers from this study stressed the significance of the social assistance programs on which they relied, including subsidized daycare and the baby bonus, a federal benefit granted to parents of newborn children. Sarah, a married immigrant racialized mother of one from Toronto, relied on subsidized daycare. She tried to obtain further social assistance but was informed that because of her husband's employment, she could not access welfare. Sarah[1] explained, "I was told about emergency funds ... need to physically go with your husband for an appointment. My husband said, 'No way, sit there all day for a possible "no" and lose income for the day.'" The main goal for Jessica was to obtain employment, so she returned to work without subsidized daycare. She explained that there was a six-month waitlist for such daycare. Sarah was hopeful that her son would get into a daycare facility soon, as he was on two waitlists.

The difficulties that mothers encounter also have long-term effects, as one way for these women to make ends meet is to rely on grey-sector employment,[2] which does not add to their pensionable income. To meet their needs in the absence of personal supports or government assistance, many mothers in this study relied on undocumented work. Two participants in Toronto worked in unreported jobs to fill financial gaps. Jessica, for example, expressed her desire to do unreported work, although every time she tried, her need to care for her son prevented it:

I was looking into working under the table ... but what happened was every time that I had to start a shift . . . about to go, [my son] got sick with a fever and a cold, so

I stayed home. One [time] I found a babysitter, but then I found out that the babysitter does not start until after 7:30 [a.m.], but I had to be at work at 7:30, so it does not work…. Since school is out, my aunt's daughter is willing to watch him since she is fourteen and not fifteen[3] and can't work now. She has actually told me that she cannot find a job and is willing to watch him. I have been thinking about it, calling agencies, but I need to do more calling. Even if it is minimum wage, it is something, better than nothing.

Being a mother, common-law partner, or a wife as well as being an immigrant women are identities difficult to separate. In relation to being unemployed, these identities have a significant role in ones' dependency. The overall impact of these identities leads to a reliance on a male domestic partner or if they do not have one, on the state.

FINANCIAL INSECURITY AND UNEMPLOYMENT

A key theme through this study was financial insecurity. Many participants noted that the first effect of unemployment was a lack of money. All participants suffered from the same initial difficulty in maintaining financial security through employment, since they also cared for children or other dependents. As a result, they all indicated that their dependents were their main priority, which led them to do what they had to as a means of survival. For instance, Jessica noted: "Because, I mean, he is a baby, he was not asked to be born to this world to suffer." Through this example, it is clear that being a caregiver played a significant role in these mothers' daily lives. To achieve financial security, they also had to be able to support their children or other dependents.

Similar to what was noted by the participants of Yu-Ling Hsiao's study (in this volume), both Ann and Nancy expressed difficulties with the immigrant settlement period, which had been further compounded with the low-income situation in which they lived. Ann noted that she first had to worry about basic retraining. As she explained, "I take English class to improve my English. I have to pay." Margaret Little has noted that compared to lower-income women workers, a "resource-rich middle-class mother has some flexibility to choose when and under what circumstances they will participate in the paid workforce" (140). To achieve this, however, adequate childcare and access to the labour market for all women are required.

It is important to note that there is a need to explore more than just motherhood for access to retraining. Other identities—notably immigrant and racialized status and low-income backgrounds—affect an individual's employment, which impacts the ability and desire to retrain. These intersectional identities limit mothers' resources in their daily lives and are also a barrier to any potential retraining (Little). Low-income status significantly implicates their opportunities for retraining and improvement of labour market outcomes.

UNEMPLOYMENT AND ITS HEALTH IMPLICATIONS

Many studies have shown that serious negative health outcomes are associated with difficult employment situations because individuals obtain their "basic life requirements" through the income and benefits accrued from working (Linn et al.; Mikkonen and Raphael). Unemployment often makes people "more anxious, depressed and concerned with bodily symptoms than those who [have] continued to work" (Linn et al. 504; Artazcoz et al.). Being unemployed can also lead to negative coping mechanisms, including drug use and excessive alcohol use (Mikkonen and Raphael).

The mothers in my study also experienced the negative effects of precarious employment. Many mothers like to ensure the health of their children through a variety of means, including healthy preventative diets. Unfortunately, providing such diets is difficult for resource-poor unemployed women workers. Jessica described such a situation:

I know it is not about going to the gym because there are other things that I can do, but I mean vegetables and stuff are pretty expensive. When you go to the grocery store with not enough money, you cannot be on that kind of special stuff like the fish and salmon, all the good things which is healthy for you. It is very pricey. Now I am buying for two. When I do have money, it is not enough. I do have to think about my son first because he has to eat, so if it is about him getting his formula over me, then so be it. Because I mean, he is a baby, he was not asked to be born to this world to suffer. It is my responsibility to take care of him to make sure he is doing well.

Thus, Jessica's case illustrates how being unemployed or precariously employed can leave women in a situation in which it is difficult to prevent health problems. In addition, there are hidden costs associated with healthcare, including commuting to healthcare appointments, childcare expenses, and the cost of healthy food. For the Canadian population, particularly mothers surviving on unemployment benefits, the associated costs are often out of reach.

Maintenance of one's health is complicated by the identities of being a woman, a mother, a wife or common-law partner, a single mother, and an immigrant. These identities cannot be pulled apart but rather act together to compound the situation and affect one's health, most notably during unemployment.

CONCLUSION

The purpose of this chapter was to explore the experience that immigrant mothers have in relation to unemployment in Canada. Fifteen participants with diverse identities took part in semistructured qualitative interviews. The interviews were analyzed through an intersectionality approach; they revealed that not everyone has been affectted by the change from UI to EI in the same way. Identities related to gender, immigration status, motherhood, marital status, socioeconomic status, age, and race compound and intersect to impact one's experience while unemployed.

Findings from this study demonstrate some of the consequences of adhering to a false model of a generalized, self-sufficient woman, which is in line with the neoliberal paradigm. Women in privileged positions have the greatest ability to purchase childcare, whether through a daycare facility or by hiring a nanny (Little, 140). The resources that some privileged women possess enable them to make choices about whether to enter the labour market. But for mothers who do not fit this model, the neoliberal policy paradigm has limited their decisions on how to complete the role of motherhood. Immigrant mothers face additional barriers during the settlement period and beyond that limit their resources and, thus, implicate their experience while being unemployed.

NOTES

[1] All names are pseudonym names chosen by the participant.

[2] Grey-sector employment is also referred to as informal employment. This work generally occurs under the table without any records. As well, it is usually paid in cash.

[3] The minimum age for employment in Canada is fourteen years old in all industries, except window cleaning, logging, construction, factory operations, repair shops, and the mining industry (Ontario, Ministry of Labour, "Minimum Age"). This was Jessica's interpretation of the minimum age for work.

WORKS CITED

Acker, Joan. "Gendered Organizations and Intersectionality: Problems and Possibilities." *Equality, Diversity and Inclusion: An International Journal*, vol. 31, no. 3, 2012, pp. 214-24.

Artazcoz, Lucía, et al. "Unemployed and Mental Health: Understanding the Interactions Among Gender, Family, and Social Class." *Research and Practice*, vol. 94, no. 1, 2004, pp. 82-88.

Battle, Ken, et al. "The Forgotten Fundamentals." *Caledon Institute of Social Policy*, 2008, www.caledoninst.org/Publications/Detail/?ID=727&IsBack=0. Accessed 10 Aug. 2016.

Bezanson, Kate, and Susan McMurray. "Booming for Whom? People in Ontario Talk About Income, Jobs and Social Programs." *Caledon Institute of Social Policy*, 2000, www.caledoninst.org/Publications/Detail/?ID=181. Accessed 10 Aug. 2016.

Bezanson, Kate. *Gender, the State and Social Reproduction: Household Insecurity in Neo-Liberal Times*. University of Toronto Press, 2006.

Cooke, Martin, and Amber Gazo. "Taking a Life Course Perspective on Social Assistance Use in Canada: A Different Approach." *Canadian Journal of Sociology*, vol. 34, no. 2, 2009, pp. 349-372.

Ferraro, Vincent. "Paid Work." *Women in Canada: A Gender-Based Statistical Report*, prepared by the Social and Aboriginal Statistics Division under the direction of Cara Williams, Statistics Canada, 2010.

Gordon, David M. et al. *Segmented Work, Divided Workers.* Cambridge University Press, 1982. Print.

Canada. "Amount of Weekly Benefits." Service Canada: People Serving People.: Government of Canada, 2014, http://www.servicecanada.gc.ca/eng/sc/ei/sew/weekly_benefits.shtml. Accessed 10 Aug. 2016.

Canada. Statistics Canada. "Table 276-0022: Employment Insurance Program (EI), Beneficiaries Receiving Regular Income Benefits by Province, Declared Earnings, Sex and Age, Seasonally Adjusted, Monthly (Persons)." Statistics Canada, Government of Canada, 2014, http://www5.statcan.gc.ca/cansim/a26?id=2760022. Accessed 10 Aug. 2016.

Kershaw, Paul. "'Choice' Discourse in BC Child Care: Distancing Policy from Research." *Canadian Journal of Political Science*, vol. 37, no. 4, 2004, pp. 927–950.

Krahn, Harvey J. et al. *Work, Industry and Canadian Society.* 5th ed., Nelson Education, 2008.

Linn, Margaret, Richard Sandifer, and Shayna Stein. "Effects of Unemployment on Mental and Physical Health." *American Journal of Public Health*, vol. 75, no. 5, 1985, pp. 502-506.

Little, Margaret H. *If I Had a Hammer: Retraining That Really Works.* University of British Columbia Press, 2004.

MacDonald, Martha. "Income Security for Women: What about Employment Insurance?" *Public Policy for Women: The State, Income and Labour Market Issues*, edited by M. Griffin Cohen and J. Pulkingham, University of Toronto Press, 2009, pp. 251-270.

MacDonald, Martha. "Women and EI in Canada: The First Decade." *Women and Public Policy in Canada*, edited by A. Dobrowolsky, Oxford University Press, 2009, pp. 65-86.

McGregor, G. "The Myth(s) of Globalization: Gender Basis in 'EI' Policy as a Case in Point." *Canadian Women Studies/les cahiers de la femme*, vol. 23, no. 3/4, 2004, pp. 30-39.

Mendelson, Michael, et al. "EI Financing: Reset Required." Caledon *Institute of Social Policy*, 2010, www.caledoninst.org/Publications/ Detail/?ID=902&IsBack=0. Accessed 10 Aug. 2016.

Mikkonen, J. and Raphael, D. *Social Determinants of Health: The Canadian Facts.* Toronto: York University School of Health Policy and Management, 2010, http://www.thecanadianfacts.org/ The_Canadian_Facts.pdf. Assessed 22 Aug. 2016.

Nichols, Leslie J. "Analyzing Policy Frames for Unemployed Workers' Supports within Canada." *AG: International Journal of Gender Studies*, vol. 2, no. 3, 2013, pp. 219-245.

Nichols, Leslie. "Employment Insurance in Canada: The Gendered Implications." *International Journal of Gender and Women's Studies* vol. 2, no. 2, 2014, pp. 357-385.

Nichols, Leslie, and Vappu Tyyskä. "Immigrant Women in Canada and United States." *Immigrant Experience in North America*, edited by H. Bauder and J. Shields. Canadian Scholars' Press, 2015, pp. 248-272.

Ontario. Ministry of Labour. "Minimum Age." *Health and Safety.* Queen's Printer of Ontario, Aug. 2015, www.labour.gov.on.ca/ english/hs/min_age.php. Accessed 10 Aug. 2016.

Peck, Jamie. *Work Place*, Gilford Press, 1996.

Reich, Michael et al. "Dual Labour Markets: A Theory of Labor Market Segmentation." *The American Economic Review*, vol. 63, no. 2, 1973, pp. 359-365.

Silver, Susan, et al. "Job Restructuring and Worker Displacement: Does Gender Matter?" *Canadian Women's Studies/les cahiers de la femme*, vol. 23, no. 3/4, 2004, pp. 7-13.

Silver, Susan et al. "The Excluded, the Vulnerable and the Re-integrated in a Neoliberal Era: Qualitative Dimensions of the Unemployment Experience." *Socialist Studies: The Journal of the Society for Socialist Studies*, vol. 1, no. 1, 2005, pp. 31-56.

Teghtsoonian, Kathy. "Promises, Promises: 'Choices for Women' in Canadian and American Child Care Policy Debates." *Feminist Studies*, vol. 22, no. 1, 1996, pp. 118-146.

Townson, Monica, and Kevin Hayes. *Women and the Employment Insurance Program. Canadian Centre for Policy Alternatives*, 2007, www.policyalternatives.ca/sites/default/files/uploads/pub-lications/National_Office_Pubs/2007/Women_and_the_EI_Program.pdf. Accessed 10 Aug. 2016.

Tyyskä, Vappu. *Action and Analysis: Readings in Sociology of Gender*. Nelson, 2007.

Tyyskä, Vappu. *Long and Winding Road: Adolescents and Youth in Canada Today*. 3rd ed., Canadian Scholars' Press, 2014.

6.
Mothering at the Margins of Health

Syrian Mothers in Istanbul

NURCAN OZGUR BAKLACIOGLU

SINCE THE BEGINNING OF THE twenty-first century, wars in various regions of the world have led to a feminization of forced migration. Although there is a growing literature on immigrant mothers (Samira 969-1003; Chang; Parreñas), studies on refugee mothers remain insufficient. The experiences of refugee mothers are partly mentioned in the reports on forcibly displaced children, parents, or women in cases of war. These include reports on mothers from Bosnia (Korac 249-272), Rwanda (UNIFEM), Somalia, Mynamar (Women's Commission for Refugee Women and Children 9-21), Chechnya (International Crisis Group 33-34) and Syria (Peace and Security).

Both migrant and refugee women undergo similar processes of illegalization, criminalization, marginalization, and victimization during their transit or stay in a destination country (Pickering). However, the reasons and conditions for leaving the country of origin have a great impact on the future experience, challenges, and opportunities of the refugee mothers abroad. Whereas immigrant mothers are always capable of returning to their country of origin as well as benefiting from family networks there, the refugee mothers do not have such opportunity. Situations of war or conflict and threats of persecution, death, or inhumane treatment do not leave any safe space for return for the refugee mothers. The impossibility of returning home, which is underlined in the first article of the 1951 Refugee Convention, is the most basic structural condition that creates the challenges confronting Syrian refugee mothers in Turkey.

The following study investigates the role of war, transit, and asylum on the motherhood experiences and coping strategies of Syrian refugee mothers living in Istanbul. It is based on observations, interviews, and qualitative data representing fifteen Syrian mothers who live in eight diverse districts of Istanbul: Bagcilar, Bayramtepe, Fatih, Eyup, Sirinevler, Sariyer, Kucukpazar, and Tarlabasi.[1] The experiences, challenges, and opportunities under the conditions of war, transit, and temporary protection are shaped by intersections of class, religion, race politics, migration security policy, and hegemonic power relations. In this way, the politics of temporary protection—which is supported by prioritization of public security, discriminative stereotypes, and negative hegemonic constructions of the refugee mother as a primitive and powerless "Other"—play an important role in the formation of experiences and opportunities of the Syrian refugee mothers in Turkey.

Grounded on a strict precondition of administrative registration, the temporary protection system[2] provides access to legal residence, education, and health services only to registered Syrian refugees. Under the Temporary Protection Directive of 2014, only the registered Syrian mothers might be provided services, including free primary and emergency health as well as reproductive health services, but only at the hospitals within the province of registration. This reality means that Syrian refugee mothers registered in the Turkish border provinces with Syria do not have access to free medical care in Istanbul or other cities of residence. Syrian refugee mothers without registration have access to only emergency health services and health services for the prevention of communicable diseases. In fact, because of the lack of registration, language problems, lack of accessible translation services, and the discriminative approach of the hospitals and medical personnel (Kivilcim), the majority of Syrian refugee mothers and children cannot benefit from free health services and have to pay high amounts for both consultation and medicines. As one forty-year-old Syrian mother said:[3]

> We went to a hospital for our baby. They asked for an identity card. We had to pay 150 TL [Turkish Lira; approximately 66 Canadian dollars] to the hospital for the consultation. We paid a lot to the pharmacy too. Now I have a pain in

my kidneys, but I don't want to go to the hospital. There is a Syrian association here. The consultation is for free, we go there.

In this way, not only does the precondition of registration limit access to health, legal residence, and education, but it also puts Syrian mothers within the limbo of structural violence and irregularity. Stuck within the administrative boundaries of temporary protection, the Syrian refugee mothers in Turkey are confined to the narrow stereotyping and criteria of patriarchal motherhood, as constructed by hegemonic motherhood discourses in both Turkey and Syria. The patriarchal institution of motherhood in Turkey casts the model of "good mother" under the representation of the Turkish stereotype of motherhood: heterosexual, loyal, morally clean, religious or modern, hardworking, sacrificing, and civilized. Bounded under this ideal image of motherhood, Syrian mothers, who are often accused of irresponsibly giving birth to additional children while living under conflict and poverty, are excluded by both the secular and the conservative prevailing discourses of good mothering in Turkey. The Islamic media often portrays Syrian mothers mourning their dead babies, children, and husbands. Although most of the news is visualized through a photo of a Syrian refugee mother holding her baby and other kids, the news usually talks about Syrian women as victims of forced marriages and sexual violence. Thus, there is a prevalent image of the Syrian woman in Turkey: she is victimized as an object of sexual trafficking and disempowered through being seen as only a suffering mother.

1. MOTHERING, SAFETY, AND SHELTER

Because of its close distance to Syria, Turkey is a favoured destination country for homeless, nomadic, and low-income Syrian refugees from the northern border regions. Refugees who do not have resources to go to relatively far and high per capita income countries—such as the United Arab Emirates, Kuwait, or Saudi Arabia—travel to Turkey. However, despite the relatively short distance, refugees have to pay bribes and high prices for shelter and travel on their way to Istanbul; thus, they often arrive in Istanbul in deep poverty. Istanbul is favoured by Kurdish, Alawi, Turkmen, Dom, and LGBTI Syrian refugees and single Syrian women who look for escape in this metropolitan city. Ezidis usually prefer to gather together at their own camps close to the Syrian border, whereas Suryanies and Christians have close links with the local populations of cities such as Mardin.

Istanbul is also a favoured city because of its opportunities for employment. Single or transgender women and women of Kurdish or Alawi origin have faced violence and discrimination at the small border cities, where it is hard to avoid the locals' gaze and their discriminatory attitudes. Thus, many single, Kurdish, or Allawi refugee mothers prefer moving to Istanbul, where they hope to find better employment opportunities and conditions for self-sustainability.

About 77 percent of the Syrian refugees in Turkey are women and children (UNHCR Regional Data). The majority of the Syrian refugee mothers have three to four children. According to official data, approximately 20 percent of the registered women are the heads of their family. Around 66 percent of the Syrian women in the eastern provinces are married, whereas 27 percent are single. Around 53 percent of the women in the eastern provinces hold primary or secondary school degrees. About 87 percent of the interviewed Syrian women do not have an income-generating occupation, and 97 percent have not been able to earn an income in the past month (AFAD, *Türkiye'de*).[4] There is no accessible data about the number of Syrian mothers and their marital situation because they are always cited together with their children or within the category of "women."

The issue of accommodation is one of the most pressing problems facing Syrian refugee mothers in Istanbul because it is closely related to the issue of poverty and safety. Since Turkey's approach to the mass influx of Syrian refugees is built on the principle of encampment, there are no public accommodation programs or assistance provided to the urban refugees, except for the unaccompanied refugee children. Thus, urban Syrian refugee women must find and cover their own accommodation. Almost all of the interviewed women refugees pay exaggerated prices for small rooms lacking basic sanitary conditions. All Syrian refugee women fear forced encampment, as a mother in Fatih said: "Better die in Syria, than go to camp." Indeed, out of more than 2.5 million Syrian refugees in Turkey, only 261,141 lived in camps as of June 2015 (AFAD, *Barınma*).

The majority of the urban Syrian refugee mothers can only afford living in abandoned semiruined houses. Nomadic and homeless refugee families used to live in self-made tents established in the city parks. According to officials, these homes violated public order and hurt the touristic image of the city; thus, local municipal government burned and prohibited the construction of such tents in the tourist-intensive districts. As a result, since 2014, Syrian refugees have avoided establishing shelters in the central city areas. Many poor refugee newcomers rent rooms at the one-bedroom apartment districts. These are old neglected rooms in districts rife with black markets, such as Tarlabasi, Yenikapi, Kumkapi, and Küçükpazar. These districts are known as places where criminals, sex workers, burglars, and traffickers reside. Single refugee mothers who find themselves living in these quarters, especially the Kucukpazar district of the city, are at risk of various forms of sexual violence and exploitation. In their struggle for safe and affordable accommodation, many single mothers prefer sharing accommodation with extended family when possible (Kesgin and Ozturk).

The high cost of accommodation constitutes a major structural source of poverty, which affects the health of refugee mothers and children. Living on the street or in a semiruined house or room does not make much difference with regards to the overall lack of basic sanitary conditions, clean water, heating, electricity, and fresh food. "We do not need refrigerator, there is nothing to put in," a refugee mother pointed out while looking at the old refrigerator, which was donated by a neighbour, in her apartment in Şirinevler. She continued, "I look for an old bed for my four kids who sleep on the ground." Children and mothers constitute the majority of the refugee population that spend most of their time in these miserable conditions.

The World Health Organization's definition of health is about not only the lack of disease but also the presence of mental and physical health and social wellbeing. This means that shelter, food, self-sustaining independent livelihood, education and safety—from all forms of physical, legal, social, and sexual violence—are all elements of wellbeing and health (Hynes 431-445). Approached through this definition, it is difficult to talk about available safe shelter, clean food and water, and safety from various forms of violence in the case of the Syrian refugee mothers in Istanbul. Instead, structural insecurity and violence affect the mental wellbeing of the Syrian refugee mothers, as they create a constant sense of insecurity and fear of death, injury, violence, and the loss of their children. Poverty, insecurity, and deprivation from safety, health and education pose harsh challenges to the physical, mental, sexual, spiritual, and social lives of the Syrian refugee mothers in Istanbul.

Safety from violence and fair access to health services are the most basic human rights defined under the international human rights law. Both rights are under the responsibility of the states in order to protect the people living within the borders of their sovereign territory. Nevertheless, the globalizing regimes of temporary protection has provided many receiving states with opportunity to discriminate and limit refugees' access to some basic rights and public services. The discriminatory nature of the temporary protection policies work through the externalizing mechanisms of health services that have a great impact on the refugee mothers, who are usually responsible for the health of their children, too. Concern about health and safety is the major sign of the structural violence embedded in the lives of these Syrian refugee mothers in Istanbul.

2. STRUGGLING FOR HEALTH AND SAFETY UNDER STRUCTURAL VIOLENCE

Mothering Health across War, Hospital, and Work Place

Because of registration problems, poor resources, or language problems, refugee mothers have difficulty accessing the free health services. As one thirty-one-year-old Syrian refugee mother said:

> We went to the health care center when my son got high fever. They did not care about us. We went to Haseki Hospital, my son got worse when we arrived at the hospital. The doctors in this hospital did not care about us. My son lost consciousness, I started to cry. A Turkish patient waiting

in the hospital was speaking Arabic. He helped us with the translation and also paid all the costs in the hospital. My son stayed in the hospital for three days.

Facing discrimination at hospitals, Syrian mothers often prefers homebirths. One nurse explained feel overloaded with many patients:

Doctors consider Syrians as a burden, because they don't get the provision payment for them. Most of the doctors hate Syrians; they don't refuse to have Syrian patients, but they mistreat them like second or third class individuals. The pregnant women are insulted. The doctors accuse them and say "you are pregnant, you had sex even in these circumstances." I think that's why Syrian women prefer homebirths. (qtd. in Kivilcim)

Maternal health is an important problem for Syrian refugee women in Turkey. Both official reports and NGO studies point to the high percentage of pregnant women and breastfeeding mothers in Syrian households in Turkey. Households with breastfeeding mothers are estimated at between 17 and 19 percent. Similarly, the number of Syrian babies born in Turkey between 2011 and 2014 is estimated at 34,792 (AFAD, *Türkiye'de*). Nevertheless, this number includes only the registered deliveries in the hospitals; no available data about home births exist. Refugee mothers tell of their difficult experiences in Syria, including enduring physical violence, inhaling noxious chemicals, and consuming trash and dirty water to survive. As a thirty-year-old woman living in Fatih explained:

Our house was bombed [in Syria]. Everything was destroyed, and the roads were blocked. We had to boil and eat the trash food. When I gave birth to my baby, the muscles around his belt were melted, the brain full of water. Doctors said this baby will not live. But I did not give up! God gave his life; God will take it. He is in the emergency unit. I will do my best to save him. My other kids sell water and napkins. We spend all money on him.

Their stories also indicate that the physical and psychological trauma of the war continues during their life in exile: "While running from Halep, my small son and I, we were hit by a gun and injured. The kids are afraid. The one-and-a-half-year-old son is still afraid when he hears an airplane or gun. My retina of my son's eye shifted during the bombing; the small one was crying for hours," recalled a thirty-year-old mother in Tarlaba ı. Unhealthy living conditions—which are based on a lack of heating, of electricity, and an inability to access clean food and water—persist in exile. Micronutrient deficiencies and anemia observed among children and pregnant and lactating women in the camps is common among the refugee children and mothers in Istanbul, too (United Nations 4-6).

There is no available study reporting on the health of the refugee women or mothers in Turkey. The obtainable official reports usually investigate the rate of access to health services, lately estimated at 59 percent among the refugees in some of the Anatolian provinces. The Emergency Affairs Directorate (AFAD) survey found that 10 percent of refugees report problems with noncommunicable diseases (NCD), including hypertension, diabetes, cancer, asthma, and renal failure (AFAD, *Türkiye'de* 55-59). There are few academic studies about the most common health problems in some of the border cities, such as Hatay (Karakuş et al. 429) and Gaziantep (Alpak et al. 1-6). Most of the available studies involve cases about disability, health complications, and epidemic diseases among the Syrian refugees, and aim at estimating the cost of the health services provided to the Syrian patients. Most of the studies are done by male academics or researchers, and lack any gender perspective.

The only data about the health situation of the Syrian refugee women in Istanbul is provided in the health report by TOHAV (Society and Law Research Foundation). TOHAV's health check among 480 Syrian refugees (240 children, 180 women, and 100 men) in Istanbul shows that Syrian refugee women suffer mostly cardiovascular, endocrinological, gynecological, neurological, and urogenital problems. As the health effects of the war continue, additional health problems are approaching because of fourteen-hour-long work days at low-paying jobs (one hundred to three hundred Euros per month). These jobs typically entail inhumane conditions at illegal work places, which often become spaces of sexual violence and discrimination.

Mothering with Honour amid Sexual Violence and Discrimination

Crossing borders, finding refuge, and starting a safe live from the very bottom of the society are the main challenges facing Syrian mothers in Istanbul. As heads of their families, more than half of the Syrian mothers undertake a heavy responsibility to protect the family, the children, and the honour of the extended family, which is a hard task to achieve in a region where masculinity rules. The body of the women represents the honour and unity of the nation, the fatherland, the society, the family, and the man. The women, not the men, are responsible for protecting these values. The honour of the man is governed through the politics over the body of the women. As seen in the Bosnian war, contemporary conflicts include widespread sexual violence aimed at dishonouring the enemy and its future through women's bodies. The rape and sexual torture against women during war victimizes not just the affected women, but their menfolk and their entire community (Indra).

The conflict in Syria constitutes one of the most violent examples of massive sexual and gender-based violence (SGBV). Stories of rape and sexual violence follow the lives of the Syrian mothers across the Syrian-Turkish borders, define their everyday lives, and affect their return projections. Indeed, more so than the bombings, the threat of sexual violence and exploitation become major threats during their flight across the masculinized borders. Accepting sexual violence as a bribe for survival, passage, accommodation, or employment is not uncommon for some Syrian refugee mothers (International Federation for Human Rights). There are stories of penniless mothers who were forced to leave their daughters as bribes to warriors, armed groups, or border guards on their way to Turkey. One Syrian woman living in Tarlabasi provided one such example: "While approaching the Turkish border, an armed group of men bribed all of us. They wanted one hundred American dollars. Those who could not pay, were not allowed to pass. One of the families did not have money. They were asked to leave one of their young daughters." Our research team has also heard many accounts of forced marriages of child daughters among refugee communities. During the interviews, the mothers used to talk about "finding a Syrian husband" for their thirteen-to-fifteen-year-old daughters. The family is the one who decides on the appropriate partner for marriage. This hierarchical decision-making process is fostered by fears of rape and the dishonouring of the family. Although forced marriage contains various forms of violence in the private sphere, it is being normalized through stories of women victims of SGBV and sex slavery circulating in public and private spaces.

The most difficult mothering task in exile is to guard the honour of the family and the daughters. Living in tents and semiruined houses without doors and windows necessitates long sleepless nights. As an eighteen-year-old girl from Ceylanpınar tent camp said: "I am happy now in Istanbul, because after four years in a tent camp, for the first time I am living between four walls and with a locked door. We have a private toilet, now; I can sleep and go to the toilet alone, without any company, whenever I want."

The burden of protecting family honour is further exacerbated by posttraumatic stress disorder (PTSD). According to a recent study, the probability of PTSD among Syrian women in Gaziantep tent camps is estimated as 71 percent and is higher among those who have undergone two or more traumatic events or have a personal or family history of psychiatric disorder (Alpak et al. 1-6). As twenty-eight-year-old Mukrime stated:

> Now we don't feel safe anywhere. We are noticed in many places; on a bus, in a hospital, everywhere. When I start talking, they immediately understand that I am a refugee and when you are a woman ... you can guess the rest. An incident happened a while ago. It also happened to other people like me. I was sitting on a chair in the hospital, waiting for my turn, talking with my sister-in-law. One man approached me and gave me his phone number. He told me that he could help me and that he could find me a job and things like that.... The way he looked at me showed me his ill intentions. His look.... (qtd. in Toplu 12)

In some of the families, men of working age were at home, while mothers had to find employment as well as care for the family. These women mentioned some muscular and bone system problems that prevented their husbands from working; some also had psychological problems. However, healthy or not, the men in the family bring enormous social and security privileges. As a Syrian Alawi mother said: "I am lucky because my husband is with me. Let god bless the lonely women! Their situation is really hard!" Men, then, could be perpetrators of violence on the one hand but a source of security and honour on the other. As twenty-six-year-old Sena said: "A lonely woman is easy prey for men. I lived for my honour, but now nobody respects me because there is no man with me" (qtd. in Toplu 15).

Among the Syrian mothers, few opportunities for socialization exist, especially for the single ones. Their image of Istanbul is limited to within the district because the majority are afraid or do not have the means to leave the district and move around Istanbul. As twenty-eight-year-old Keriman said:

> Our money is finished. We are starving. We have a security problem; we are under threat every day and there is no other guilty person except us. We are treated as alien people, as prostitutes, just because we have lost our husbands. This is embarrassing. Whether we are Kurdish or Arab, it doesn't matter. Nobody respects us. (qtd. in Toplu 14)

Patriarchal hierarchy also places psychological pressure on the young and single mothers living under the gaze and rule of the oldest women or man in the extended family. Decisions about pregnancy are under the control of the husbands. Women who prefer to work for a better life instead of giving birth to a baby do not have much say on this decision. Thus, enforced motherhood rises as the main handicap in the front of the refugee women who aim at self-realization. A twenty-year-old-mother in Sariyer explained it this way:

> I did not want to have a baby. We are still very young. I wanted to work and collect money for making our own

home. My husband decided that we have to do it. I asked the mother-in-law to care after the baby, but she wants to work herself. Now I have to stay at home, look after Hossein and cope with our poor living conditions.

Only five months after her first Caesarean section, she was pregnant with her second baby: "I told my husband that we should protect ourselves, but he said that God brings the fortune of each baby. It will be hard for me. The doctor said that it is a risk to become pregnant so soon." Now, she has to handle the responsibility for any problems during her risky pregnancy as well as the stresses associated with a second Caesarean birth.

The masculine hegemony within private and public spheres deteriorates the health of refugee mothers. With or without husbands, Syrian mothers have to struggle with various hierarchies of power. Mothering in poverty opens various channels for exploitation and marginalization in both the private and public sphere. Besides the male pressure in the family, single mothers have to cope with social discrimination and even violence under the shelter of the broad family. All or this is normalized under the search for safety for the children. Refugee mothers with preschool-aged children are especially dependent on the hierarchical relations in the extended family, and are, thus, open to violence and exploitation in the private space. Poverty is the main factor that normalizes violence in the private sphere: "It was very easy to live in Syria before the war. The men were working, and the women were taking care of the kids. Everything was cheap. We used to have our own houses. It is very hard to live here in Istanbul. If you do not have money you go on the street," explained a twenty-eight-year-old mother in Fatih.

The major fear among the Syrian mothers in Istanbul is to be put in the camps. "Because of the widespread rape and sexual exploitation in the camps, the women in the camps are considered as dirty," said a young woman in Taraba 1. At the beginning of the interview, her small child was hiding behind the door because he thought we were going to drive them to the camp or to Syria. "My greatest fear is to not be able to pay the rent and loose this home," said a mother in Bagcilar. Without a bathroom, kitchen, windows, or even a washbasin, the ten-by-fifteen-metre-squared storeroom provided a "safe home" during the night. None of the interviewed mothers wanted their children to work, for example, by selling napkins on the streets, but this was often the only way to pay the rent and find some food.

Moreover, child "marriages" have become a survival strategy to save young daughters from sexual violence and exploitation, and also to save the honour of the family. A mother in Fatih said: "I pray for my daughter to have her menstruation as late as possible, otherwise I will have to marry her ... in order to save her." The cross-border circulation of their exile experiences and the rumors about their private life, aggravates the fears and uncertainty about a future return to either their extended family networks or their home communities in Syria: "Our neighbours and relatives ask and learn about our experiences in Turkey. What if they hear something wrong about us?" wondered a mother in Fatih. These cross-border fears and the prevailing masculine violence in exile construct each Syrian mother as an agent of masculine hegemony. In order to protect their daughters, they establish hierarchical relations, follow security-based survival strategies, increase control over their daughters, and narrow their chances for self-sustaining strategies.

CONCLUSION: MOTHERING IN EXILE— STRUGGLING AGAINST STRUCTURAL VIOLENCE

Since the beginning of the century, the access to international protection has been replaced by temporary protection regimes, which often lack gender sensitivity and externalize the women and LGBTI refugees. These temporary, masculine, and often religious forms of protection construct hierarchical relations between the modern norms of good mothering (i.e., white, middle-class, and modern refugee mothers) and the "Other" forms of mothering (i.e., Eastern, poor, and primitive). This dichotomy not only leads to the construction of refugee mothers as a threat to public welfare but also promotes policies of social and economic discrimination, marginalization, and sexual exploitation of the refugee women and mothers. Although many receiving countries avoid cross-border deportations of refugee mothers, many do reside in conditions of fear in temporary and insecure housing. This affects Syrian refugee mothers, as they are perceived as protracted guests without any rights, including little access to health services. Through constraints on the basic rights to security, fair employment, and accommodation, the temporary protection policies and practices systematically undermine the economic wellbeing of the refugee mothers.

Focusing on women's experiences, feminist motherhood studies argue that feminist women can consciously choose their own way of mothering that moves beyond the narrow confines and demands of patriarchal motherhood and its institutions (O'Reilly). As with the case of the Syrian refugee mothers, the violence of displacement and war changes the structure and social power relations in the traditional Syrian family, and provides the opportunity for the refugee mothers to control their private, family lives, to make their own decision, and to create their own self-sustaining lives. (See Connor, Ayallo, and Elliott in this volume for further research on mothering survival strategies among African refugee mothers in New Zealand.)

The mothers' strong desire for employment free of SGBV, fair wages, and safe education for their daughters and sons demonstrates the power and enthusiasm for emancipation prevalent among most of the interviewed Syrian refugee mothers. Mothering seems to strengthen the desire for establishing and managing a separate family space and future. Such a desire is exemplified in the case of the twenty-year-old Syrian mother in Sariyer, who decided to live separate from the extended family and expressed her desire to work instead of giving birth to another baby. Angry at her husband, she protested: "Since he insisted on making kids, he will have to work more and harder to cover their expenses! I told him, but he does not understand! I could work anywhere. I can cook, clean, sew.... It would be better if I could work too; we could collect money for a house and then make kids!"

Nonetheless, as the experiences of Syrian refugee mothers show, the political, administrative, social, and cultural boundaries of the modern, temporary and masculine protection regimes narrow the living spaces and opportunities for self-sustaining and emancipated motherhood. The legal and structural mechanisms of social marginalization and victimization of the refugee women make Syrian refugee mothers vulnerable to ethnic discrimination, sexual violence, and social exploitation. Blind to the high rates of rape and sexual violence in the war, in the camps and during the flight, many middle-class women dismiss refugee mothers as conservative in their unwillingness to use birth control; as irresponsible and incompetent for having the numerous kids; and as social exploiters who allow or use child labour alleviate their poverty. In this way, as Val Gillies points out, the poor outcomes for children are associated with the "bad" mothering of the Syrian refugee mothers. In fact, the perception of the refugee mothering practices is much more contested than the mothering practices of impoverished Turkish mothers because it is intertwined with geography, race and temporary "guest" status of the refugee mothers.

Under this perspective, the crowded families of the refugee mothers are seen as both an opportunity for charity as well as a social burden on the welfare system in Turkey. Some Islamic mothers have advised Turkish mothers to teach their own children about the poverty of the Syrian children and mothers, to give charity to Syrian children and to strengthen the Turkish children's Islamic morality (Reyhane).

Through those disciplining discourses, modern Islamic middle-class Turkish mothers marginalize and subject Syrian mothers to their "good" mothering projects on child education and morality care. There are some class-based similarities between the poor refugee and Turkish mothers, as both experience rising violence and deepening poverty in their respective communities. Nevertheless, impoverished Turkish mothers have clear legal access and a voice, albeit a limited one, to debate public schooling and welfare policies. Refugee women, on the other hand, are overwhelmed by the struggle for legality, fair and human shelter, clean water and food, and safety from sexual violence and exploitation, which has followed them from the war, to the border, to the camps and onto the streets, and, finally, into their new apartments and workplaces.

The fear of sexual harassment and rape is so deeply present in the memories and daily articulations of the refugee mothers that it constructs their overall experience in Turkey within the frame of constant insecurity and never-ending poverty. This fear is extremely profound in the experiences of the single mothers.

The lack of access to official documents because of the war leaves Syrian women vulnerable to illegal religious forms of marriage, which often involve sexual exploitation as sex workers or deeper poverty and vulnerability as single mothers.

Similarly, Syrian refugee mothers who lost their husbands during the war or flight across the borders become economically worse off in refuge and also at peace because of their single motherhood. Unwanted or forced motherhood profoundly changes women's perceptions, goals, and ambitions in exile, too. Goals and dreams are postponed until the children are grown; the struggle to survive now takes precedence.

Nevertheless, in a constant divergent collision between their memories, responsibilities, and desires as women and mothers, and the responsibilities, demands, and constraints of both local and Syrian neighbours, women, men, employers, and so forth, the Syrian refugee mothers succeed to resist, subvert, and survive the material and social marginalization of the temporary protection regime. There are numerous success stories. A woman named Najlaa, for example, gathered forty-five Syrian mothers in Kilis, Turkey and established a handcrafts and knitting community centre of Syrian mothers. Thus she created a sustainable business model to make ends meet for forty-five families (Unal). Echoing the sentiments of Ruth Sidel, single or not, refugee mothers are courageous, resilient, creative, and strong enough to survive and undertake the burden of the family and mothering by constructing ways of mothering that express their values and preserve their sense of emancipation beyond the narrow confines and demands of patriarchal motherhood (Edin and Lein).

NOTES

[1]Further analysis, interviews, and outcomes of the fieldwork study on Syrian women and LGBTI refugees in Istanbul can be found in my and Zeynep Kivilcim's book, *Sürgünde Toplumsal Cinsiyet (Gender in Exile)*, Istanbul: Der Publishing, 2015. Based on the analyses of the interviews and observations related only to the Syrian refugee mothers interviewed, the following chapter brings new and different perspective to the Syrian refugee crisis.

[2]This system is designed under the Temporary Protection Directive entered into force in October 2014.

[3]The interviews were hold in Arabic or Kurdish, simultaneously translated into Turkish, and later on in English.

[4]This official study is based on interviews with Syrian women in the following provinces: Adana, Adıyaman, Gaziantep, Hatay, Kahramanmaraş, Kilis, Malatya, Mardin, Osmaniye and Şanlıurfa. Thus, it does not represent the Syrian women in Istanbul.

WORKS CITED

Afet İşleri Daire Başkanlığı (AFAD) [Emerency Affairs Directorate]. *Barınma Merkezlerinde Toplam Suriyeli Sayısı*. Ankara, 24 Haziran 2015.

Afet İşleri Daire Başkanlığı -AFAD. [Emerency Affairs Directorate], *Türkiye'de Suriyeli Kadınlar*. Report, Ankara, 2014.

Alpak, G. et al. "Post-traumatic Stress Disorder among Syrian Refugees in Turkey: A Cross-Sectional Dtudy." *International Journal of Psychiatry in Clinical Practice*, vol. 19, no. 6, Oct. 2014. *Taylor & Francis*, doi: 10.3109/13651501.2014.961930. Accessed 11 Aug. 2016. Baklacioglu, Nurcan Ozgur, and Zeynep Kivilcim. *Sürgünde Toplumsal Cinsiyet [Gender in Exile]*. Der Publishing, 2015.

Chang, Grace. *Disposable Domestics: Immigrant Women Workers in the Global Economy*. South End, 2000.

Edin, Kathryn, and Laura Lein. *Making Ends Meet: How Single Mothers Survive Welfare and Low-Wage Work*. Russell Sage, 1997.

Gillies, Val. *Marginalised Mothers: Exploring Working-Class Experiences of Parenting*. Routledge, 2006.

Hynes, H. Patricia. "On the Battlefield of Women's Bodies: An Overview of the Harm of War to Women." *Women's Studies International Forum*, vol. 27, 2004, pp. 431-445.

Indra, Doreen Marie. *Engendering Forced Migration: Theory and Practice*, Berghahn Books, 1999.

International Crisis Group. "Chechnya: The Inner Abroad. Report N°236," International Crisis Group, 30 June 2015, www.crisisgroup.org/europe-central-asia/caucasus/north-caucasus/

chechnya-inner-abroad. Accessed 11 Aug. 2016.

International Federation for Human Rights. "Violence against Women in Syria: Breaking the Silence," *FIDH: Worldwide Movement for Human Rights*, FIDH, April 2013, www.fidh.org/en/region/north-africa-middle-east/syria/13134-violence-against-women-in-syria-breaking-the-silence. Accessed 11 Aug. 2016.

Karakuş, Ali, et al. "The Reflection of the Syrian Civil War on the Emergency Department and Assessment of Hospital Costs." *Ulusal Travma ve Acil Cerrahi Dergisi*, vol. 19, no. 5, 2013, pp. 429.

Kesgin, H. and Ali Ozturk. "The Bitter Truth Behind Syrian War: Desperate Widows." *Anadolu Agency*, Anadolu Agency, 10 Feb 2014, www.aa.com.tr/en/news/285989--the-bitter- truth-behind-syrian-war-desperate-widows. Accessed 11 Aug. 2016.

Kivilcim, Zeynep. "Legal Framework and Problems of Access to Health Care." Columbia Global Centers-Istanbul Panel: Prioritizing Women-Adapting Refugee Health Services for Twenty-First-Century Health Challenges, 7 Mar. 2015, Istanbul, Conference Presentation.

Korac, Maja. "War, Flight, and Exile: Gendered Violence Among Refugee Women from Post-Yugoslav States." *Sites of Violence: Gender and Conflict Zones*, edited by W. Giles ad J. Hyndman, University of California Press, 2004, pp. 249-272.

O'Reilly, Andrea. *Rocking the Cradle: Thoughts on Feminism, Motherhood, and the Possibility of Empowered Motherhood.* Demeter Press, 2006.

Parrenas, Rhacel Salazar. *Children of Global Migration: Transnational Families and Gendered Woes*, Stanford University Press, 2005.

Peace and Security UN Women. *Inter-agency Assessment Gender-Based Violence and Child Protection among Syrian Refugees in Jordan, with a Focus on Early Marriage*, United Nations, 2013.

Pickering, Sharon. *Women, Borders, and Violence: Current Issues in Asylum, Forced Migration.* Springer, 2011

Reyhane, Ummu. "Suriyeli muhacirler bizim için kulfet mi, Nimet mi?" [Are Syrian Migrants Burden or Profit?]. *Müslüman anneler* [Muslim Mothers], www.muslumananneler.net. Accessed 11 Aug. 2016.

Sidel, Ruth. *Unsung Heroines: Single Mothers and the American*

Dream. University of California Press, 2006.

Toplum ve Hukuk Ara;tirmalari Vakfi (TOHAV) [Foundation for Social and Legal Research]. *Suriyeli Mültecilerle İligili Sağlık Tarama Raporu* [Syrian Refugees Health Report], Istanbul, TOHAV, 2013

Toplu, Reyhan. "Immigration of Discrimination: Syrian Asylum-Seeker Women, Istanbul Experiences." Unpublished collection of interviews with Syrian Women, Istanbul, 2014.

United Nations. *2014 Syria Regional Response Plan Turkey.* United Nations, 2014.

Unal, Selin. "The Syrian Refugee Mother Transforming Women's Life in Turkey." *UNCHR News Stories*, UNCHR, 30 July 2015, unhcr.org/55b9f4689.html. Accessed 11 Aug. 2016.

United Nations High Commissioner for Refugees (UNCHR). *UNCHR Regional Data on Syrian Refugees*, UNCHR, data.unhcr.org/syrianrefugees/regional.php. Accessed 11 Aug. 2016.

United Nations Development Fund for Women (UNIFEM). *Baseline Survey on Sexual and Gender-Based Violence in Rwanda.* United Nations, 2008.

Women's Commission for Refugee Women and Children. *Abuse without End: Burmese Refugee Women and Children at Risk of Trafficking.* Women's Refugee Commission, 2006.

7.

Changing Places, Changing Bodies

Reproducing Families through Food

HELEN VALLIANATOS

FOOD IS A HIGHLY SALIENT TOOL used to signify identity. It is a social object, laden with social values that are consumed; in turn, through digestion, people incorporate a food's meanings and morals. A food's meaning comes from its analogous physical properties, its association with particularly symbolic festivals, and its connection to long-standing traditions. The latter two meanings are well illustrated by harvest festivals, such as Thanksgiving in the United States, where fall foods, such as pumpkins as well as the conspicuous roast turkey, are central elements. Furthermore, certain kinds of food make allusions to gender, and men may be censured from consuming foods associated with women and vice versa. The gendering of foods is exemplified by Hua men of Papua New Guinea, who at initiation avoid eating mushrooms aesthetically associated with women (i.e., because they sprouted during women's menstrual cycle) (Meigs). Gendered food meanings continue in contemporary North America through the inherent meanings embodied in certain foods (McPhail et al.), in food consumption practices (Counihan), and in food work (Beagan et al., *Acquired Tastes*; DeVault).

Similarly, consumption and avoidance of particular foods symbolizes group boundaries of inclusion or exclusion. Mary Douglas's classic study of Jewish food categories, albeit imperfect, illustrates how and why certain foods are fit for offerings, others for everyday consumption, whereas others are proscribed. Food taboos can be effective markers that separate "us" from "others," when "others" consume those tabooed foods. Thus, the food practices of immigrants can reveal gendered social norms and values as well as serve as a tool to mark insider and outsider status. Furthermore, proscribed foods may also mark one's current status within the group; this includes food rules placed on women while pregnant and breastfeeding. In many societies, social rules govern what an expectant or new mother can and cannot eat.

As a key component of everyday life, food is inextricably linked with reproduction, where reproduction is defined as a combination of social and biological propagation. The process of eating mirrors reproduction, wherein one incorporates the "other" (i.e., food) to (re)create self (Fischler) both physically and socially. For instance, through consumption of particular foods in particular ways, people not only sustain themselves biologically but also (re)create current and desired social selves (Beagan et al., *Acquired Tastes;* Korseymer). Pregnant women embody this process of digestion and creation, as they are constructing not only their own but their child's body. Consequently, they are subject to a heightened social gaze—either self-imposed or from family, community, and the body politic (i.e., social structures such as medical, educational and legal institutions that regulate, scrutinize, and control both individual and social bodies—see Scheper-Hughes and Lock). Indeed, what a pregnant woman eats, how she eats, and how she behaves are of interest to many.

Pregnant immigrant women are of particular significance to the body politic. Since many may be ignorant of hegemonic messages of appropriate food practices and others may simply defy them, these women become targets for intervention (e.g., treatment and understanding of culturally based ideas of food, body, and gender by biomedical institutions or practitioners). Because birthing is not only physical reproduction but also critical to social propagation and to the continuation of the family and community, pressures to alter customary practices to conform to hegemonic medical discourses and practices are a potential source of tension. For immigrant women, this tension accentuates other stressors associated with migration and settlement (e.g., financial and linguistic challenges). The need to become literate of new reproductive contexts and rules—in conjunction with the anxiety of not having the means, knowledge, or skills to ensure that traditional practices for social reproduction are followed—is a source of pressure and strain for immigrant mothers. Nevertheless, migration can also offer opportunities previously unavailable to pregnant women.

This chapter examines the experiences of thirty-eight immigrant mothers who migrated from South Asia—primarily from northern India and Pakistan—and finally settled in an urban centre in Western Canada. These women represented diverse religious affiliations—Muslim, Hindu, Sikh, Jain—ages, and socioeconomic backgrounds; all, however, experienced a downward socioeconomic shift consistent with contemporary immigrant experiences in Canada (McDonald and Kennedy). For example, one mother explained how tough the initial years in Canada were, even though both she and her husband were highly educated: "Even now, he has a job of his own field, but it is a very initial level job; the pay is not what I expected. In Pakistan, you live together in a family house, expenses are shared, everybody pitches in. There is always some support. Hard times are much harder here, as you have nobody." Individual and focus group interviews were conducted in women's homes in English, Hindi, or Urdu and ranged in length from one and a half to three hours. A community research assistant who could provide clarification and translation during the interview process as needed accompanied me. Food was always shared. I provided food for the focus group interviews, as hospitality norms dictate the offering of food to guests, and I was always offered food when conducting individual interviews. In the following section, I provide a contextual background on reproductive food practices, before examining how these food beliefs and practices shifted after these women migrated.

FOOD RULES FOR MOTHERS IN SOUTH ASIA

The basis for rules governing mothers' food consumption in South Asia is humoral medicine. Humoral medical systems are based on the idea that balance of bodily elements must be maintained for good health; the number and type of these elements vary by humoral medical system. In South Asia, Unani and Ayurvedic medicine exemplify this system, with the latter being most widespread. To maintain health in Ayurvedic medicine, the three *doshas* (*vata, pit-*

ta, and *kapha*) must be in balance. Simply put, the body can vary in state from "hot" to "cold." This classification is not a bipolar categorization but rather a continuum from one end ("hot") to the other ("cold"). One of the ways to maintain everyday health (i.e., balance) is through diet. Just as a body can be classified in the "hot-cold" continuum, foods are also categorized along this spectrum. Foods, however, do not change their categorization; thus as the body state shifts, people modify their diet by taking into account the season, presence and type of illness, and life stage, including pregnancy or lactation.

Pregnancy is classified as a "hot" condition; consequently, to maintain balance and health, women must avoid "hot" foods and consume "cold" ones. If too much heat builds in the body, the consequences can be severe. As one mother explained, miscarriage may result: "We give less meat to pregnant women because meat has a tendency to increase body heat, which may cause miscarriage, this is what we believe." Such "hot" foods include meat, eggs, dried fruit or nuts, and vegetables and fruits, such as eggplant (brinjal), papaya, and mango. One Pakistani mother recalled avoiding not only meat but bitter melon and dates as well. Typical "cold" foods include other vegetables and fruits and dairy products. However, it should not be assumed that all women strictly follow these rules. Even in India, I found that generalities were quickly qualified: one could eat proscribed foods if the pregnancy was going well in the third trimester, and idiosyncratic bodily differences meant that foods such as fish and chicken were acceptable for some but not for others (Vallianatos, *Poor and Pregnant*). There was also a fair amount of debate among women with whom I spoke on the classification of foods along the "hot-cold" spectrum, outside of a few agreed-upon categorizations (e.g., meat was a "hot" food). Furthermore, I found that prior reproductive experiences and women's family structure in India influenced how closely their behaviour aligned to these food norms. For instance, if a woman had not followed the rules in a previous pregnancy and experienced a negative outcome, she was more likely to follow the food rules the next time. I also noted that the presence of other family members, particularly mothers-in-law, influenced the likelihood of a woman abiding by the food norms in India (Vallianatos, "Placing Maternal Health").

With birth, the state of the body changes, and instead of avoiding "hot" foods, mothers consume them and avoid "cold" ones. Heat provided by "hot" foods is required to heal and strengthen the body after birth, which is especially important for the forty days after birth, but consumption of "cold" foods continues at least through the early months of breastfeeding. While breastfeeding, mothers also avoid "windy" foods, such as cauliflower, as these foods would produce gas and pain in the infant's stomach.

CHANGING PLACES, CONTINUING PRACTICES?

In India, the women with whom I had worked were mostly migrants from rural areas surrounding New Delhi. Just as there was variation among those women on whether the food norms were followed, my work with migrant mothers also found variations in practices. A few women made sure to continue food proscriptions after migration, as one woman shared: "we are not allowed to eat bitter melon, dates and avoid meat also.... I took the same precautions here." Similarly, after birth, effort was made to eat the "hot" healing foods traditionally provided: "I called my mother in India, [my mother noted I had] never made those things in India, [but] now my friends are making me eat traditional things [laughs]." The mother-in-law of this participant's friend, who was in Canada, made one of the traditional snacks consisting of nuts fried in butter (*panjery*) for her. Mixing turmeric in milk was a common postbirth remedy; in fact, the consumption of liquids (e.g., milk, juice, and water) was highly recommended.

But continuation of customary food practices can also be challenging, as immigrant women in Canada reported receiving different advice from biomedical practitioners that conflicted with customary food norms. This is an interesting finding, since biomedicine (known as allopathic medicine) is also practised in South Asia. I was told that women in Canada preferred to visit an allopathic doctor who was of South Asian origins, who would incorporate Ayurvedic concepts into biomedical practice, including using food to heal prior to turning to allopathic pharmaceuticals. Such discordant advice received from non-South Asian allopathic doctors was particularly well illustrated by one participant's experience receiving the recommendation to consume meat. Anemia during pregnancy is not uncommon, and a good dietary source of iron is lean red meat. One Sikh mother recalled being told by doctors that "meat gives you strength." Meat eating was possible in her family, but its consumption is gendered. Men often do eat meat, including her husband, who wanted her to feed their son meat: "my husband wants him to be a strong boy, so he wants him to eat meat." Despite a biomedical doctor's advice to eat meat during pregnancy, this immigrant mother never did, as she had not eaten meat and eggs since the day she was married. As she explained: "after marriage, at my in-laws, ladies don't eat eggs and meat, so I had to follow ... according to our religion, men are not allowed, but we can't stop them." The normative practices established by her affinal kin continued to shape her pregnancy dietary choices after migrating, even over the advice of biomedical experts. Elders in an extended family, particularly the mother-in-law, play a key role in controlling a woman's diet during pregnancy.

The role of family members in propagating dietary knowledge is further illustrated in focus-group debates. For example, one recent immigrant mother, Asha,[1] opined that "There is a lot of pressure from mother and in-laws, husband, that you should drink a lot of milk and healthy food when you are pregnant." This well-meant pressure, combined with gendered household tasks, compelled women to behave in ways that made them uncomfortable or ill; they could not solely meet their own desires. The discomfort women reported experiencing was exacerbated by pregnancy sickness (aka morning sickness). Another mother, Chandra, responded to the Asha by saying, "Back home when I used to make meals I never felt like eating it [sic] because the smell of food made me not [like] eating it." And Asha agreed. These women still had to prepare meals for their families that they did not like or desire, as their particular food aversions associated with pregnancy were ignored in order to put other family members' needs first. Living on their own away from extended family allowed these women more freedom to alter practices to suit their own needs.

Moving to a place far from family networks did provide some women with the opportunity to eat as they wished while pregnant or breastfeeding, without considering traditional norms. Yet many did continue to follow dietary dictates as best they could, especially as they navigated alterations in underlying beliefs that shaped normative practices.

CHANGING BODIES, CONTINUING BELIEFS?

Understanding the bodily changes in mothers requires understanding the belief systems that women use to make sense of their (and their baby's) needs. Medical systems on which dietary recommendations are based are still cultural systems. Thus, how biomedicine is practised in different places is culturally influenced. As previously noted, for these women, moving to Canada was not the first time that they experienced biomedicine; it is a medical system also integral to the wellness practices in their home countries. However, how biomedicine integrates with Ayurveda and beliefs rooted in long cultural histories of diet and health practice did seem to lead to some disjunctions for these women after migrating. In this section, I further delineate the underlying beliefs that influence food practices of mothers as their bodies change with reproduction.

Two forms of authoritative knowledge have shaped food consumption practices for mothers. The first kind is the customary and embodied knowledge—shared through elders' teaching—that enforces traditions. This type of knowledge is to be respected, for as one woman said, "what older people say there is some truth and benefit." Another woman noted that respect for one's elders and their teachings is reflected in women's food practices before birth and in the postpartum period: "our elders tell us to do it, so we just follow the tradition." But not all women agreed with their elders' advice. A mother who had a professional degree was frustrated with the inaccuracies, from her standpoint, of her mother-in-law's advice: "I couldn't do things in my way. If the child cries then it is mom's fault. If I would hold her, they had problems like you're spoiling her and stuff like that." This woman felt that she could not voice her own opinions and beliefs, including how to feed her infant, and that she was being forever criticized for mothering

129

practices; at root of her problem was her inability (or perceived inability) to voice her thoughts. For her, migration provided an opportunity to act on her beliefs and behave in a manner that she thought to be correct.

The second kind of authoritative knowledge is that of medical systems (both Ayurvedic and biomedicine). These medical systems are grounded in beliefs and traditions based on histories of ideas, experiences, and practices, with Ayurveda rooted in the Vedic period[2] (between 1500 and 500 BCE) and biomedicine rooted in Western scientific traditions. Although both knowledge systems are used in India, the dominance of biomedicine in Canada did seem to influence the practices of some women, who began to view dietary traditions as myths, not scientific ideas, which must, therefore, be incorrect. Others found inconsistencies between biomedical healthcare practitioners in South Asia and Canada confusing, as one recent immigrant woman explained:

In Pakistan, doctors say don't eat cauliflower, potatoes, basmati rice if you're breastfeeding or especially if you have a C-section, but here in Canada, there is no diet restriction. I don't know if the vegetables, nutrients are different here than back home ...Vegetables like cauliflower, potatoes and rice tend to make you fat back home but not here.

Another Pakistani mother exasperatedly said, "Here, they don't stop you from eating anything when you are sick. In Pakistan, if you have a fever people say don't eat wheat. Here, there is no restriction on food when you're sick, but there, back home, people put restrictions on food. Even if you have diarrhea, [in Canada] they don't stop us from eating." Mothers' experiences in hospital after giving birth illustrated the disjunction between the two systems practiced in Canada, as illustrated in this exchange:

Asha: Here, when my third child was born they gave me cold food like ice cream, but in India, that would be unthinkable, no cold food. It depends on your thinking. Eashi: I remember when I was having labour pains, my mom called and told me, "don't eat ice cream or sit on

cold mat and take spa bath after birth."
Ghaada: In Pakistan, they don't give you bath after delivering at least for two or three days. Here they make you take bath right away. People say drink warm water, stay inside the house, if you drink cold water your tummy will bulge out. All say this, yes, yes.

The embodied knowledge of the women themselves is also important in shaping beliefs (and practices) during pregnancy (Vallianatos, *Poor and Pregnant*) and also while breastfeeding. A recent immigrant woman explained, "If you eat cauliflower it will cause acidity in stomach and my baby used to cry, so my diet became limited." Thus, certain foods are avoided because of perceived effects on the women and, hence, on their infants.

Medical pluralism—the simultaneous practice of different health beliefs and practices—is well documented in diverse places around the world, including India and Pakistan (Leslie; Nichter and Lock; Samuel; Shaikh et al.). This is no difference in Canada, where people routinely try "home" or "familial" remedies. Working with South Asian immigrants in the United States, Deepa Rao has documented how beliefs on the effectiveness and appropriateness of different medical systems and treatments affected these immigrants' health practices. I suggest "medical pluralism" is a useful concept for understanding these immigrant mothers' beliefs and practices. Their simultaneous use of traditional medical systems with new understandings of bodies, particularly pregnant bodies, in Canadian biomedical practices suggests expectant and new mothers were balancing the authoritative advice received from professionals, their families, and their own embodied ways of knowing. These behavioural choices and resultant practices were important not only for their own sense of well-being and identity but because of the symbolic power and meanings that these choices evoked. In the following section, the multiple meanings of reproduction and the pressures placed on mothers are explored.

OUR BABIES, OUR SELVES: REPRODUCING IN A NEW PLACE

Food work is central to contemporary women's roles and responsibilities in Canada, as it is elsewhere in the world among different ethnocultural groups (Beagan et al., "It's Just"). In her chapter in this volume, Meredith Stephens explores this cross-cultural responsibility by sharing her personal experiences on the importance for mothers to provide a high quality lunch in Japan. Reproducing the family through their food work is central because of the need to both nourish the family and feed the soul of the family. It is through food that mothers transmit their love and values to the next generation. An elder Sikh woman advised, "put all your efforts, time, skill, the food will turn good." It is through the "good" food she prepared that her affection for her family was shown. Because of their food-related responsibilities, mothers bear the responsibility to transmit familial customs and values in order to ensure ethnocultural identities are not lost after migrating (Vallianatos and Raine). It is also through their food work that mothers may be judged as being inadequate. As one mother noted, "They do say that she doesn't cook well; she doesn't cook in our style."[3]

Mothers also have a special position in their communities, especially so in migrant communities. Because of the social and physical role that pregnant women have in propagating the family and community, pregnant women are especially cared for. One recent immigrant mother recollected that "My husband looked after me. He bought special cheese, yogurt for me and made me eat it." In a group interview with recent immigrant women, the women stated that being catered to while pregnant was done, in part, out of consideration for the infant's future. One woman related that in her region of origin, "If the baby drools, [it means that] the mom didn't get the food she craved during the pregnancy; it's in our culture." Another mother replied that in her traditions, "If the mother is not happy during pregnancy, the baby cries a lot." Thus, the state of the infant after birth is a reflection not just of the mother's self-care during pregnancy but also of the care that her family provided.

Beyond the physical act of reproduction, mothers also nourish the infant and birth a new social member into the community. The act of feeding growing children is a venue for teaching, implicitly and explicitly, what it means to a member of a particular family and ethnocultural community. Mothers may feel pressure, self-imposed or from other family members, to cook traditional foods for their children, yet at the same time, those children eventually become conduits for new food items and practices. For example, children of various sociocultural and ethnic backgrounds may be influenced by food advertising on television or by peer interactions (Kotler et al.; Webber Cullen et al.). Some mothers indulged their children by taking them to chain restaurants on a monthly basis. Other mothers attempted to incorporate some new food items. For instance, when I asked one mother if her children asked for food that they had seen on television or elsewhere, she replied, "pizza pops, Oh Henry [chocolate bars], they see white friends eating, and they ask me to buy. But I prefer to buy fruits. I try to give them less ice cream, less candy, not every day; sometimes it's okay.... [I buy] sometimes when I am in a rush, I have no time to argue, and it's hard to explain to them."

In some families children may begin to resist traditional foods and begin to prefer new "Canadian" foods, which can be tantamount to rejecting traditional cultural values (see Beagan et al., *Acquired Tastes*; Vallianatos, "Migration, Mothers, Meals"). Most mothers tried to accommodate their children's preferences, despite being saddened by their implicit shifting values. As one mother eloquently reflected: "But here with my kids, they have complaints, dislikes and likes. I think it is my fault; I never set any limit, like that's it—you have to eat or stay hungry. So I have spoiled them. I should have set the limit, the way my mom and dad did." She noted that children's preferences were not catered to in the same way back home, yet this seemed to be more common after she migrated. She hypothesized that this was in part due to her and husband's downward social shift after arriving in Canada. Thus, to compensate for that, they spoiled their children: "We give them not only what they need but also what they want."

As I mentioned above, some mothers negotiated and interpreted different types of authoritative knowledge in concert with the embodied knowledge of their own dietary practices (e.g., disjunctions around consuming red meat while pregnant); some also extended this belief to their children's dietary practices, as exemplified in the words of one Punjabi mother:

I make them eat beef as I am [in Canada], because they are not going to go back to India and they have to live here, so I don't mind them eating it. Even the doctors say that you should eat beef or meat cause if you don't, you could get a deficiency of I don't know vitamins or iron, so yeah.... Well, like, what I believe is that once you come here, you have to be a little bit like them [Canadians] 'cause, I mean, if you follow your Indian culture it's going to be hard for you, 'cause if you come here, you have to change. But there [India] you can think Indian, but here it can't be like that, so it's not easy going shopping every day.

This mother's perspectives are intriguing. She was further asked about what her family back in India thought about this, to which she replied, "I don't think they mind [that I feed my children beef] because if I tell them that there is nothing to eat, they don't mind." She also alluded to her belief on the necessity of change and to conform to Canadian hegemonic values in some ways. Furthermore, she ended her thoughts on the subject by noting the pragmatic necessities in her quotidian food provisioning for her family. In a place where beef is readily available as opposed to more traditional red meats (i.e., goat), shifting family food practices made sense for her.

Another component to reproducing the next generation through food involves fasting; through teaching, implicitly at first, how and when to fast, mothers impart gendered, religious and ethnocultural values and identities. Fasting in South Asia is predominantly women's work, although men fast as well (Pearson; Vallianatos, *Poor and Pregnant*). Many women continue to fast even while pregnant or breastfeeding, although allowances may be made for reproduction (i.e., when the woman is pregnant or breastfeeding): "I used to feel hungry and thirsty [when breastfeeding] but I still used to fast." In Canada, though, women noted that fasting was not the same, particularly because it was less of a communal affair. Fasting was less arduous back home, where women, kin, and neighbours would gather to prepare for, conduct, and break the fast. Without this sociality, some mothers found continuing traditions difficult, and instead of modelling fasting behaviour, they reduced this practice. As one woman explained, "I used to [fast], but now I don't with the kids because it's hard to focus with the kids because whenever the kids are eating they give some food to mummy and daddy."

In sum, women's bodily changes during reproduction symbolize their social and biological roles as mothers. Migrant mothers negotiate personal, familial, and ethnocultural beliefs in their everyday food practices. Arguably, this ability to negotiate is particularly important after migration when mothers impart what it means to be a member of their respective communities through food practices. Immigrants typically connect with home through food, but during reproduction, food practices become more fraught with meaning; these tensions were particularly evident in group interviews, as mothers debated their distinct ways of reproducing communities—who reproduced "good" future citizens versus those who altered customary practices.

Thus, reproductive food beliefs and practices altered with migration, but how they altered reflected individual life histories, particularly women's education, family structure, and reproductive experiences. Postmigration stress centred on lack of support networks, particularly those of kin. Yet opportunities also existed, and these centred on the freedom to behave in accordance with personal beliefs, informed by authoritative or embodied knowledges. Examination of the food practices of maternal migrants, therefore, is a fruitful avenue for exploring how meanings of self and place are produced, negotiated, and reproduced.

Acknowledgements: I thank all the women who took the time to speak and share food with me. I would also like to thank H. Syed who worked so closely with me and helped me in any way needed. Y. Chiu and others at the Multicultural Health Brokers Cooperative fostered the initial connections to the community.

NOTES

[1]Pseudonyms are used to protect the identity of participants, in accordance with voluntary and informed consent, which was received from all participants.

²The origins of Ayurvedic traditions are debated by scholars, as some suggest its origins are even earlier. However, written records do exist from the Vedic period.

³ For analysis on intrahousehold gender and age dynamics, see Vallianatos, "Migration, Mothers, Meals."

WORKS CITED

Beagan, Brenda, et al. *Acquired Tastes: Why Families Eat the Way They Do*. University of British Columbia Press, 2015.

Beagan, Brenda, et al. "'It's Just Easier For Me to Do It': Rationalizing the Family Division of Food Work." *Sociology,* vol. 42, no. 4, 2008, pp. 653-671.

Counihan, Carole M. *The Anthropology of Food and Body: Gender, Meaning and Power*. Routledge, 1999.

DeVault, Marjorie L. *Feeding the Family: The Social Organization of Caring as Gendered Work*. University of Chicago Press, 1991.

Douglas, Mary. "The Abominations of Leviticus." *Food and Culture: A Reader*. 3rd ed., edited by Carole M. Counihan and Penny Van Esterik, Routledge, 2013, pp. 48-58.

Fischler, Claude. "Food, Self and Identity." *Social Science Information*, vol. 27, no. 2, 1988, pp. 275-292.

Kotler, Jennifer A., et al. "The Influence of Media Characters on Children's Food Choices." *Journal of Health Communication*, vol. 17, no. 8, 2012, pp. 886-898.

Leslie, Charles. *Asian Medical Systems: A Comparative Study*. University of California Press, 1976.

McDonald, James T. and Steven Kennedy. "Insights into the 'Healthy Immigrant Effect': Health Status and Health Service Use of Immigrants to Canada." *Social Science and Medicine*, vol. 59, no. 8, 2004, pp. 1613-1627.

McPhail, Deborah, et al. "I Don't Want to Be Sexist But..." *Food, Culture & Society*, vol. 15, no. 3, 2012, pp. 473-489.

Meigs, Anna. "Food as a Cultural Construction." *Food and Culture: A Reader*, edited by.Carole M. Counihan and Penny Van Esterik, Routledge, 1996, pp. 95-106.

Nichter, Mark and Margaret Lock, editors. *New Horizons in Medical Anthropology*. Routledge, 2002.

Pearson, Anne M. "Because It Gives Me Peace of Mind." *Ritual Fasts in the Religious Lives of Hindu Women.* State University of New York Press, 1996.

Rao, Deepa. "Choice of Medicine and Hierarchy of Resort to Different Health Alternatives among Asian Indian Migrants in a Metropolitan City in the USA." *Ethnicity and Health*, vol. 11, no. 2, 2006, pp. 153-167.

Samuel, Geoffrey. "Healing and the Mind-body Complex: Childbirth and Medical Pluralism in South Asia." *Multiple Medical Realities: Patients and Healers in Biomedical, Alternative and Traditional Medicine*, edited by Helle Johannessen and Imre Lázár, Berghahn Books, 2006, pp. 121-135.

Scheper-Hughes, Nancy, and Margaret M. Lock. "The Mindful Body: A Prolegomenon to Future Work in Medical Anthropology." *Medical Anthropology Quarterly*, vol.1. no.1, 1987, pp. 6-41.

Shaikh, Shahzad H., et al. "Trends in the Use of Complementary and Alternative Medicine in Pakistan: A Population-Based Survey." *Journal of Alternative & Complementary Medicine*, vol. 15, no. 5, 2009, pp. 545-550.

Vallianatos, Helen. "Migration, Mothers, Meals." Manuscript submitted.

Vallianatos, Helen. "Placing Maternal Health in India." *Locating Health: Explorations of Healing and Place*, edited by Erika Dyck and Christopher Fletcher, Pickering & Chatto Publishers Ltd., 2011, pp. 11-27.

Vallianatos, Helen. *Poor and Pregnant in New Delhi, India.* International Institute for Qualitative Methodology Series, Left Coast Press, 2006.

Vallianatos, Helen, and Kim D. Raine. "Consuming Food, Constructing Identities: A Symbolic Analysis of Diet among Arabic and South Asian Immigrant Women." *Food, Culture and Society*, vol. 11, no. 3, 2008, pp. 355-373.

Webber Cullen, Karen, et al. "Socio-environmental Influences on Children's Diets: Results from Focus Groups with African-, Euro-, and Mexican-American Children and Their Parents." *Health Education Research*, vol. 15, no. 5, 2000, pp. 581-590.

I.

MOTHERING IN A FOREIGN LAND II
Generational Dynamics in Settlement and Mothers' Responsibilities

8.
An Immigrant Mother's "Revolt against Silence" in Edwidge Danticat's *Brother, I'm Dying*

JUSTINE DYMOND

"Will the war on terrorism redefine the meaning of who belongs in America?"
—Tram Nguyen, *We Are All Suspects Now: Untold Stories from Immigrant America After 9/11*

"I wanted to speak for my uncle and my father, for my family,
but also for the hundreds and thousands of families who lose loved ones in this way."
—Edwidge Danticat in an interview with Renee H. Shea

IN HER MEMOIR, *Brother, I'm Dying* (2007), Haitian American writer Edwidge Danticat recounts the stories of Granmè Melina, a figure much loved by the children in the Port-au-Prince neighbourhood of Bel Air. Danticat writes, "One of the stories she told most often was the Rapunzel-like tale of a beautiful young girl whose mother, fearful that she might be abducted by passersby, locked her inside a small but pretty house by the side of the road while the mother worked in the field until dusk" (*Brother* 69). At the end of her work day, the mother's song identifies her to her daughter, who unlocks the house to let the mother in. Echoing not only Rapunzel but also the Biblical story of the Garden of Eden, the story includes a snake "hoping to trick the girl into coming out" (*Brother* 69). Granmè Melina's tale of a mother's protection from afar clearly resonates with the young Danticat, whose parents had left her in order to (eventually) protect her and her

141

brother from the political chaos of their homeland. But perhaps more pointedly, the absent mother of Granmè Melina's story uses her voice as a metaphorical key to indicate when it is safe to open the door of the house. This aspect of the story resonates with the memoir's recurring theme of Danticat's role as the voice of her uncle throughout her childhood and into adulthood. Initially, while living with her uncle in Haiti after her parents emigrate to the U.S., she takes on this role when her uncle loses his voice to throat cancer. In writing her memoir, Danticat's voice once again stands in for her uncle and bears witness to his harrowing escape from political violence in Haiti and his sudden death in detention in Miami—the tragic and wholly preventable loss of a man who never wanted to leave Haiti but was forced to do so.

Alongside the stories of her uncle and her father, the paternal figures in her life, Danticat also recounts her experiences of becoming a mother as she is pregnant with her first child at the time of her uncle's death. In these parallel story lines, Danticat confronts mortality while creating life and also grappling with the significance of giving birth as a naturalized U.S. citizen "around the same time [her] uncle was being rejected from this country" (qtd. in Pulitano 47). Danticat notes in an interview with Elvira Pulitano in *small axe: A Caribbean Journal of Criticism* that becoming a mother "did make me think a lot about the complications of living in this country at that particular time. You have one foot that's digging in deeper and another that's being yanked out" (47). Here, Danticat describes her experience of motherhood as inextricably bound up with her identity as an immigrant, which simultaneously strengthens and fractures her sense of national belonging.

Wendy Knepper argues that *Brother, I'm Dying* performs a "maternal discourse" (193): "This ambivalent sense of mortality and natality, born of the knowledge of the imminent loss of her father and gestating life of her child, sets the stage for her political narrative, which explores the extremely precarious lives of Haitian citizens and stateless persons, particularly through the tale of her Uncle Joseph's life and death" (193). Knepper sees Danticat's narrative as constituting "a kind of natal function, bearing silenced narratives into public forums for discussion and inclusion in history" (202).

Building on Knepper's notion of the dual function of Danticat's maternal discourse (*bearing* children and *bearing* narratives), I argue that Danticat does more than add her uncle's story to the public record. In both the process of writing the memoir and its publication, Danticat performs acts of "disobedience to a directive," as she writes in *Create Dangerously: The Immigrant Artist at Work*: "There are many possible interpretations of what it means to 'create dangerously,' and Albert Camus, like the poet Osip Mandelstam, suggests that it is creating as a revolt against silence, creating when both the creation and the reception, the writing and the reading, are dangerous undertakings, disobedience to a directive" (11). From her position of fractured rootedness as a mother, Danticat disobeys the authority of the Department of Homeland Security, which actively works to silence her authorial voice and impede her access to records of her uncle's experience in detention. Similarly to Eglė Kačkutė, who views "mothering in the mother's native tongue ... as the source of maternal agency and power" (in this volume), I see Danticat's position as an immigrant mother as a source of her "revolt against silence." Once in the public record, Danticat's memoir enacts a corrective to the anti-immigration discourses that buttress legislation, such as the *USA PATRIOT Act*,[1] and acts of inhumanity perpetrated under the guise of "national security." Furthermore, as I will show, Danticat's maternal disobedience extends to the memoir's disruption of a literary tradition that idealizes the U.S. as a land of opportunity.

HISTORY, MEMORY, AND LIFE WRITING

Brother, I'm Dying is Danticat's first autobiographical book. Prior to writing the memoir, she published four book-length works of fiction for adult readers, the majority of which focus on either historical traumas—such as the 1937 massacre of Haitians living in the Dominican Republic under the rule of the despot Rafael Trujillo—or the memories of Haitian Americans who lived through such traumas. In light of her focus on such turbulent and traumatic history in her fiction, Danticat's decision to write a memoir about her uncle's death is not as much of a departure as might at first be assumed.

Nonetheless, Danticat's turn to the genre of autobiography must be understood in the broader context of life-writing studies. In *Reading Autobiography: A Guide for Interpreting Life Narratives*, Sidonie Smith and Julia Watson define life writing "as a historically situated practice of self-representation. In such texts, narrators selectively engage their lived experience through personal storytelling. Located in specific times and places, they are at the same time in dialogue with the personal processes and archives of memory" (14).[2] As signaled by Smith and Watson's definition, which informs my analysis, life writing inherently engages with the imperfect process of remembering at both a personal and a collective level. They write: "Memory is a means of 'passing on,' of sharing a social past that may have been obscured, thereby activating its potential for reshaping a future of and for other subjects. In sum, acts of personal remembering are fundamentally social and collective" (26).

Although memoir writing invokes a more rigorous ethics of remembering than fiction, it is worth pausing to note that much of the scholarly interest in Danticat's fiction focuses on history and memory. Bharati Mukherjee writes, "The question posed in her fiction: how does a citizenry, even that portion of it now relocated far from the homeland, adapt to the reality of their past, and the nightmare of familial memory?" (691). In Danticat's fiction, as Valerie Kaussen argues, the reader meets many "ghostly migrants" on the move in the wake of "the violent geopolitics of Haitian-U.S. relations, the long history of invasions, occupations, economic exploitation, puppet governments, and support of murderous dictators" (25). Nick Nesbitt writes, "History is the absent presence in Danticat's writing, where the memory of the past invades the subjective experience of those who have lived on and who struggle with writing to preserve the life that was stolen from others, erecting a small shrine in a corner of the temporal diaspora" (210). In short, Danticat grapples with the ethics of remembering and forgetting in her fiction; she gives voice to the voiceless and silenced, which makes visible diasporic Haitian communities and the history of Haiti.

The scholarly understanding of Danticat's fiction could, thus, be easily applied to her memoir. Although Danticat does not directly witness her uncle's violent treatment and suffering at the hands of Homeland Security employees, as a writer, she *bears* witness by telling his story and lending her voice to reveal the truth of his experience in the Krome Detention Center, a place that for Haitian immigrants "meant nothing less than humiliation and suffering and more often than not a long period of detention before deportation" (Danticat, *Brother* 225). In this act of witnessing, Danticat intervenes in the collective memory, the history of immigration post-9/11, and revolts against a silence created by the national hysteria of the War on Terror.

In the post-9/11 U.S. context, immigrants and immigrant writers confront a reactionary social imaginary, which has shaped U.S. immigration policy since the terrorist attacks. In the wake of 9/11 and the *PATRIOT Act*, people of Middle Eastern, Arab, South Asian, and Muslim heritage (or perceived as such) have been vulnerable to racist violence in the streets and increased surveillance, policing, and detention by the U.S. government and its agents. Increased authority and regulation, coupled with a surge in nativism, have affected nearly all immigrants, especially immigrants of colour. Daniel Kanstroom, of the Boston College Human Rights Program, notes that although immigration law and criminal law have been merging since the 1980s, "Prior to September 11th, 2001 one could have said that some legal categories were pretty clear. Immigration law was deemed to be civil, not criminal law. Non-citizens who were subject to formal criminal process retained the same rights as citizens" (640-641). In the post-9/11 context, the U.S. Attorney General has the authorization "to incarcerate and detain non-citizens on the basis of mere suspicion" (Kanstroom 650).

Although Danticat initially began writing *Brother, I'm Dying* "for therapeutic reasons" (qtd. in Pulitano 43), she realized quickly that her uncle's story had a wider appeal:

> A couple of things contributed to the nonliterary attention the book received. We were living during a period when the people who were in charge of immigration policy felt so empowered by things like the Patriot Act to do anything they wished to immigrants—legal or otherwise—because they were supposedly protecting the country, so I think

the subject of immigration-detainee mistreatment had become to some extent familiar even to people who were not involved in immigration matters. That's why there was a news element to it. At that time in Miami, where I live, people were being picked up on the street and off public transportation buses. There were raids in the middle of the night and so forth. There was a kind of persecution of immigrants after September 11, 2001, that was very intense. (qtd. in Pulitano 43-44)

It is in this context that, as she describes in *Brother, I'm Dying*, Danticat's eighty-one-year-old uncle and his son Maxo fly to Miami. They are escaping political violence in Haiti—in particular, the violence resulting from Haitian gangs protesting the removal of President Bertrand Aristide from power, and the United Nations soldiers and Haitian riot police sent in to quell the gangs. Although Uncle Joseph has a visa to enter the U.S., he requests asylum, a surprising move that Danticat later speculates about: "I can only assume that when he was asked how long he would be staying in the United States, he knew that he would be staying past the thirty days his visa allowed him and he wanted to tell the truth" (*Brother* 215). Danticat receives a phone call from Customs and Border Protection alerting her that her uncle is in custody. When Danticat goes to the airport to find her uncle, she is told that she cannot see him because he is being sent to the Krome Detention Center. Having visited Krome previously "as part of a delegation of community observers organized by the Florida Immigrant Advocacy Center" (*Brother* 211), Danticat is well aware of the horrific conditions that await her uncle:

Some detainees fought among themselves, sometimes nearly killing each other as uninterested guards looked on. They spoke of other guards who told them they smelled, who taunted them while telling them that unlike the Cuban rafters, who were guaranteed refuge, they would never get asylum, that few Haitians ever get asylum. They said that the large rooms where they slept in rows and rows of bunk beds were often so overcrowded that some of them had to sleep on thin mattresses on the floor. They were at times so cold that they shivered all night long. They told of the food that rather than nourish them, punished them, gave them diarrhea and made them vomit. They told of arbitrary curfews, how they were woken up at six a.m. and forced to go back to that cold room by six p.m. (*Brother* 212)

In Krome, Uncle Joseph is not given access to his medications, including pills for his high blood pressure. During his asylum interview, he becomes violently ill and then unconscious. Despite his condition, a medic claims "'he's faking'" (*Brother* 233), which fatally delays necessary medical attention. Eventually "transported to Miami's Jackson Memorial Hospital with shackles on his feet" (*Brother* 236), he is placed in a ward "where no lawyers or family members are allowed to visit, and where prisoners are restrained to prevent escapes" (*Brother* 238). There, on November 3, 2004, in Ward D, Danticat's Uncle Joseph died.

DISOBEDIENT MOTHERHOOD

Although Joseph's story takes centre stage in *Brother, I'm Dying*, the "maternal discourse"—in the memoir, shaped by Danticat's pregnancy and the birth of her daughter, but not exclusively so—frames the central narrative such that motherhood, national belonging, and human rights are inextricably linked.

In *Human Rights and Narrated Lives*, Sidonie Smith and Kay Schaffer focus on autobiographical narratives "from the margins, voiced by other kinds of subjects—the tortured, the displaced and overlooked, the silenced and unacknowledged" (16), and their influence on human rights discourse and policy. By naming such narratives "acts of remembering" and "alternative or counter-histories," Smith and Schaffer argue that these narratives "test the values that nations profess to live by against the actual experiences and perceptions of the storyteller as witness" (*Human Rights and Narrated Lives* 3). Moreover, the authors argue that these narratives "issue an ethical call to listeners both within and beyond national borders to recognize the disjunction between the values espoused by the community and the actual practices that occur" (*Human*

Rights and Narrated Lives 3). Although Danticat may not represent at first glance a voice "from the margins" in Smith and Schaffer's sense—after all, Danticat is an experienced literary author—she nonetheless gives voice to "the displaced and overlooked, the silenced and unacknowledged" in bearing witness to her uncle's story. As Danticat indicates in the epigraph of this chapter, she also sees the writing of *Brother, I'm Dying* as an opportunity to speak "for the hundreds and thousands of families who lose loved ones in this way" (qtd. in Shea 188). In speaking for her uncle and countless others, Danticat presents a counter-history, one that conflicts with the immediate post-9/11 discourses calling for increased security to protect U.S. borders against terrorists and, most recently, with the anti-immigrant rhetoric of Republican presidential candidates.

Despite occupying a position of agency as a renowned author, Danticat still speaks from a marginalized position as an immigrant mother. Although Danticat never explicitly states her position of fractured rootedness in the memoir, she frames and envelops her father's and uncle's stories with her own story of pregnancy and young motherhood, and of Granmè Melina's stories. Furthermore, embedded within the framework of Danticat's emerging motherhood is another story of motherhood that Danticat recounts about her cousin Marie Micheline in a short chapter titled "Giving Birth." Occurring a little over a third of the way into the memoir, this chapter perhaps surprises the reader who expects to hear about Danticat's experience with childbirth. Instead, the reader learns that in Haiti in 1974, Marie Micheline hides an illegitimate pregnancy from Uncle Joseph and his wife, Denise, until she is two months from term. When Tante Denise discovers Marie Micheline's secret, she banishes her adopted daughter who, rejected by her baby's father, marries a Tonton Macoute, a violent and abusive man who hides Marie Micheline from her family. Worried about her, Joseph finally sets off to find her and frees her from the village where her husband has hidden. There, in a tiny house, she lies "covered with pus-filled blisters, open and discolored wounds" (*Brother* 85). As he helps her out of the village, Marie Micheline says, "'Papa, even though men cannot give birth, you just gave birth tonight. To me'" (86). In Marie Micheline's story, there is a narrative of disobedient motherhood—Marie Micheline's pregnancy flies in the face of familial and cultural norms during that time—that also portrays Uncle Joseph as a maternal figure who disobeys the prevailing political forces to rescue his daughter.

In telling Marie Micheline's story of disobedient motherhood, Danticat underscores her own disobedient "maternal discourse" in telling her uncle's story. To find the truth of Joseph's experience in detention and to bring his story to print, Danticat had to overcome the objections of the Department of Homeland Security and employ journalistic research strategies. Except for two phone conversations with her uncle during his detention, Danticat was not present in Krome or the hospital to directly witness her uncle's ordeal. In fact, the Department of Homeland Security refused to let her visit her uncle "for what [she] was told were 'security reasons'" (Danticat, "Foreword" x-xi). After filing "Freedom of Information requests that went nowhere" (qtd. in Shea 189), Danticat pursued a lawsuit with the help of the Florida Immigration Advocacy Center to recover transcripts and other records that documented her uncle's experience in detention. In a chapter titled "Alien 27041999," Danticat reports verbatim from some of these documents, such as the transcript of her uncle's interview with an officer from the Bureau of Customs and Border Protection. The chapters that recount Uncle Joseph's detention and rely on official documents exist in stark contrast to the rest of the memoir in which Danticat's empathic style and voice dominate. This contrast mirrors Joseph's dehumanizing experience, yet Danticat's humanizing consciousness still prevails. Although her uncle's responses, as transcribed, suggest that any health issues he had were minimal, Danticat reminds the reader that his responses were mediated by a translator who was not his own son, Maxo, "a fluent English speaker" (*Brother* 216). Danticat also explains what was not linguistically trans- latable, namely the cultural inflections of her uncle's responses: "'How would you describe your current health status?' Officer Reyes continued. According to the transcript, my uncle answered, 'Not bad.' He had probably said, 'Pa pi mal,' just as my father continued to, even as he lay dying" (*Brother* 218). In her cultural translation of her uncle's misunderstood understatement for her readers, not only does Danticat fill the gaps and silences left by official records, she also reveals the inhumanity of the processes and authority wielded by the Department of Homeland Security, a counter-history to prevailing claims that such processes are necessary to prevent and root out terrorism.

THE RELUCTANT IMMIGRANT

Brother, I'm Dying also enacts a counter-history to the exceptionalist narrative that has dominated the tradition of immigrant literature in the U.S. and has emphasized full assimilation into the host country as the immigrant's ultimate goal. In the post-9/11 context, however, there has been a noticeable surge in stories of reluctant or ambivalent immigration and narratives of return.[3] Early twentieth-century immigrant narratives— primarily featuring European immigrants, such as Anzia Yezierska's *Bread Givers* or Willa Cather's trilogy about Nebraska—also wrestle with the reluctance to leave home and divided loyalties, and are sometimes represented by older generations' resistance or inability to assimilate, but the overarching theme favoured assimilation. David Cowart describes the earlier trend and the recent shift in the following terms:

> After first novels set in America, these writers tend to shift their focus toward their native lands—unlike their predecessors, who had perforce to turn their creative backs on the homeland to tell American or international stories. In the older model (itself an aspect of the assimilationist ideal), immigrants with literary aspirations suppressed their ethnicity and moved swiftly toward being perceived as thoroughly American. (128-129)

However, racialized difference can prove to be an insurmountable barrier to assimilation in some immigrant stories. Such racialized ideologies have historically worked to exclude migrants, especially when embedded in law, such as the anti-Asian climate that led to the Chinese Exclusion Act of 1882 and its successive reinstatements until 1943. The climate in the U.S. since 9/11, despite claims of it being a postracial era, has reinvigorated racial profiling in the name of "national security." In his introduction to *We Are All Suspects Now: Untold Stories from Immigrant Communities After*

9/11, Tram Nguyen notes, "Upon arrival in the new country, they [immigrants and refugees] set out to make a home and remake an identity. But in the loaded terrain of a post-September 11 nationhood, that identity is increasingly tricky to navigate" (xv). Howard Winant offers an explanation for why: "Race offers the most accessible tool to categorize the American people politically: who is 'loyal' and who is a 'threat,' who can be 'trusted' and who should be subject to surveillance, who should retain civil rights and who should be deprived of them" (130). While those of Arab and Middle Eastern descent may be the primary targets of such suspicion, all immigrants of colour become suspect.

As Winant, Nguyen, and others have noted, then, the exceptionalist narrative of the U.S. as a land of opportunity for immigrants willing to assimilate has not always been an equal-opportunity story. The more recent move towards narratives of the ambivalent or reluctant immigrant marks an interesting though not wholly abrupt shift in immigrant literature. In her essay "Immigrant Writing: Changing the Contours of a National Literature," Mukherjee calls for the development of a new category of immigrant literature that she names "Literature of New Arrival" (683), which she uses "to distinguish it from traditional—canonical—US immigrant literature" and to recognize "a literature that centers on the nuanced process of *rehousement* after the trauma of forced or voluntary *unhousement*" (683 emphasis in original). This shift, according to Mukherjee, is also marked by "broken narratives of disrupted lives, proliferating plots, outsize characters and overcrowded casts, the fierce urgency of obscure history, the language fusion (Spanglish, Chinglish, Hinglish, Banglish), the challenging shapelessness, and complexities of alien social structures" (683-684).

The retreat from the "assimilationist ideal" may have begun, as Cowert notes, during the era of "'roots' awareness and multiculturalism in the mid-seventies" (128), but more recent geopolitical conditions, such as the economic recession in the U.S. and the Syrian refugee crisis, have perhaps fueled the reluctance of both real and fictional immigrants. Although the root causes of the turn from an emphasis on the goal of assimilation are too numerous to detail here,[4] it is important to note that critics also embrace "ambivalence" as a theoretical framework. In the words of Arupama Jain, "The concept of ambivalence emphasizes the range of possibilities available to individuals contending with both Americanization processes and transnationalism, as well as signaling the variability of stories" (24). Ambivalence allows for an understanding of variability not only across different stories but even within the same story.

The seeds of Danticat's reluctance and future ambivalence were already sown by the time she was twelve. Although she would eventually be reunited with her mother and father in New York, she had no desire to leave her uncle in Haiti. Moreover, she sensed the betrayal implied in seeking to live in a country that once occupied Haiti.[5] In *Brother, I'm Dying*, she recounts this sense of divided loyalty in a scene in which she and her brother go to the American consulate to see if their paperwork will be approved. As the consul sits behind his desk with their immigration file before him and his authority over their lives nearly palpable, he asks if they miss their parents. Danticat writes:

> Hanging on the wall behind him was a large American flag, the stars literally bursting from the corner square, their spiky edges merging into the wall. Sensing that it was the right thing to do, we both nodded, as if bowing to the flag that our grandfather had once fought against, that our mother and father had now embraced for nearly ten years, that we were about to make our own. As my head bobbed up and down, I felt my old life quickly slipping away. I was surrendering myself, not just to a country and a flag, but to a family I'd never really been part of. (*Brother* 105-106)

Notably, Danticat frames her reluctance in martial terms—"surrendering myself"—which renders her experience of immigration as one of military defeat. Immigrating to the U.S., thus, represents a loss of monumental proportions to Danticat's twelve-year-old self: a loss of family and country.

Given the reluctance of Danticat to leave her home in Haiti to live in the U.S., the reader can understand her uncle's even greater resistance to leaving and how dire the circumstances were in Haiti for him to request asylum in the country that once occupied his homeland.[6] Uncle Joseph's reluctance to emigrate was born out of his love for his homeland and commitment to his work—first politically and later as a church minister—towards better conditions in Haiti. As both a temporary immigrant (he held a valid visa) and a refugee, Uncle Joseph sought asylum from political violence; however, although he had travelled to the U.S. previously for medical reasons and to visit his family, he never wanted to emigrate there prior to his final trip to Miami. Perhaps in asking for asylum, he was signalling the desperation of his act, an urgency otherwise obscured by the planning implied in a visa. That his prospective adoptive country treats him as a criminal and an enemy takes on greater tragic irony in light of his asylum request.

Danticat's ambivalence grows more salient after she becomes a naturalized U.S. citizen. In *becoming* a mother at the same time that her uncle dies while attempting to gain asylum in the U.S., as I have noted, she experiences a fractured rootedness ["You have one foot that's digging in deeper and another that's being yanked out" (qtd. in Pulitano 47)]. In a 2004 interview with *The Guardian*, Danticat also said, "I live in a country from which my uncle was catastrophically rejected, and come from one which he had to flee.... I'm wrestling with the fact that both places let him down" (qtd. in Jaggi). At the funeral home, when Danticat views her uncle's body, she imagines his last thoughts: "Did he think it ironic that he would soon be the dead prisoner of the same government that had been occupying his country when he was born? In essence he was entering and exiting the world under the same flag. Never really sovereign, as his father had dreamed, never really free" (*Brother* 250).

Indeed, in the post-9/11 context, the processes of immigration resemble a militarized criminal justice system. The fear and jingoism of the post-9/11 climate in the U.S., however, is not as sudden a development as it first seems. As Danticat indicates, in the wake of the *PATRIOT Act* and the War on Terror, the indignities and inhumanities conducted at the Krome facility reproduce and exacerbate a long history of racial discrimination in immigration, U.S. law, and American culture more generally. Danticat explicitly asks if racism was at the root of her uncle's treatment:

I suspect that my uncle was treated according to a biased immigration policy dating back from the early 1980s when Haitians began arriving in Florida in large numbers by boat. In Florida, where Cuban refugees are, as long as they're able to step foot on dry land, immediately processed and released to their families, Haitian asylum seekers are disproportionately detained, then deported. While Hondurans and Nicaraguans have continued to receive protected status for nearly ten years since Hurricane Mitch struck their homelands, Haitians were deported to the flood zones weeks after Tropical Storm Jeanne blanketed an entire city in water the way Hurricane Katrina did parts of New Orleans. Was my uncle going to jail because he was Haitian? This is a question he probably asked himself. This is a question I still ask myself. Was he going to jail because he was black? (*Brother* 222-223)

In questioning the racism at the core of her uncle's treatment and tying the post-9/11 criminalization of immigration to a history of racist exclusion, Danticat bears witness to the confluence of injustices that culminate in her uncle's death. No longer a "ghostly migrant," Uncle Joseph nonetheless haunts the American social imaginary—a counter-history to the master narratives of suspicion and fear of foreign others in the War on Terror and the image of the U.S. as the land of milk and honey for immigrants.

At this point, I could turn to suggestions of hope and renewal in Danticat's memoir, but in the wake of her uncle's (and father's) death, hope is hard to find. By the end of the memoir, she has given birth to a girl she names Mira after her father, and her father gets to meet his granddaughter before he dies. In the last chapter, Danticat once again references a story by Granmè Melina, in which a grieving daughter refuses to hold the joyful wake customary before a funeral. She asks an old woman who "had the gift that the ancestors granted to only a chosen few, of being able to journey between the living and the dead" (*Brother* 266) to find her father in the land of the dead and bring him back to the land of the living. The old woman returns to report that the father has now claimed the land of the dead as his home and urges his daughter to accept his refusal to return. The daughter then agrees to hold a celebratory wake: "'We will eat. We will sing. We will dance and tell stories. But most importantly, we will speak of my father. For it is not our way to let our grief silence us'" (*Brother* 267).

As Danticat explains earlier in the memoir, "Granmè Melina's stories didn't always have happy endings" (*Brother* 70). The tale of the girl locked into her house by her mother certainly does not end well. After the snake's many failed attempts to imitate the mother's voice, it realizes it can simply kill the mother. As an allegory, the snake represents the external political forces that can prove fatal to one or more family members. In the final story of the grieving daughter, however, Danticat reprises the theme of "revolt against silence"—in this case the painful silence of loss and the necessity of continuing to speak for the dead and bearing counter-histories into life.

Brother, I'm Dying opens with the news of Danticat's pregnancy and closes with Danticat's imagining of her father and uncle enjoying a walk together, a reunion in the afterlife. By framing her memoir with a maternal discourse—Danticat's pregnancy and Granmè Melina's stories—Danticat roots her uncle's story in a literary landscape where bearing witness and telling the stories of the silenced hold sway. In this landscape, she disobeys various directives that aim to silence her and her uncle's voice, and she calls us—the readers—to listen and to act.

NOTES

[1]Signed into law on October 26, 2001, the *USA PATRIOT Act* is an acronym that stands for Uniting and Strengthening America by Providing Appropriate Tools Required to Intercept and Obstruct Terrorism.

[2]Autobiographical narratives imply a different degree of "truth" than fiction, but, of course, memory—personal or otherwise—is notoriously unreliable. Smith and Watson note that autobiographical truth "is an intersubjective exchange between narrator and reader aimed at producing a shared understanding of the meaning of a life" (13), yet "life narrative is indeed a moving target of ever-changing practices without absolute rules" (7).

[3]Although my focus here is primarily on the reluctant or ambivalent immigrant, Danticat's fiction and even her memoir include characters and figures who are emblematic of return. In *Brother, I'm Dying*, some of the gang leaders who chase Uncle Joseph from his church and home are "U.S. deportees" (182). "Return" is, of course, a problematic, catch-all term that disguises the wide-ranging circumstances of those who return to their birth country—from jet-setting transnationals, whose economic status enables them to move relatively freely across borders, to those forcibly deported and repatriated, including those who may have no memory of their native country because they immigrated as infants or young children.

[4]For example, see Jorge Duany, *Blurred Borders: Transnational Migration Between the Hispanic Caribbean and the United States* (Chapel Hill: North Carolina, 2011); Daniel Martinez Hosang, Oneka LaBennett, and Laura Pulido, eds., *Racial Formation in the Twenty-First Century* (Berkeley: California, 2012); Alejandro Portes and Rubén G. Rumbaut, *Immigrant America: A Portrait* (Oakland: California, 2014).

[5]U.S. marines occupied Haiti for nineteen years from 1915 to 1934.

[6]As I write in this article, the news is full of desperate Syrians and Iraqis escaping the violence in their home countries, a violence also rooted in the history of military occupation.

WORKS CITED

Cowart, David. *Trailing Clouds: Immigrant Fiction in Contemporary America*. Cornell, 2006.

Danticat, Edwidge. *Create Dangerously: The Immigrant Artist at Work*. Princeton, 2010.

Danticat, Edwidge. *Brother, I'm Dying*. Vintage Books, 2008.

Danticat, Edwidge. "Foreword." *We Are All Suspects Now: Untold Stories from Immigrant America After 9/11*, edited by Tram Nguyen, Beacon, 2006, pp. vii-xi.

Duany, Jorge. *Blurred Borders: Transnational Migration Between the Hispanic Caribbean and the United States*, University of North Carolina Press, 2011.

Jaggi, Maya. "Island Memories." *The Guardian*, Guardian News

and Media Limited, 19 Nov. 2004, www.theguardian.com/
books/2004/nov/20/featuresreviews.guardianreview9. Accessed
12. Sept. 2015.

Jain, Arupama. *How to Be South Asian in America: Narratives of
Ambivalence and Belonging*, Temple, 2011.

Kanstroom, Daniel. "Criminalizing the Undocumented: Ironic
Boundaries of the Post-September 11th 'Pale of Law.'" *North
Carolina Journal of International Law & Commercial Regulation*,
vol. 29, no. 4, Summer 2004, pp. 639-670. Print.

Kaussen, Valerie. "Migration, Exclusion, and 'Home' in Edwidge
Danticat's Narratives of Return." *Identity, Diaspora and Return
in American Literature*, edited by Maria Antònia Oliver-Rotger,
Routledge, 2015, pp. 25-43.

Knepper, Wendy. "In/justice and Necro-Natality in Edwidge
Danticat's *Brother, I'm Dying.*" *The Journal of Commonwealth
Literature*, vol. 47, no. 2, 2012, pp. 191-205.

Martinez Hosang, Daniel, et al, editors. *Racial Formation in the
Twenty-First Century*. University of California Press, 2012.

Murkherjee, Bharati. "Immigrant Writing: Changing the Contours
of a National Literature." *American Literary History*, vol. 23,
no. 3, 2011, pp. 680-696.

Nesbitt, Nick. *Voicing Memory: History and Subjectivity in French
Caribbean Literature*. University of Virginia Press, 2003.

Nguyen, Tram. *We Are All Suspects Now: Untold Stories from
Immigrant America After 9/11*. Beacon, 2006.

Portes, Alejandro, and Rubén G. Rumbaut, *Immigrant America:
A Portrait*. University of California Press, 2014.

Pulitano, Elvira. "An Immigrant Artist at Work: A Conversation
with Edwidge Danticat." *small axe: A Caribbean Journal of
Criticism*, vol. 15, no. 3, 2011, pp. 39-61.

Shea, Renee H. "A Family Story: Danticat Talks about Her Newest—and Most Personal—Work." *Edwidge Danticat: A Reader's
Guide*, edited by Martin Munro, University of Virginia Press,
2010, pp. 187-193.

Smith, Sidonie, and Kay Schaffer. *Human Rights and Narrated
Lives: The Ethics of Recognition*. Palgrave Macmillan, 2004.

Smith, Sidonie and Julia Watson. *Reading Autobiography: A Guide
for Interpreting Life Narratives*. University of Minnesota, 2001.

Winant, Howard. *The New Politics of Race: Globalism, Difference, Justice.* University of Minnesota, 2004.

9.
Isolation and Negotiation

A Case Study of Chinese Working-Class Immigrant Women's Mothering Experiences

YU-LING HSIAO

"Without knowing English, I feel imprisoned in this restaurant and isolated from what is going on in the town. However, I cannot do anything about it."
—Chinese Mother, Mei, 2013.[1]

ACCORDING TO PIERRE BOURDIEU, cultural capital refers to a wide range of nonfinancial assets related to culture and language, from mannerisms and education to linguistic competency (Bourdieu 84; Reay 26). Social capital is a social network that develops based on how family and society interact (Bourdieu 84; Reay 26), whereas Tania Das Gupta and her colleagues define social class as "a set of relations that has to do with how people (re)produce their livelihood in the everyday world" (57) and "traits" (57) that immigrants bring and reproduce across national borders and societies. These three concepts—socioeconomic status, cultural, and social capital—shape immigrant families' lives in important ways. Class resources can shape who has access to networks, education, and social-cultural capital that can propel acculturation in the new culture (Suarez-Orozco and Suarez-Orozco 22). The daily lives of working-class immigrant women are often challenging because many have limited education, skills, and exposure to the English language in their country of origin, which makes the process of adjusting to life after migration arduous. The cultural capital that they have in their home communities does not transfer to the host society. Such losses in capital can cause immigrant women to feel insecure and alienated while working and raising children in the host society (Salaff and Greve 155). Thus, working-class immigrant mothers endure the double burden of lacking cultural and social capital, and turn their attention to the matter of "survival" in the larger economic structure (Zhou and Nordquist 190, 189).

As Leslie Nichols discusses in her chapter in this volume, the working-class immigrant mothers' lack of resources has left them little choice but to enter the labour market, which has further challenged their mothering roles. Gender and migration scholars Pierrette Hondagneu-Sotelo and Ernestine Avila note that "motherhood is not biologically predetermined in any fixed way but is historically and socially constructed" (549). In this sense, immigrant mothers must negotiate and contest their mothering approaches through the acculturation process and contend with the challenges of fulfilling the work and family responsibilities in their new social and living environment' they must also negotiate and accommodate their mothering roles shaped by both the cultures of their country of origin and host country.

Immigrant mothering often involves the task of educating children in unfamiliar social contexts. Because of working-class immigrant mothers' often limited understanding of the new culture's norms and practices (Bourdieu 84), they experience parental difficulties regarding their children's education (Cheah et al. 3; Hondagneu-Sotelo and Avila 549; Reay, 59). With the disadvantages of rearing their children in the mainstream society, working-class Chinese immigrant parents in United States sometimes develop a sense of guilt, isolation, and powerlessness in regard to their children's educational lives (Qin 24).

Many studies on Chinese immigrants and education focus on the relationship between parental aspiration and academic achievement; however, few studies have focused on the interplay of class and ethnicity that shape working-class Chinese mothers' parenting challenges and strategies (Louie xxx; Qin 1) and negotiating the acculturation process shapes childrearing and children's educational experience. In this study, first, I explore three mothers' feelings of powerlessness and isolation living in a Midwestern community in the United States because of their limited cultural and social capital. Second, I explore how inadequate access to these forms of capital

(Bourdieu 84) shapes three mothers' ways of interacting with local school culture. Lastly, I show how these mothers form parental strategies based on their interpretations of local community and school cultures.

PARTICIPANTS AND CONTEXT

The three working-class Chinese mothers I highlight in this chapter are Fanny, Ching, and Mei (all pseudonyms). I chose these mothers because each represents different roles—waitress, housewife, and waitress-restaurant owner, respectively—that provide insights into working-class women's experiences in the local ethnic economy.

Fanny immigrated to the United States almost twenty years ago. She graduated from middle school in China. At the time of this study, she worked at a Chinese restaurant in Oakville (pseudonym) and spoke a little conversational English. A relative introduced Fanny to her husband before she migrated. He came from a nearby village and was already working in the United States. Once Fanny decided to marry him, she joined him in Oakville and began to work at a restaurant as a waitress. After migrating, the family experienced a variety of citizenship and financial issues leaving Fanny with little of her own savings on which to rely. Fanny and her husband have one daughter, Daisy, who was born in the United States.

Ching is Fanny's older sister. She had been in the United States for seven years at the time of this study and has an elementary school education. She was a married housewife, and the main caretaker of her three children and Fanny's daughter. She does not speak any English. When she was in China, she helped her father tend their fish pond. Ching and her husband are from the same village, and her husband was a technician in China. Their first daughter, Christine, was born in China. When Christine was about one year old, Ching's husband left to work in the United States. Fanny had two other children, Victor and Hope, after migrating.

Both Fanny's daughter, Daisy, and Ching's daughter, Christine, were placed in English Language Learner (ELL) programs throughout their elementary school years. Both daughters not only struggled in learning English but also felt frustrated by other academic subjects, such as math and social studies.

Similar to Ching's migrant experiences, Mei's husband also came to the United States when their firstborn son, Steven, was around one year old. The family reunited in Oakville seven years after Mei's husband's migration. Mei and her husband owned a restaurant at the time of this study. Mei worked as a waitress and sometimes a cook at this Chinese restaurant. After living in the United States for five years, Mei was able to speak a little conversational English and make small talk with customers. She had three additional children after settling in Oakville. She sent those three children back to China in the care of their grandmother while Steven remained in the United States. Mei and her husband think Steven is old enough to take care of himself after school while they work in the restaurant. Steven came to the United States with Mei when he was in second grade. Steven was first placed in an English Language Learner Program, left the program when he was in fourth grade, and performs well academically.

The ethnographic research study was conducted in the town of Oakville. The population of Oakville is approximately 35,750 people; the Asian population in this town is 1.4 percent (United States, Census Bureau). There are about 110 Chinese immigrants in the town, which constitutes about 60 Chinese families, and accounts for 0.3 percent of the total population in this region (United States, Census Bureau). Several international companies in the area offer white-collar positions and employ approximately forty to fifty middle-class Chinese immigrant families originally from China, Hong Kong, and Taiwan; the restaurant business in Oakville employs about ten working-class Chinese immigrant families from Fuzhou, China. The participants in this study held positions of working class status[2] both before and after migration. In China, they worked in farming, in fishing, as technicians, and in other manual jobs. In contrast, the middle-class Chinese population in the community began immigrating in the 1970s to work in local international companies. Working-class Chinese from Fuzhou started migrating to Oakville in 1990 (Hsiao 16). Prior to settling in Oakville, most of them worked in Chinatown in New York City. On average, working-class Chinese families have settled in

Oakville for ten years. Most of them live within family networks. For example, there may be two or three families working together in a restaurant and also living together under one roof.

Many working-class Chinese families (Guest 25; Fu 9) are new immigrants from the Fuzhou area, who migrated for economic and social reasons (Fu 21). Since most of these Fouzhounese immigrants in the U.S were from class-disadvantaged and education-deprived areas in China, they comprised the majority of workers performing long-hour, semiskilled, or manual jobs in the ethnic enclave (Fu 19; Guest 35). Under patriarchal Confucius thought, women are supposed to remain at home to care for their children while men work as the family breadwinners (Sheng 133). Contemporary Fuzhounese couples continue to hold these common gender roles; women stay in the village taking care of the children while their husband works in the United States (Guest 30). However, among Fuzhounese women who migrate to join their husbands, these traditional gender roles often change in order to meet household economic needs.

RESEARCH DESIGN

This study[3] employed the methodology of an ethnographic case study and explored the lived experiences of three working-class Chinese immigrant mothers in Oakville. It focused on their interactions with their children's educators and the strategies that they used to navigate school and community activities. The analysis was based on data drawn from participant observation; for three years, I was immersed on a weekly basis in the community, where I conducted ongoing informal conversations as well as formal, one-hour interviews with each participant. I put emphasis on the participants' observations and on understanding their feelings and thoughts through casual conversation about their aspirations and struggles.

I translated the transcripts from Chinese to English and then coded and categorized the data into different themes. I applied several techniques of data analysis, including the use of members' stories to identify critical incidents and determine their significance, to construct case records, and to generate themes (Emerson et al 68, 157; Patton 572).

FINDINGS AND ANALYSIS

Isolation and Helplessness

The most prominent theme that surfaced from inductive data analysis was the mothers' feelings of isolation from the dominant English-speaking and Caucasian community. The women's limited English ability and demanding working schedules interfered with learning English and the culture of their new home, Oakville. In most cases, when the Fuzhounese mothers united with their husbands in the Unites States, they suddenly had to change their housewife role relying on their husband's salary to become equal economic contributors (Shi 365). Moreover, the three families still owed money on debts that they incurred from migrating. Mei and Fanny worked twelve hours a day, six days a week in their family business to help their husband pay off the debts, and Ching took care of four children at home while her husband worked twelve hours per day.

Although these three mothers realized that limited English was the main problem to connecting with other women and families in the town, they were not able to take free ELL classes available in the community because of the demands of their work schedules and the lack of social and logistical support for attending (Hsiao 59, 61, 76). Yet Mei believed that if she knew English, it could help her business. She said, "I want to learn English badly. If I knew English I could communicate with the townspeople and understand what [food] they really like so we could adjust our menu."

As previously mentioned, Mei and Fanny had to work to help their husbands pay off existing debts. Both of their experiences reflect Leslie Nichols's statement that working-class women were compelled to become economic supporters for their families because of financial difficulty. My research found that Fanny and Mei' choices were limited in the labour market to ethnic businesses after migration. Fanny, especially, had heavy economic burdens because her husband not only owed debts from migrating to the United States but also had financial stressors because of unsuccessful business ventures. Fanny's case supports Xiaoming Sheng's research that although immigrant Chinese women have changed their role as equal economic contributors after migration, their role in the family as wife or mother is still subordinated to their husband based on Confucius patriarchy (134). Even though the participants did not share detailed feelings about their role changes, Fanny expressed she had no freedom for herself because of the long hours working in the restaurant as well as the restrictions that her husband placed on her. For example, Fanny's husband did not allow her to attend a friend's wedding because he thought her money was better spent on the family than on the expensive plane ticket.

The women's language barriers and long work hours and constraints prevented them from engaging in and understanding the community activities and culture, which further led to isolation from their children's school activities and events. For example, Fanny felt disconnected from the town and her daughter's education: "I thought the life would be better here in the U.S, but it is not. I never got the chance to rest as I continuously work at the restaurant. I never feel connected to [the community] here and never know what's going on in Daisy's school." These three Chinese mothers' feelings of isolation and powerlessness without knowing English also caused feelings of frustration and panic once they began to encounter problems related to their children's school matters. Ching expressed that she wanted to call me for help at the beginning of each school semester because she had difficulty understanding the chaotic bus schedule. One time, her son did not catch the school bus home, and she received a voice message from the school but did not understand it and did not know what to do. Ching felt desperate and scared that she was going to lose her son. When I told her that Victor was still at school and she could ask her husband to pick Victor up, she sounded relieved and told me that she was going to call her husband right away.

A hectic work schedule and language barriers were not the only obstacles that alienated these working-class mothers from their children's educational experiences and practices. Working-class Chinese mothers in general may also face frustration, and self-critique given their limited school education and literacy ability of both their country of origin and the migrated country, which can-generate a sense of helplessness in how to become involved in their children's education (Qin and Han 15). In my study, for example,

Ching held a meeting with school officials to discuss the state's decision to reject the school's request for her daughter's Individualized Education Program (IEP). The school asked her to write in Chinese why she disagreed with the state's rejection. However, Ching's Chinese fluency is stronger verbally than in writing, and she was embarrassed to have to write Chinese characters during the meeting. Ching held the pen awhile and asked me, "Ms. Yu-Ling, could you write it for me? I am not good at Chinese writing either."

After I helped her to write down her opinions about the state's rejection, she asked me, "What then? Who is going to help Christine [her daughter]? Nobody at home can help her." The data reveals that working class mothers often attempt to become involved with their children's school matters but can feel overwhelmed and helpless because their limited cultural capital in the migrated society and confusion about their children's educational system can further exacerbate their frustrations and struggles as immigrants. They often turned to me, as a Chinese speaker, to translate and facilitate their understanding.

Dominant Messages and Negotiations

The previous theme shows three working-class Chinese mothers' feelings of paralysis and isolation as members of a linguistic and ethnic minority with busy schedules, limited English ability, and limited education. A further complicating factor for working-class mother's lived experience is that class barriers limit the social interaction between middle and working-class Chinese in the community. The middle-class community members displayed frequent examples of intragroup class prejudice against working-class Chinese, often based on differing parenting styles and beliefs about parenting (Hsiao 168, 172). Even with these limitations, the mothers attempted to help their children academically and socially based on their comprehension of the messages from the school. Their interpretations were not only shaped by their migration background but also formed through their "dissonant acculturation" (Portes and Rumbaut 53-54; Qin 164), which refers to the gap between the immigrant children's acculturation to the mainstream society and that of their parents. In this sense, children usually acculturate faster than their parents, especially when the parents lack the cultural capital of the country to which the family migrated (Portes and Rumbaut 53-54; Qin 164). For example, based on her understanding of the Chinese culture of education, Fanny interpreted the school directive to "work with [her] children at home" to mean that she should provide their children with extra work to practice independently. In a parent-teacher meeting, Daisy's teacher told Fanny that Daisy's overall English ability was still below average and encouraged the parents to work with their children at home. After the meeting, Fanny said to me, "Unlike China, the school in the United States never gives students homework. The reason that Daisy is behind in English is because she does not practice enough in writing characters and spelling." Fanny interpreted the school messages through her understanding of the educational norms and practices in her country of origin.

A similar situation happened to Ching when the school informed her that they were considering forming an IEP for Christine because of her slow progress in English learning. During the meeting, Ching asked me: "Is Christine considered for that class [Individualized Education Program] because she does not work hard in school? I knew it. She is very lazy. She watches TV all the time.... I told her to do homework, and she always told me that she did not have homework." Ching did not understand the idea of an IEP, so she interpreted the incident to mean that the school considered her daughter for an IEP because of laziness. At the same time, Ching was not aware of the academic difficulties that her daughter experienced as an English language learner and that these difficulties are sometimes unrelated to students' efforts. Ching's structural positioning as an immigrant mother and a Chinese working-class woman informs her conviction that her daughter's academic performance is related to her daughter's lack of diligence—a situation that makes her vulnerable to misinterpretation and that potentially interferes with making fully informed decisions for her daughter.

Mei also developed her understanding about the school messages in ways that have shaped her mothering toward Steven's school matters. Steven performed well academically; however, Mei was worried about her son's social life, especially in the context of him receiving free lunch. For example, the ELL teacher brought a free lunch application to Mei's restaurant for Steven to fill out and for Mei to sign. Mei did not sign it and told me:

> I think that if Steven applies for free lunch, it will have a bad influence when he applies for college ... something like ... it is more possible for colleges to turn him down if they know he applied for free lunch before. You know what ... the government always knows what you are doing. Those [governmental institutions'] computers are connecting with each other.

Mei's approach to supporting her child's school activities was shaped by her limited understanding of the messages from school, and her immigrant status rendered her vulnerable to governmental surveillance and control. Although the ELL teacher told her that no one other than school personnel would reveal Steven's application for free lunch, Mei still believed that applying for free lunch would leave a negative, permanent record for Steven in his social life and would diminish his chance to attend college.

Ultimately, Mei's understanding of educational and governmental institutions was limited. Her social status and lack of trust and knowledge of dominant cultural and schooling practices prompted fears regarding how to protect her children in the dominant society. In turn, such fears continue to shape her mothering practices.

ACTIVE STRATEGIES

These three Chinese mothers formed their educational strategies to assist their children's education based on their experiences, cultural background, and their understanding of society through the interactions with the dominant educational institutes. For example, Fanny devised a strategy of copying the Bible to help her daughter learn and acculturate to Protestant Christianity, which is the dominant religious affiliation in Oakville.

Combined with her understanding of the Christian culture in the small town and her educational experiences in China, Fanny believed that copying the Bible could improve her daughter's English literacy ability. She said, "I told Daisy to copy the words from the Bible. I think that Bible has better and meaningful words that she can learn. By copying the Bible, she not only can learn spelling but also can learn how to apply it ... which may improve her learning." Although Fanny is not a Christian and has little understanding of Biblical content, she believed that the Bible is a "good" text that can influence her daughter morally and academically and also aid in the acculturation process. However, given Fanny's language barrier in reading English and limited understanding of the Bible's content, she could only ask her daughter to copy texts from the Bible (see Figure 1) as a literacy exercise.

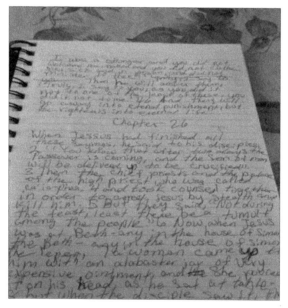

Figure 1. Daisy's Hand Copying of the Bible." By Hsiao, Yu-Ling. Aug 11, 2014.

Like Fanny, Ching also embraced the "drilling" approach, which was influenced by her schooling experience in China. Following this approach, she believed the way to improve her daughter's learning was to assign her daughter more homework to practice based on her interpretation that Christine's slow learning progress was due to a passive attitude or behaviour toward learning: "I told Christine that she has to bring assignments home, but she kept lying to me that she doesn't have homework. Please ask Christine's teacher to give her more homework ... it's better to give her homework everyday ... so that her learning will be better off." Considering the lack of information about IEP or about the concept of special education in China and the U.S., Ching has not had the knowledge base to assist Christine's learning. Also, similarly to Fanny, Ching's lack of knowledge about academic institutions in the host society diminished their ability to help her children. In Fanny and Ching's examples, they both created strategies to help their children succeed in school but it was difficult for them to actually engage in the learning process or practices of their children given the gap between their school's communication strategies and their limited knowledge base of schooling norms in the adopted culture.

Mei's strategy was to protect Steven by not applying for free lunch and by not accepting the school's offer to give Steven more food for breakfast because of the poor economic situation in the family. She said,

> No matter what, we'll squeeze money out for Steven's lunch.... Or he can eat more breakfast at home in the morning.... We do not want his friends looking at him differently ... we cannot risk Steven's future with this free lunch thing.

It seems that Mei formed this strategy based on her fear of her family being labelled low income, which reflects her recognition that low-income status shaped how others view her family and her child while also shaping her reactive strategies towards Steven's social life at school.

DISCUSSION AND IMPLICATIONS

Three primary themes emerged from the data. The theme of "isolation and helplessness" shows that the three mothers feel isolated and powerless without knowing English and understanding the culture of the community, which, in turn, leads them to feel a sense of uncertainty and a lack of confidence in educating their children. The theme of "dominant messages and negotiations" illustrates how the women interpreted messages from their children's schools and the community at large. The theme of "active strategies" reveals how the women strategize with limited understanding of cultural and schooling norms to protect their children and to advance their children's academic success with the skills that they do have. These themes help to capture the varieties and complexities of the formation of mothering and cultural practices among working-class Chinese immigrants.

The emergent findings reveal that the complexities of working-class Chinese mothering are shaped through these women's relational position and their experiences interacting with mainstream society and highlight the multidimensional forces involved in mothering practices. Based on these three mothers' experiences in navigating work, family life, and dominant schooling messages they have shaped and reshaped their mothering practices through a process that is constantly contested. The factors of this process include migrant experiences, interactions with the community, new information, and cultural interpretations of the new society. For example, Ching's mothering practice was reshaped when she started to read English children's books in Chinese to her toddler children. (She told a story in Chinese by looking at the pictures in an English children's book. She still did not know the book's real content.) Although she did not know English, she tried her best to increase her younger children's literacy given the messages that she received from the school about her older daughter's academic struggles.

Evelyn Nakano Glenn argues that "Mothering is not just gendered, but also racialized ... [and] differentiated by class" (qtd. in Hondagneu-Sotelo and Avila 551). Fanny, Ching and Mei's cases expose the gendered vulnerabilities immigrant women can experience due to their social-class status and limited social and cultural capital, as well as their isolation from middle-class Chinese speakers and the broader English-speaking community. Their efforts to mother in ways that support their children's educational success are constrained by their educational background, working hours, and limited understanding of the educational processes their children navigate in the public schools. Even though the three mothers have noticed their vulnerabilities, they still constantly strategize and navigate their mothering within and outside their limits in order to help and protect their children in educational institutions of the dominant society.

NOTES

[1]The transcript of Mei is transcribed and translated from Chinese to English by Yu-Ling Hsiao.
[2]The category of working-class I am using here is based on the occupations Chinese immigrants hold and their position in the economic structure.
[3]This article draws in part from content in my unpublished dissertation (see Hsiao).

WORKS CITED

Bourdieu, Pierre. "The Form of Capital." *Sociology of Education*. edited by Alan R.Sadovnik. Taylor & Francis, 2007, pp. 83-95.

Chea, Charissa, et al. "Understanding 'Tiger Parenting' through the Perceptions of Chinese Immigrant Mothers: Can Chinese and U.S. Parenting Coexist?" *Asian American Journal of Psychology*, vol. 4, no. 1, 2013, pp. 30-40.

Emerson, Robert M, et al. *Writing Ethnography Fieldnotes*. The University of Chicago Press, 1995.

Fu, Danling. *An Island of English: Teaching ESL in Chinatown*. Heinemann, 2003.

Gee, James Paul. *Social Linguistics and Literacies: Ideology in Discourses*. Routledge, 2015.

Guest, Kenneth J. "From Mott Street to East Broadway: Fuzhounese Immigrants and the Revitalization of New York's Chinatown." *Journal of Chinese Overseas*, vol. 7, no.1, 2011, pp. 24-44.

Gupta, Tania Das, et al. "Class Borders: Chinese and South Asian Canadian Professional Women Navigating the Labor Market." *Asian and Pacific Migration Journal*. Vol. 23, no. 1, 2014, pp. 55-83.

Hondagneu-Sotelo, Pierrette, and Avila Ernestine. "I'm Here, But I'm There: The Meanings of Latina Transnational Motherhood." *Gender and Society*, vol. 11, no. 5, 1997, pp. 548-571.

Hsiao, Yu-Ling. "Brave Settlers in a Model Minority Land: A Ethnography Exploring Dynamics of Social Class and Educational Experiences Among Chinese Immigrants in a Midwest Town." Diss. Oklahoma State University, 2016.

Louie, Vivian S. Compelled to Excel: Immigration, Education, and Opportunity among Chinese Americans. Stanford University Press, 2004.

Patton, Michael Quinn. *Qualitative Research & Evaluation Methods*. Sage Publication Inc, 2015.

Portes, Alejandro, and Ruben G. Rambaut. *Legacy: The Story of the Immigrant Second Generation*. University of California Press, 2001.

Qin, Desiree Baolin. "'Our Child Doesn't Talk to Us Anymore': Alienation in Immigrant Chinese Families." *Anthropology and Education Quarterly*, vol. 37, no. 2, 2006, pp. 162-179.

Qin, Desiree Baolin., and Eun-Jin Han. "Tiger Parents or Sheep Parents? Struggles of Parental Involvement in Working-Class Chinese Immigrant Families." *Teachers College Record*, vol. 116, no. 8, 2014, pp. 1-32.

Reay, Diane. *Class Work: Mothers' Involvement in Their Children's Primary Schooling*. UCL Press, 1998.

Salaff, Janet W., and Arent Greve. "Can Women's Social Networks Migrate?" *Women's Studies International Forum*, vol. 27, no. 4, 2004, pp. 149-162.

Sheng, Xiaoming. "Cultural Capital and Gender Differences in Parental Involvement in Children's Schooling and Higher Education Choice in China." *Gender and Education*, vol. 24, no. 2, 2012, pp. 131-146.

Shi, Yu. "Chinese Immigrant Women Workers: Everyday Forms of Resistance and 'Coagulate Politics.'" *Communication and Critical/Cultural Studies*, vol. 5, no. 4, 2008, pp. 363-382.

United States, Census Bureau, U.S. Dept. of Commerce. "Profile of General Population and Housing Characteristics: 2010 Demographic Profile Data." United States Census Bureau, Government of the United States, 2010. Accessed 30 Sept. 2015.

Zhou, Min., and Regina Nordquist. "Work and Its Place in the Lives of Immigrant Women: Garment Workers in New York City's Chinatown." *Applied Behavioral Science Review*, vol. 2, no. 2, 1994, pp. 187-211.

10.

Foreign Mothers, Native Children

The Impact of Language on Cultural Identity among Polish Americans in Chicago

ANNA KUROCZYCKA SCHULTES

FOR IMMIGRANTS, BECOMING ACCULTURATED to living abroad can be a very difficult process—one that becomes even harder when the wellbeing of children is involved. In this chapter, I focus on whether Polish mothers living in the Chicago metropolitan area find this experience challenging. From the perspective of cultural anthropology, women have been the ones traditionally charged with the task of cultural (re)production (Walks). To borrow from Faye Ginsburg's and Reyna Rapp's analysis, I find mothering a vital "entry point to the study of social life ... [because it allows one to] see how cultures are produced (or contested) as people imagine and enable the creation of the next generation, most directly through the nurturance of children" (1-2). I am particularly interested in how culturally significant contexts are signified through language and how the use of a given language shapes the viewpoint of children who are raised abroad and find themselves navigating between two cultures. For Polish mothers living in and around Chicago, home culture reproduction may be an easier undertaking because of the pronounced active presence of the Polish community in this part of the United States.

Regardless of one's location, however, mothering abroad is a problematic task due to its cultural and historic implications. The conflict between the ideals of intensive mothering[1] and the demands of global migration (Ehrenreich and Hochschild) places women in a precarious position: whether to "perform" motherhood based on the cultural norms of the host country or whether to abide by their own definitions of motherhood. Pierrette Hondagneu-Sotelo

174

and Ernestine Avila state that women who emigrate engage in a
" radical gender-transformative odyssey" (552). Through migration, "they are initiating separations of space and time from their
communities of origin, homes ... [and] in doing so, they must cope
with stigma, guilt, and criticism from others" (Hondagneu-Sotelo
and Avila 552). Polish mothering in Chicagoland,[2] thus, cannot
be discussed without examining the historical ties linking Poland
to the United States first, which will then allow me to ascertain
how the presence of this ethnic community affects Polish women's
mothering choices.

POLISH IMMIGRATION TO THE UNITED STATES

With between nine and ten million Polish Americans living in
the United States, Poles constitute one of the largest white ethnic
groups[3] in America—3.2 percent of the total population (Greene).
Of those, nearly one million are first-generation emigrants from
Poland. Scholars have traditionally divided Polish migration to the
United States into three waves: the so-called "for bread" migration
at the turn of the nineteenth and twentieth centuries; World War II
émigrés; and the "new immigrants" arriving after 1969 (Erdmans;
Greene). The majority of Polish immigrants, about one million,
came through Ellis Island between 1880 and 1920. The exact number is unknown, as many were mistaken for citizens of countries
that partitioned Poland: Russia, Germany, and Austria-Hungary.

Polish immigration continued throughout the 1990s, even after
the downfall of the communist system in 1989, mainly because of
the economic instability facing the nation.[4] As Western companies
moved into Poland, however, employment opportunities increased
for the young, urban, and well-educated population, who had
previously immigrated to the United States in high numbers. In
the 1990s, young and well-educated Poles could take advantage
of "new business initiatives; jobs in new technology markets (e.g.,
computers and telecommunications); economic and development
aid provided by the United States, Sweden, and Germany; and
managerial, skilled, and unskilled positions in Western companies
like Pepsico and Bell Telephone" (Erdmans 116). Nonetheless,
certain groups of the population, including retirees and those

less educated, fared better under the socialist system, which had provided state subsidies. Without these state subsidies, many industries failed: textiles in Łódź, mining in the Lower Silesia region, and shipbuilding along the Baltic Sea. Farmers and artists (writers, sculptors, actors) also lost state subsidies, which lead to unemployment rates as high as 12 to 15 percent in the 1990s and served as precursors for continued emigration (Erdmans 116).

Starting in the mid-1990s, the nature of Polish immigration to the United States changed. New categories of temporary visitors were introduced, among them the au pair and summer work travel programs, which allowed a number of students and scholars to stay in the U.S. on a short-term basis, whereas prior to the 1990s, many Polish tourists ended up seeking employment and making their stays permanent. According to the U.S. Department of State, the overall number of both temporary and permanent Polish migrants decreased substantially from its peak of 108,000 in 2000 to 68,000 in 2011.[5] Increased educational attainment, including English proficiency, has also affected the geographical mobility of the Polish community and led to a decline of distinctly Polish neighbourhoods in the United States. Poles now choose to resettle in the suburbs rather than remain in traditionally Polish areas in cities such as Chicago and New York because they perceive suburban life to be synonymous with social mobility (Erdmans; Leven and Szwabe). As one immigrant said: "You made it in America, you move to the suburbs" (qtd. in Erdmans 123). Polish immigrants have, thus, contributed to greater cultural variation in white suburbia.

It is in one of these suburbs on the North Shore of Chicago where I conducted research for this study. All of the thirty-one women—mothers—surveyed were born in Poland, more than half were between thirty-four and forty-one years of age, and more than three quarters of them have been living in the United States for over ten years.[6] Since language and culture are inextricably intertwined (Walks 11), it was my goal to discern how these mothers maintain their heritage, specifically based on their approach towards passing their native language onto their children.

As a Polish immigrant married to an American who does not speak my native tongue, I made the conscious decision together with my husband that I would speak solely in Polish to our daughter, and he would speak in English to her, as this is the only language that he is fully proficient in. We have managed to maintain this arrangement since her birth four and a half years ago. Thus, both as an immigrant and a professional who has been working with language learners for over twelve years, I am highly interested by the phenomenon of heritage language[7] maintenance and loss. I use the term "heritage language" in this chapter to refer to the language that immigrant children acquire first—the native language of their parents—but may not end up being completely fluent in because of a switch to another dominant language later in life (Kozminska 2).

THE MYTH OF THE *MATKA POLKA*

The question of how Polish women ought to raise their children cannot be examined without going back to the nineteenth century when the Polish Mother (*Matka Polka)* figure appeared as a model of female identity leading the fight for Polish values.[8] She was an integral part of Polish Romantic poetry, especially in the work of poet Adam Mickiewicz, who wrote a poem titled "To the Polish Mother,"[9] in which he describes *Matka Polka*'s role as a mother and supporter of the Polish cause during the partitions. As Bogusława Budrowska writes, "Women were faced at the time with many different tasks. Adequate child rearing, thus, became political because it was the only guarantee of maintaining a national identity" (my trans.; 193). When men were at war, it was the woman's job to raise the children—preferably a patriotic son with a "light of genius"[10] in his eyes—and mind the house while, at the same time, finding the means to provide for her family. The burden of managing this led to the creation of the myth of the heroic *Matka Polka*: a devoted mother who symbolized the strength of the nation.

The fact that the *Matka Polka* emerged in a time of political unrest underscores her direct link to the Polish nation state: having a family and raising children was now a public matter. Anna Titkow details this intersection of gender and nation in the following passage:

Losing independence and statehood created the cultural ideal of the Polish woman as hero, capable of dealing with any pressures ... On her shoulders rested the responsibility of maintaining national heritage: *language, culture*, faith. It is this difficult time of loss of independence which created the social genotype of the ideal woman, who is capable of taking on the most difficult of circumstances which exist to this day. (qtd. in Budrowska 193; my trans; emphasis added)

This quote highlights how closely parenting choices for Polish women are connected to the idea of being a good mother, a good patriot, and a good representative of the nation state. In the foreign context, this myth can also serve to at least partially explain how by choosing to speak Polish to her children, a mother living abroad may also be fulfilling her culturally engrained duty of being a good *Matka Polka*.

"POLISH ABOVE ALL ELSE"
(*"PRZEDE WSZYSTKIM JĘZYK POLSKI"*)

Of my research participants, 80 percent responded that they speak Polish with their children, whereas 100 percent agreed that it is important for them that their children speak Polish. The two main reasons mothers gave for maintaining the language are the following: they want their children to be able to communicate with their family in Poland—grandparents, aunts, and uncles—and they want their children to be able to identify with Polish culture and maintain an understanding of their heritage.

The need for children to speak Polish in order to communicate with their family is a matter of primary concern for mothers. Within the Chicago Polonia—the term commonly used to refer to the Polish diaspora—it is a frequent occurrence to see families visit relatives in Poland on an annual basis, especially during summer vacations and other times off school, such as at winter break. When I asked the mothers whether it was important for them that their children speak Polish, many of them referred to the family that they left behind in Poland. Karolina commented,

"We have family in Poland and I want [my children] to be able to understand their cousins." Kasia also stressed that she would like her children to understand their relatives: "Since my entire family speaks Polish, and they live there, I would like for my child to be able to communicate with them." Not to mention, speaking Polish makes traveling around the country a much smoother process. As Ela said, "I would like my children to know and use the mother tongue and be able to easily communicate in Polish during our trips to Poland."

Studies have revealed that Eastern European immigrants, in particular, value extended family relationships as the mothers above clearly expressed (Nesteruk and Marks). Moreover, Olena Nesteruk in her research on heritage language maintenance and loss among Eastern Europeans found that the relationship with grandparents is especially crucial for immigrant families and plays a very important role in childrearing: "the grandparents visit the USA, often staying for several months at a time to help with child-care" (278). As a result, all the participants in Nesteruk's study, and nearly all of the participants in my study as well, emphasized the importance of maintaining their native language to "facilitate communication across generations" (Nesteruk 278).

Moreover, interacting in Polish allows mothers to impart a sense of Polish cultural belonging[11] onto their America-born children. Karolina, a mother of two children, aged four and six, expressed the connection of language and culture most profoundly by forbidding them to speak English at home: "I always tell [my children] that they are Poles born on American land." Beata, an architect in her mid-forties with two children aged four and twelve, elaborated on this important cultural connection with the following: "*Polish [is] above all else*. We speak English only on occasion, when it is necessary, which is at parties or playdates with kids who only speak English. I would call this 'using English to be polite'" (emphasis added). The myth of the *Matka Polka* could certainly be partially responsible for these decisions. By choosing to use their native language, mothers take the responsibility for passing this important element of cultural capital onto their children (Hryciuk and Korolczuk 11). However, unlike Polish migrant mothers who adhere to the myth of the *Matka Polka* in the United Kingdom and Germany and "actively act towards preventing children from becoming citizens or feeling at home in their destination country" (Pustulka 159), Polish mothers in Chicagoland do not bar their children from integrating with English-speaking kids at school or from developing ties to their place of upbringing. The Chicago *Matka Polka* wants her children to become fully bicultural: to acculturate into the host society and maintain a strong sense of belonging to the mother's ethnic background.

Moreover, by speaking their native language at home, mothers arm their children with a form of cultural capital, which Pierre Bourdieu identifies as a set of social assets beyond financial means that can aid social mobility. Cultural capital can appear in three forms:

> in the *embodied* state, i.e. in the form of long-lasting dispositions of the mind and body; in the *objectified* state, in the form of cultural goods (pictures, books, dictionaries, instruments, machines, etc.), which are the trace or realization of theories or critiques of these theories, problematics, etc.; and in the *institutionalized* state, a form of objectification which must be set apart because ... it confers entirely original properties on the cultural capital which it is presumed to guarantee. (3; emphasis in original)

Mothers, aware of the importance of upward mobility, believe that the "good mother" not only loves her child but also transmits what Pierre Bourdieu has termed "habitus"—"systems of durable transposable dispositions" (72) that are transformed into cultural capital as children age. Such "dispositions" can pertain to anything from how children speak, to the schools that they attend, the habits and views they express, and the sports they practice. Immigrant mothers have the opportunity to confer the embodied state of cultural capital to their children, especially in the form of language, by engaging with them solely using their native tongue.[12]

Maintaining the native language, however, is an especially challenging task for women who either have lived in the United

States for the majority of their adult lives, like three quarters of the women in this study, or have partners who are non-Polish speaking.[13] In those instances, speaking English or the combination of both languages sometimes becomes a necessity in order to communicate complex topics to older children, who already attend English-speaking schools. Such was the case for Monika, whose fourteen-year-old American-born daughter sometimes had a hard time expressing herself in Polish: "We mix both languages because it is easier for my teenage daughter to understand a given topic or problem. Her Polish vocabulary is not sufficiently developed." Even though firstborn children of immigrant parents receive more exposure to the heritage language and often speak the native language of their parents essentially as their first language, speaking the heritage language becomes increasingly more challenging as children begin school and the main language of instruction is English. Furthermore, English is frequently used at home among siblings (Nesteruk 273). In this way, the parents' native language becomes the "limited" language of basic interpersonal communication, whereas English is essential for their success at school (Cummins). English, thus, is used for practical purposes: to communicate quickly and effectively.

Sometimes using English also becomes a life-saving measure. Both of Natalia's boys, aged five and nine, were born in the United States but spent three years of their childhood in Poland after Natalia and her American husband decided to return to her hometown. Although repatriation proved too challenging and Natalia moved back to Illinois, her sons have an excellent command of Polish as a result. Natalia mentioned, therefore, that when it comes to the boys' safety, she frequently repeats Polish commands in English to make sure that her sons can express themselves properly in both languages:

> Since Polish is my native language, I feel ill at ease speaking to my own children in English. However, when I conduct serious conversations with them—the understanding of which could impact their safety (i.e., about not talking to strangers or not opening the front door)—I frequently repeat myself in English as well.

Several women in my study also alluded to the emotional discomfort that they feel when speaking English to their children. Kate Hammer and Jean-Marc Dewaele have argued, for example, that the native language is likely to remain the language used to express emotion when the second language is learned later in life (180).[14] Barbara, who has lived in the United States for twelve years and has a four-year-old son, eloquently explained this phenomenon: "I came to the U.S. from Poland as an adult—I was twenty- years old. Therefore, my Polish was, and still is, the only language that I know best, the language that I think and "feel" in and the language that allows me to express myself most accurately." Beata expressed a similar sentiment in relation to deciding what language to speak with her children: "For me as a mother, talking to my children does not only serve as a means of communication but also allows me to express my emotions, both positive and negative. It would be difficult for me to express them in English; the spontaneity is not there." Hence, the interplay of the native language and the foreign context poses an interesting dilemma for mothers. Not only would speaking the language of the dominant culture erode the cultural intricacies that are conveyed through language (e.g., the use of idiomatic expressions), but it would also eliminate the "spontaneity" and emotional fluency that mothers rely on to communicate with their children.

BILINGUALISM AS A MOTHER'S "GIFT"

Much research has been devoted to the cognitive benefits of being bilingual and the ability to be culturally proficient in multiple settings (Bialystok et al). Mothers also perceive bilingualism as a skill that will arm their children with many advantages in the future. Studies conducted with bilingual children suggest that their executive functioning skills, which are responsible for higher order thinking (i.e., skills needed to control their attention, working memory, and multitasking ability), are already more highly developed than monolingual children at two and a half years of age (Bialystok et al. 486). Moreover, cognitive and language development professor Ellen Bialystok and colleagues point out that bilingual children more rapidly acquire new word meanings because of their ability to assign multiple labels for the same objects and concepts (504).

The mothers in my study expressed an awareness of the developmental benefits of bilingualism and used it as a reason for speaking Polish to their children. Hania stated that learning languages "stimulates the brain," whereas Zosia commented that being bilingual is an important aspect of one's "intellectual development." Another mother declared: "[speaking] a second language is a bonus! It means that a child will have better brain development and greater general knowledge." Yet another mother remarked that bilingualism affects the "plasticity of the brain." Moreover, it is worth emphasizing that seven mothers noted that it is important for them that their children speak Polish in order to further their future opportunities. As Natalia explained:

> My own research has shown that the children of immigrants often regret it when they are older if their parents didn't pass on their native language because *knowing "foreign" languages is very helpful nowadays*. In addition, in old age, these children often feel the need to discover their parents' culture on their own, and knowing the language is crucial in this endeavor. (emphasis added)

Whether in school or on the job market, Ola concluded that "knowing languages increases one's chances of having a successful career." Being proficient in one or more languages also makes it easier for kids to acquire others. Barbara observed, "[It's important for me that my child speaks Polish] in order to maintain his heritage … but also because I'm cognizant of the fact that a solid foundation in Polish will make it easier for him to absorb any other language [in the future]."

It is crucial to note that bilingualism among children of immigrants has been linked to high parental education levels (Portes and Rumbaut). Interestingly enough, both of the women who reported using "mostly English" at home with their children were, in fact, well educated—one possessed a bachelor's degree and the other a master's;[15] however, while their children understood Polish, they oftentimes stumbled for words when speaking it and preferred to use English. One of these two women, Zosia, who is in her mid-fifties and whose eighteen-year old daughter was born in the United States to an American father, also commented on the importance of language learning: "Knowing as many languages as one can opens one's window to the world. It develops and strengthens one's belief in him/herself, allows for one to develop more interpersonal contacts and stimulates an interest in learning other cultures." As a Polish woman raising her child in the United States, it was important for Zosia that her daughter learned how to speak Polish and participated in events organized by the Polish community. As with many other Eastern European immigrant children, Zosia's daughter grew up going to Saturday School to learn how to read and write in Polish and travelling to Poland, several times by herself even, to maintain a connection to her family and her roots. Nevertheless, Zosia emphasized that she speaks mostly English to her daughter because "children born in the United States should speak English fluently first and foremost but not neglect Polish at the same time." Zosia's daughter is, therefore, a true heritage speaker of Polish—one who was raised with a strong cultural connection to the language through family and community interaction but who switched almost solely to using the dominant language over time (Kozminska 2).

Polish mothers raising children in Chicagoland may rely on many community-based resources to aide in teaching their children the native language and culture, such as ethnic-based daycare centres and schools, which serve as an effective means of transmitting the heritage language (Nesteruk 279-80). Of the thirty-one women I surveyed, the vast majority—twenty two—reported sending their children to an ethnic school.[16] It is evident, therefore, that parents rely heavily on this resource to help cultivate their Polish heritage and to promote and protect the ethnic culture, language, and traditions[17] (see Strzelecka-Misonne's chapter in this volume for a critique of Polish schools). Being in close proximity to such schools clearly contributes to the language learning process.

CONCLUSION

The aim of this study was to ascertain how Polish migrant women's backgrounds affect their mothering practices and whether the culture of the home country gets transmitted to children through the use of the mother's native language. It is clear that Polish mothers find it critical to teach their children about their ethnic backgrounds. In the context of migration, language becomes one of the most effective means of doing so but also one that is within their ability to control, either by speaking it themselves or making sure that their children have access to the language through contact with family, ethnic friends, or resources, such as schools. Depending on the mothers' ages at time of migration, their native language is also the one that comes more naturally when discussing emotions or disciplining their children. With language transmission being only one of the many responsibilities that fall on women's shoulders, some Polish mothers also perceive this duty in a very practical way—as a benefit to children's intellectual growth and development and as a potential boost on the job market. The pragmatic approach to speaking Polish to one's children, thus, speaks to how the myth of the *Matka Polka* is perpetuated in a foreign context and contributes to the retention of ethnic culture, traditions, and values.

NOTES

[1]Intensive mothering is a late twentieth-century ideology that regards mothering as a "child-centered, expert-guided, emotionally absorbing, labor-intensive, and financially expensive" task (Hays 8), which requires the mother to be the child's primary care provider until the child is at least three or four years old.

[2]This term is frequently used in the Midwest when referencing the metropolitan area linked to Chicago, Illinois, and its suburbs as a result of geographic, social, economic, and cultural ties.

[3]Poles constitute the fifth largest white ethnic group after the Germans, Irish, English, and Italians (Leven and Szwabe).

[4]It is important to note that not all newly registered immigrants were new arrivals. Many undocumented immigrants of the 1970s and 1980s were not officially accounted for until the Immigration Reform and Control Act amnesty of 1986.

[5]The main factor contributing to the decline in Polish migration

to the U.S., however, is Poland's accession to the European Union in 2004, which lowered the role of U.S. pull factors.

[6]I use pseudonyms when referring to all of the research participants quoted in this chapter in order to protect their anonymity. All surveys and interviews were conducted in Polish and translated by me.

[7]"Heritage language" is a relatively recent term in linguistics. Heritage speakers in the American context were either born in the United States or left their place of birth before the age of eight.

[8]I discuss the concept of the *Matka Polka* in great depth in my article "On the Margins of Religion/On the Forefront of Culture: The Image of the *Matka Polka* (Polish Mother) in Contemporary Poland."

[9]The original Polish title is "*Do Matki-Polki.*"

[10]This phrase stems from Adam Mickiewicz's poem.

[11]Since the term "Polishness" has often been associated with pejorative, nationalistic tendencies, I consciously avoid using it here. When referring to Polish cultural belonging, I emphasize the elements of Polish culture that mothers choose to pass on to their children, such as language and traditions.

[12]School-aged children who are fluent bilinguals may also socialize their mothers through interactions in the language of the host country.

[13]Three women in this study were married to other immigrants from Lithuania, Bulgaria, and Hungary.

[14]Nevertheless, Hammer and Dewaele also found that in situations of migration to the U.S., migrants who frequently interact with native speakers may experience emotional acculturation and switch to their second language in order "to approximate their emotional expression to match that of their companions" (180). For Polish migrants in Chicagoland, emotional acculturation may not be quite as common because of the presence of the Polish community. Out of thirty-one research participants, eight of them—approximately one quarter—responded that they participate in activities organized by Polonia groups in the area.

[15]Two other women reported using both Polish and English in the home; one had a Hungarian husband, whereas the other needed to sometimes use English to help her teenage daughter understand complex topics.

[16]This number includes those women who send their children to a Polish preschool or Saturday School.

[17]Although Polish culture has been inextricably intertwined with Catholicism, Polish schools in the Chicago Area—such as the Fryderyk Chopin School in Buffalo Grove, Illinois, or Polska Szkoła Jana III Sobieskiego in Prospect Heights—offer catechism as an extracurricular, unlike the schools mentioned by Strzelecka-Misonne.

WORKS CITED

Bialystok, Ellen, et al. "Word Mapping and Executive Functioning in Young Monolingual and Bilingual Children." *Journal of Cognition and Development*, vol. 11, no. 4, 2010, pp. 485-508.

Bourdieu, Pierre. "The Forms of Capital." *Handbook of Theory and Research for the Sociology of Education*, edited by J. Richardson, Greenwood, 1986, pp. 241-258.

Budrowska, Bogusława. *Macierzyn´stwo Jako Punkt Zwrotny w Zyciu Kobiety* [*Maternity as a Turning Point in the Woman's Life*]. Wydawnictwo Funna, 2000.

Cummins, Jim. "Basic Interpersonal Communicative Skills and Cognitive Academic Language Proficiency." *Research Gate*, Research Gate, Apr. 2014, www.researchgate.net/publication/242539680_Basic_Interpersonal_Communicative_Skills_and_Cognitive_Academic_Language_Proficiency. Accessed 5 Dec. 2015.

Ehrenreich, Barbara, and Arlie Russel Hochschild, eds. *Global Woman: Nannies, Maids, and Sex Workers in the New Economy*. Metropolitan Books, 2003.

Erdmans, Mary Patrice. "New Chicago Polonia: Urban and Suburban." *The New Chicago: A Social and Cultural Analysis*, edited by John P. Koval. Temple University Press, 2006, pp. 115-27.

Ginsburg, Faye D., and Rayna Rapp. "Introduction." *Conceiving the New World Order: The Global Politics of Reproduction*, edited by Faye D. Ginsburg and Rayna R. Rapp, University of California Press, 1995, pp. 1-18.

Greene, Victor. "Poles," *Harvard Encyclopedia of American Ethnic Groups*, Harvard University Press, 1980, pp. 787-803.

Hammer, Kate, and Jean-Marc Dewaele. "Acculturation as the

Key to the Ultimate Attainment? The Case of Polish-English Bilinguals in the UK." *Cultural Migrants and Optimal Language Acquisition*, edited by Fanny Forsberg Lundell and Inge Bartning, Multilingual Matters, 2015, pp. 178-202.

Hays, Sharon. *The Cultural Contradictions of Motherhood*. Yale University Press, 1996.

Hondagneu-Sotelo, Pierette, and Ernestine Avila. "'I'm Here, but I'm There': The Meanings of Latina Transnational Motherhood." *Women and Migration in the U.S.-Mexico Borderlands: A Reader*, edited by Denise A. Segura and Patricia Zavella, Duke University Press, 2007, pp. 388-412.

Hryciuk, Renata E., and Elżbieta Korolczuk. "Wstęp. Pożegnanie z Matką Polką." *Pożegnanie z Matką Polką?: Dyskursy, Praktyki i Reprezentacje Macierzyństwa We Współczesnej Polsce*, edited by Elżbieta Korolczuk and Renata E. Hryciuk, Wydawnictwo Uniwersytetu Warszawskiego, 2012, pp. 7-20.

Kozminska, Kinga. "Language Contact in the Polish-American Community in Chicago." *International Journal of Bilingualism*, vol. 19, no. 3, 2013, pp. 239-258.

Leven, Bozena, and Michal Szwabe. "Migration Policies and Polish Labor Responses—A Tale of Two Countries." Proc. of European Trade Study Group, University of Birmingham, 2013, http://www.etsg.org/ETSG2013/Papers/320.pdf. Accessed 23 Aug. 206.

Nesteruk, Olena. "Heritage Language Maintenance and Loss Among the Children of Eastern European Immigrants in the USA." *Journal of Multilingual and Multicultural Development*, vol. 31, no. 3, 2010, pp. 271-286.

Nesteruk, O. and L.D. Marks. "Grandparents across the Ocean: Eastern European Immigrants' Struggle to Maintain Intergenerational Relationships." *Journal of Comparative Family Studies*, vol. 40, no. 3, 2009), pp. 77-95.

Pustulka, Paula. "Child-Centred Narratives of Polish Mothers: Cross-generational Identity Constructions Abroad." *Studia Migracyjne-Przegląd Polonijny*, vol. 3. 2014, 151-170.

Schultes, Anna Kuroczycka. "On the Margins of Religion/On the Forefront of Culture: The Image of the *Matka Polka* (Polish Mother) in Contemporary Poland." *Mothers and History. Journal of the Motherhood Initiative for Research and Community*

Involvement, vol. 5, no. 1, 2014, pp. 263-274.

Walks, Michelle. "Identifying an Anthropology of Mothering." *An Anthropology of Mothering*, edited by Michelle Walks and Naomi McPherson, Demeter Press, 2011, pp. 1-47.

11.
Mothering Duties Come First

Professional Immigrant Filipinas' Career Reconstitution Dilemmas

CIRILA P. LIMPANGOG

CHILDCARE REMAINS THE PRIMARY responsibility of women even when there is evidence of increased involvement of men. Although men's lack of participation in childcare is problematic, I argue in this chapter, however, that women's inability to modify their self-expectations as mothers continues to be a problem. Caring for children exceeds the categories of labour usually captured in time-use research. Arlie Hochschild ("The Culture") works with a more capacious meaning of care that encompasses time, depth, a sense of duty, and urgency. "Care" she says is "an emotional bond, usually mutual, between the caregiver and cared-for, a bond in which the caregiver feels responsible for other's well-being and does mental, emotional, and physical work in the course of fulfilling that responsibility" (*The Commercialization* 214). Because care involves feelings, "we rarely imagine it to be work" (*The Commercialization* 218), Hochschild emphasizes that "care is a result of many small subtle acts, conscious or not" (Hochschild, "The Culture of Politics" 333). Married women in full-time paid work who have delegated—fully or partially—this caregiving role have been plagued by what Hochschild ("The Culture") calls a "care deficit." Unless what I call "care-share deficit" between parents is also addressed, I argue that women are likely to endure guilt for not accomplishing their mothering duties well, stress from men's lack of care participation, and delayed career reconfiguration in the destination country.

Childcare and housework renegotiation between spouses is a strategy to reconstitute women's careers. It is one of the main themes that emerged from my doctoral research, which examined identity reconstruction of professional immigrant Filipinas in Melbourne. From 2006 to 2008, I conducted in-depth interviews with twenty women recruited through a snowball approach. Aged twenty-five to forty-five, these women had arrived in Australia in the last twenty-five years. They obtained their university degrees in the Philippines and from first-world countries, including Australia and the United States of America. The participants were highly urbanized, and all but two were from Manila, having been born, raised, educated, and employed there. They occupy a middle-class status in the Philippines terms of educational qualifications and employment. Participants emphasized education as a highly important asset; some stressed its overriding value to achieving money and political influence. Participants claimed that their parents instilled in them the value of a high-quality education, and they wanted to pass this onto their children. I explored the lived experiences of these women during a period when Filipina immigration to Australia was previously studied within the framework of marriage. From the 1970s to the early 1990s, women predominantly migrated as "mail-order brides," partners and spouses, and the domestic violence some of them encountered was a legitimate agenda for academic and popular media inquiry. Yet the scope of their investigations—with few exceptions (Roces; Tibe-Bonifacio)—always focused on women's domestic lives, which omitted their citizenship and worker identities. Elsewhere, I have explored the participants' resistance against workplace discrimination (Limpangog, "Racialized and Gendered"). The reductionist and contradictory images of mail-order brides as manipulative and gold digging versus virginal and family orientated stuck in people's imagination, especially the media's (Saroca), although the actual matchmaking industry had radically weakened following stricter measures imposed by the Australian and Philippine governments in the late nineties. This current chapter surveys Filipino cultural expectations of women in the family, particularly their childcare strategies.

This research uses cultural identity, agency, and the intersectionality of gender, race, and class as analytical lenses. Kathy Davis posits intersectionality as "the interaction between gender, race, and other categories of difference in individual lives, social practices, institutional arrangements, and cultural ideologies and the outcomes of these interactions in terms of power" (68). Intersectionality acknowledges the multidimensionality of women's lives, in which ethnicity and class entangle with gender to illuminate diverse and different identities and approaches. At the familial and social networking level, I argue that immigrant Filipinas' carework and careers in Melbourne are negotiated within their families, especially with their spouses. Sharing household responsibilities with extended family is not rare among the participants, but this arrangement is only temporary. It occurs during the infrequent visits of family members from the homeland and the arrival of new immigrants needing short-term accommodation. Occasionally, a sibling or parent who has immigrated previously but are members of a different household would also extend care. Power is negotiated in all these arrangements within the extended family, but the main focus of this analysis is the power between the participants and their spouses, precisely because they share the parenting role. Gender and ethnic framing of mothering is enacted, resisted, and revised within domestic power relations. As a process of both being and becoming, Stuart Hall has asserted that histories, power, and culture place people in certain positions, which, in turn, frame their identity. I maintain, however, that certain aspects of gender identity within culture are more than mere behaviours or performances. These are deeply embedded as proper ways of being and, therefore, change is heavily resisted.

GENDER EGALITARIANISM AND PARADOXES WITHIN THE FILIPINO FAMILY

Different social and cultural contexts and ideologies of family life encode different rights, expectations, norms, responsibilities, and needs onto families and their members. Although it does not make much sense to speak of one type of Filipino family, there exists a Filipino family ideal that incorporates its own ideology. Part of the problem surrounding the power of the family ideal is that often the ideal is very different from the circumstances of a lived family life. Yet the ideal of the family still has enormous regulative power on family members. It embeds ideologies that control the functioning of the household. For example, all the participants lived with their respective families (mostly nuclear) and thought of themselves as a family with the exception of Ligaya,[1] an economist, who insisted that without marriage her live-in partner was not family. The following section outlines some of the enduring ideals of Filipino family life and emphasizes, in particular, those around motherhood and mothering that regulate through compliance, resistance, or negotiation, the lives of these women.

Philippine sociologist Belen Medina describes the Filipino family as a "shock absorber," "wailing wall," and "refuelling station," with the mother "usually [being] the main source of emotional support in the family" (64). The Filipino family is also noted for its family-centred and personalized care "from cradle to grave," so much so that it rejects institutionalized care (Wilks). The precolonial myth "*Si Malakas at si Maganda*" (literally, "The Strong and the Beautiful") imitates gender complementarity as the first woman and the first man emerged together from the split bamboo pole. They would share equal powers but they would also have specific roles. This assertion for equality was suppressed but was not forgotten, despite the three hundred years of Spanish colonial rule, the fifty years of American occupation, and then the nine years of Marcos dictatorship. Filipinas have the right to inherit and own property, acquire an education, access credit and capitalization, travel, be employed, and pursue careers without having to get their parents' or spouse's consent, according to the 1987 Family Code of the Philippines. The 2015 World Economic Forum ranked the Philippines as seventh among countries closing the gap in gender inequality. Improving women's rights in the Philippines, however, continues to be marred by a rigid gender division that limits women from succeeding in their careers.

Despite increased women's participation in paid work and contractual overseas labour, which has led to a global trend towards the feminization of labour, the Filipina is still expected to embody the "*ilaw ng tahanan*" ("light of the home") role. Thus, she is the carer and spiritual nurturer of children, and her carework is extended to the elderly and other family members. She also acts as family manager and fund custodian. In the event of family breakdown, the woman is often blamed. The man is expected to be the *"haligi ng tahanan"* ("pillar of the home"). As the family leader, he acts as the breadwinner and protector of its members. The switching of gender roles is still disliked, even with more men participating in carework; traditionally, they did so only when women were sick (Parreñas).

The maintenance of family is highly valued by Filipinos, and mostly relies on women's reproductive roles. Among the participants, the performance of their idealized mothering is fundamental in the (re)construction of their Filipino identity. The societal pressure for women to feel or behave maternally is not unique to Filipinas. Within the Australian migrant population, insisting on the greater value of the family and mothering duties is a way that immigrant groups separate themselves from the native population, as in the case of the Italians (Baldassar, "Transnational Families"; Baldassar, *Visits Home*) and Greeks (Bottomley, *After the Odyssey*). Their assertion of putting family and mothering duties first is also a way of maintaining their moral distinctiveness (even superiority) and of preserving ethnic honour (Bottomley, *From Another*). Family-centeredness and mothering identity reinforce each other, and these identities overlap as immigrant women reconstitute their careers, community, and housework arrangements.

MOTHERING DUTIES COME FIRST

I asked participants how they balanced being the *ilaw* as well as succeeding in their careers. To relinquish the maternal role of childcare to strangers and institutional facilities appears unacceptable to most. They unanimously affirmed that mothering duties come first, ahead of their own needs and career aspirations, especially when the children are young. This appears to be in contradiction to the care crisis in the Philippines, where the "left-behind" children are cared for by family members and not by strangers (Parreñas)—family members and nannies hired within one's immediate kin network appear to be the only legitimate proxies in care giving. I, however, see this as an assertion of the participants' idealized mothering modality within a family-migration context, in which unlike their contract-worker sisters, my participants took their children with them to Australia. "With whom will you leave your children, with the white people?" asked Leah, whose two children were four years and seven months old when they arrived in Melbourne. In the Philippines, they had a nanny and a maid. These live-in, full-time helpers were recruited from the kinship network and were, thus, trusted. With scarce kin support in Australia, Leah decided to forgo employment and focus on looking after the children.

Rosanna, whose two children were born in Melbourne, had a similar viewpoint. Instead of putting a brake on her career, she delegated childcare to a co-national. Rosanna chose her because "you can trust her; you know that she can be very caring to the child ... because you have heard feedback about her, and you can communicate with her easily." Rosanna's children treated Nanay Lydia, the nanny, with affection and filial respect, corresponding to the title *nanay* (mother). When her second child came, Rosanna approached another kin member. She believed that the infant needed one-on-one attention, whereas in childcare facilities, every caregiver was responsible for up to six children.

The lack of trust in white people may be partly interpreted in terms of the participants' feeling of cultural superiority. It may also be a precaution against the foreign-care practices that they were not accustomed to. Many aired that mothering was their most vital responsibility, and it should take precedence over paid work and other facets of their lives. They feared a "care deficit" if they did otherwise. They were willing to put their careers on hold in favour of the children's nurturance, which was met according to their specifications. The social and cultural displacement resulting from migration reinforces their insistence on an old, tried-and-tested notion of mothering. Yet their notion of idealized mothering was different from their practice in the Philippines, where they had nannies. Their current mothering praxis is not a faithful continuation of the past but a construction of a role that draws on the values that they hold dear.

Amy chose family over career upon arrival in Melbourne. She thought that her daughters needed full-time attention during the crucial years of adjusting to the Australian educational system. She regularly attended their school activities, assisted them with their assignments, and made their lunches. As Amy explained: "I actually did this partially in Manila. Having a full-time teaching job, a part-time insurance brokering after hours, and the heavy traffic made it impossible for me to come home early and do my mothering duties as much as I wanted. Then there were lesson planning and marking tasks that I took home." In Melbourne, by getting more involved, she said that she got to know her children's friends and their respective families; she ensured that the girls were not exposed to vices. I view her stance of intensive mothering[2] using the yardsticks of school performance and quality of peers as emblematic of her middle-class status. Though stay-at-home-mom, Amy also minded her friends' preschool children, and although they paid her, it was due to kinship-based moral duties that she extended care.

Having a baby made Sharon homebound. Her husband, Richard, was then employed as a full-time IT specialist. Sharon elaborated: "although I could work, I opted not to until Daniel was two. Everything and everyone around him was new, except me. So I thought [I would work] after six months when he's fully adjusted." During our interview, she was a full-time office administrator, whereas Richard was freelancing. She felt lucky that Richard was the one staying at home to care for their then three-year-old son Daniel, who went to childcare only once a week. Richard did not originally choose to be the day carer, but his work option made him homebound and subsequently compatible with Sharon's parents-only caring idea. When Richard had to meet clients after hours, however, childcare reverted back to her.

Luningning's children were also born after she migrated to Australia. She was ambivalent about proceeding with a newly acquired teaching job and putting her firstborn in childcare:

> I wanted to place the baby in a daycare but I couldn't do it. I kept on crying because I felt sorry for the baby. I saw the others being laid on the ground when they had to be exposed to sunlight at six or seven months.... It was very, very hard. What about the baby, he cannot yet speak? It was like five babies to one carer. Poor baby.

Mothering duties implicit in a Filipino-based orientation often left her burdened. She finally opted to hire her sister-in-law to babysit. Other participants also turned to the childcare services of co-nationals and relatives. Trust, a familiarity with culturally acceptable childcare practices, and a common language determined this option. All of these are linked the traditional practices in the Philippines, in which children of working parents are primarily entrusted to those within the family network and live-in maids. The intersection of gender and class made the participants' mothering ideology more pronounced, especially the nontransferability of care to anyone but trusted proxies.

Rosanna obtained transnational kin help during the challenging time of giving birth. Her mother stayed for six months while she transitioned from her first maternity leave to joining the labour market. After the birth of her second child, an older sister came. Although the kin's help was invaluable, it was also a source of dilemma. With another participant, Susan, her mother visited to provide emotional support when she gave birth. She was thankful but was also remorseful as their childrearing practices clashed. Susan believed in controlled crying as a method for putting babies to sleep, but her mother considered it unloving. As Susan explained:

> Usually colic babies have a pain in their tummies. They cry at a certain time at night. Controlled crying is [when] you leave the baby, and you don't give him comfort, otherwise, he will get used to it. When he cries then after a certain time, you come back to the crib and comfort him. Then you increase the interval of comforting. And that didn't work because that is not a Filipino thing. When my mom heard him crying she started to cry and accused us as being bad parents.

Carol, an IT manager, sidelined her career when her children were growing up. Being, sacrificial and at the same time successful is an image she cherished. Carol stressed: "my mother was a superwoman. She was the head of her department, but she also raised us— nine kids who are all successful in our chosen careers. She's such a martyr, I know, but she is my role model." Similarly, Luningning claimed that by shifting careers from the public relations industry to higher education, she would be assured of a more predictable familial routine. Her mother was her icon for being a highly regarded academic in the Philippines, who successfully raised her children. Indeed, my participants made huge sacrifices in being a "supermom" and a career woman, yet no one complained or reported any marital conflicts with respect to childcare roles. Carol stared at me for a full minute and broke into a tiny laughter. "It's okay," she faintly said and shook her head. It was a gesture of gentle sarcasm and an acceptance of her situation. I remained silent and did not pursue the matter anymore, out of respect. Although Susan, Carol and Luningning believed in their mothers' childrearing practices, they found these very hard to replicate in Australia. Yet they persevered. They agreed that women should put their families above their own careers and not complain. The acceptance of their mothering roles without question is best understood in terms of the intersection of their gender, class, and Filipino identities. The self-expectation of success in both career and domestic life has enabled women to hurdle hardships but with a great deal of stress.

The valorization of motherhood is both universal and culture specific. Despite the growing advocacy for shared parenting and work-life balance, mothers remain the primary caregivers in affluent countries—such as Canada (Wall and Arnold), the United States (Bianchi et al.; Mannino and Deutsch), Great Britain (O'Brien; O'Brien et al.) and Australia (Baxter; Craig, "Does Father"; Craig and Mullan, "Lone and Partnered")— although evidence shows fathers' increasing involvement over time (Craig and Mullan, "Australian Fathers'"). Even though indicators in these studies vary, with time-use as most common, some authors took into account task complexity and intensity, and amount of accountability, which, when taken as a whole, reiterates women's double day. Challenges are even more pronounced for immigrants, as they negotiate social structures and resist domestic subordination.

In her research on parenting, Lyn Craig reveals that Australian mothers provide "absolute care" to children, with higher interaction and physical activities than fathers do. The father's discretionary time with children is spent usually on "fun" activities, such as reading and playing, and is rarely done alone; thus, the mother's time is not substituted. Craig further emphasizes that "mothering involves more double activity, more physical labour, a more rigid timetable, and more overall responsibility than fathering" (76), which is akin to Sharon Hay's theory on intensive mothering. My participants constantly referred back to their idealized idea of mothering and justified it through the expression "*kasi Pinoy tayo*" ("because we are Filipinos"). Many expressed this with sarcasm, others with pride, albeit with ambivalence. Their own mothers modelled the "supermom," a mother who is successful in both family and career realms but one who endures severe hardships. Such behaviour clearly manifests the intersectionality of gender and culture.

As I mentioned above, in the Filipino cultural context, the emotional and moral duties ascribed to a mother are nontransferable, except to acceptable proxies; thus, there are limited choices when they become inaccessible. Close (female) members of the family and domestic helpers are the customary proxies and temporary relievers. Maids are rarely strangers, as they are usually recruited from the wider kinship pool. Because they become part of the organic household, they are treated like family. Trust inherent in a close relationship is an important element in relinquishing care duties to proxies, and this is rarely extended to institutional carers, who are considered strangers. In the Philippines, institutional care is consigned to orphaned or abandoned children, and when there are no members of kin to look after them. It is a stigmatized option. The participants' responses indicate that such views persisted after migration. They valued their maternal role very much, as it was their way of replicating their own mothers' style. Some expressly resisted the "supermom" model, since the absence of maids in the new context made its execution highly problematic. However, performing the idealized mother is tied up with respect and power that they might want validated within the extended family. In concurrence with Yen Le Espiritu, I view that holding onto their idealized mothering was the participants' way of framing the unfamiliar dominant white culture as "other," which, consequently, allowed them to assert their moral superiority. Motherhood often poses as an additional challenge to immigrant women wanting to adhere to societal demands of fitting in and becoming autonomous (see Sazzad, this volume).

Men's childcare participation was conspicuously absent in most of the participants' responses; their lack of participation contributed to the women's delayed labour market participation. Most of those who were employed delegated care duty to a kin member. Participants provided information about their husband's childcare involvement only when pressed. Some had a way of covering up their spouse's seemingly inadequate participation by saying "he's a great dad ... he plays with the kids ... he cooks for them occasionally" but showed resistance to follow-up questions. Some husbands, both those born in the Philippines and in Australia, participated in childcare, although many of them were described as being a "helper" or "reliever," and the woman remained as principal caregiver. Fathers' tasks were typically "fun," consistent with Lynn Craig's study ("Does Father"). According to my participants, these include reading books to children, taking them to the park or movies, playing with them, taking them to and from childcare or school. Some were also involved in bathing the kids and changing nappies. Many did not automatically take part, and it was their wives who would organize their participation. Rosanna's story highlights the difficulty in sharing carework.

THE CASE OF ROSANNA

"It is highly important that you ask him to do things," said Rosanna. She had to "demand" her husband's housework participation, otherwise nothing would happen. Rosanna's husband had a privileged upbringing. He was the only son and the youngest in their family, so his elder sisters did the housework. Besides, they always had a maid. When they were newly married, Rosanna thought that managing the household was not onerous, as she was trained to do it even though she also grew up with maids around her. She also assumed that working hard would win her husband's empathy. But he rarely offered help. The arrival of children made her more exhausted, and so she began expressing her needs: "You know, it's always off when we say the obvious [in Filipino norms] so it took me a while to express myself."[3] Rosanna was earning some money in her part-time dental practice, but her income was not a source of gender power capable of subverting their housework relationship. However, housework responsibilities shifted as she deemed that mothering duties were more demanding. This was also expressed by other participants. When the pressure intensified and she went beyond the cultural barrier, her husband listened. He was intent on helping but needed guidance as how to proceed with simple tasks. "He now washes the dishes, whereas before he did not," Rosanna said, explaining that her husband routinely cleaned up after dinner. She stressed this with a caveat, "he's asked me to remind him and not just to put up with a dirty sink, so that he can internalize his tasks." It also took a while for him to participate in childcare. He had learned to "give the kids a bath, and change a nappy," but she still did most of the work. She said that she put the children to bed, cooked, ironed their clothes, and cleaned the house. To cope with all of these responsibilities, she said that "sometimes the newly washed clothes are piling up for ironing. We have takeaway [meals]."

Rosanna's husband never offered to look after their children at least on a part-time basis so that she could further her career. Looking after their young children and keeping the house were her default responsibilities. Thus, Rosanna practised her dental profession on a part-time basis only. She and her husband could have used full-time childcare, but Rosanna was willing to compromise her career to ensure that the children's needs were attended to—and if possible—by her personally. Their ten-year-old son was diagnosed with mild autism, which was another reason why they thought that close parental supervision was necessary. On days that Rosanna was not reporting for work, she took her son for professional treatment or both children for their extracurricular activities. These were also the days when she caught up with housework. Indeed, home duties were a steep learning curve to Rosanna's husband. She decided to train her children to perform domestic chores, regardless of their gender. I saw her son cooking rice and then looking after his sister during one of my home visits.

Fathers also occasionally looked after the sick children when in extreme situations the mother could not miss work. Susan explained: "When our son is sick, by default, I am the one not sleeping through the night to monitor his condition. I am also the one absenting from work." As to why men were less involved, the women explained that their husbands, though 'willing' to provide care, had full-time jobs. But so did the women, or at least some were encumbered from getting a full-time job in some points of their career reconstitution in Australia, let alone any job, because of care duties. All except three of the participants were working full-time at the time of the interview. The couples' traditional sex-role attitudes did not manifest much until they had children. It appears that many of the participants continued to be bound by idealized gender roles and rigid cultural traditions that prescribed the husband as breadwinner, despite the demands of their own paid work. None of the participants challenged their spouse's 'helper' attitude, which normalized their role as principal care provider. Despite the women's ability to later reconstitute their career while being the principal carer, the feeling of a "care deficit" lingered. For instance, Luningning was always time poor while juggling postgraduate studies, paid work, and care duties. Obtaining the care support of a trusted kin did not seem to alleviate her feeling that she suffered from a "care deficit." She and other participants insisted on their spouses' increased participation later on, but none of them, except Kris, had attempted a radical shift towards equal care responsibilities. Although there were shifts in varying degrees to the women's advantage, their parenting roles on the whole bore an uncontested care-share deficit.

One exceptional case of role reversal was that of Kris, whose husband agreed to be the housekeeper and carer of their six-year-old son. Although her immediate family members were in Melbourne, they still lived too far away to be able to regularly help. As Kris explained:

Steve and I made a commitment that if we're going to have a child, one of us should be there for the child.... So we decided that whoever between us is available that person takes care of the child. We thought that he could have an early retirement.... If I were to stop working, by the time I go back to employment I'd be old already, whereas Steve started working at age fifteen, so he'd been working for forty years already. He was willing to continue working full time, but he also understood that I'd like to work. At that time, there was an opening for teachers after a long recession in the '90s. Our son was already two and a half years old. We decided that it was time for me to go back teaching.

This switch of caregiving roles boosted Kris' teaching career, which she claimed did not threaten her spouse's position at home. Her spouse did the cooking and housecleaning, which Kris happily relinquished. She still did a considerable amount of home duties after returning from work to assure Steve that she was doing her equal share. It is possible that Kris was offsetting what Bittman et al. call "gender deviance." She was sensitive that stay-at-home fathers could be stigmatized for assuming a feminized role (Rochlen et al.). Steve appeared to be comfortable being the housekeeper during my interview visits. He cooked and served us meals and came out only during breaks; he never once spied on my conversations with Kris. His involvement in their son's upbringing was clear, as he chatted about his son's school progress at the dinner table. Though generally rare, this male-centered care and housework arrangement fulfilled their individual and family desires without compromising Steve's self-esteem.

After a few years, when the participants had adjusted to Australian practices, and their children had reached at least three years old, many decided to use childcare centres. Although this may suggest a process of acculturation, their decision had more to do with having limited options, as trusted co-nationals and kin were themselves employed or did not live close by, and their kin in the Philippines could not easily acquire a tourist visa. The participants eventually found full-time jobs, which necessitated a more organized childcare routine. Those who had children in preschool depended on a child-care centre as a last resort. Because participants consider being a mother their primary role, many felt guilty about this choice, which closely appropriates Hochshild's "care deficit."

CONCLUSION

The centrality of mother-child relationships conforms to the traditional Filipino notion of childcare. Mothering from the Filipino perspective emphasizes physical presence and emotional attachment with the child and the ability to provide focused and one-on-one attention. In the Philippines, childcare is only relinquished to close relatives and live-in maids, who are treated as family. The belief that the nearest kin has the moral responsibility to do proxy care-work often follows women emigrating from the Philippines. To entrust the child to institutional childcare facilities and to strangers would be to renounce the participants' primary duty as "*ilaw ng tahanan*." Although the lack of childcare placement is a structural barrier to working women in Australia (Leahy and Doughney), the participants in my study did not put the blame on the placement scarcity. They only considered childcare centres as a last option. The women did not oppose their husband's sharing of carework; in fact, it was appreciated. However, the women's choice of prioritizing their children was made within their gendered realities, in which their husbands refused to reconfigure their careers to help their spouses with the carework, which left the women burdened with a double shift (Hochschild, *The Second Shift*). These conflating factors help frame the women's persistent definition of their maternal identity in terms of their ideas of traditional Filipino femininity, which can be appreciated through the intersection of gender, race, and class.

I view these women's efforts of replicating their own mother's caregiving templates as linked to respectability in the family and pride within the ethnic community. It was also their way of asserting cultural superiority over the dominant white Australians, which is consistent with Gillian Bottomley's idea (*From Another*). To my participants, hands-on childcare is very Filipino and may be relegated only to trusted kin. They felt that this was better compared to the popular centre-based care practice in Australia. Laminated education diplomas hang in the participants' living rooms. They would proudly show photos of their children and stress their extracurricular activities and academic achievements; and to those with older kids, the well-paying jobs their children took. Almost all home visits I made included receiving a tour of their homes without my prompting. These are symbols of respectability within the Filipino culture; they speak volumes about the women's accomplishments in their careers and their role as mothers. This reasoning, however, tends to obscure carework as an area for gender reconfiguration. Although the principal role of carer gave them fulfilment, participants felt that it was sometimes self-defeating. I have argued that an uncontested care-share deficit helped reassert the women's principal care role, which ironically left them feeling guilty for not resembling their ideal form of mothering. Addressing this deficit requires an understanding of not only gender but also cultural dynamics, and in this instance, beliefs and practices of mothering within the Filipino frame are seen as both a source of respectability and a form of intense pressure for the women. Still, it is important to stress that carework and housework remain the predominant responsibility of women in general in Australia (Bittman et al.), and this may reinforce the women's mothering ideal as well as their spouses' "helper"-only attitude (Craig).

This chapter has looked at carework within the capacious definition by Hochschild, which involves time, emotion, sense of duty, and urgency (*The Commercialization*). For the men to transition to a co-principal carer, men must think and define themselves as such. This shift could be a focus of future studies of migrating Filipino couples. Elsewhere, I have suggested that ongoing advocacy towards parity in the household must be encouraged through school- and family-oriented programs, such as boy and girl scouting, premarriage and prenatal courses (Limpangog, "Gender Equality"). I extend this suggestion by specifying the need for new heroes and models and for having them documented well and widely disseminated. Fathers' increased participation in usually women-led parent school councils and playgroups must be encouraged; the destigmatization of stay-at-home dads must also be supported (Rochlen et al.). Enlisting older children in carework should also be explored. All of these are practical ways to address the care-share deficit.

Rhacel Salazar Parreñas has argued for the need to expand gender boundaries beyond the context of the *ilaw* role of women and the *haligi* role of men, as both equally fulfill the *haligi* role (164-166). Indeed, the social construction of carework among Filipina immigrants is slowly changing towards egalitarianism. It can even be improved with more concerted change in gender relations as well as with the ability of women to let go of the "supermom" ideal and revise their principal care role that brought them guilt, severe stress, and career reconstitution difficulties. New models and heroes of gender equality are needed.

NOTES

[1]Pseudonyms were used to protect the privacy of research participants. The interviews were done in a mixture of English and Tagalog. I translated the interviews in English and had these validated by the women.

[2]Sharon Hays in *The Cultural Contradictions of Motherhood* contends that the ideology of "intensive mothering"—depicted by her as the dominant contemporary mode of parenting in the U.S., which demands the devotion of great resources of time, energy, and finances to raising and nourishing children—systematically serves patriarchy, the state, and capitalism. The exhortation of mothers to become child centred, to accept guidance from parenting experts, and to be emotionally absorbed in parenting has become normalized among the middle class. In this sense, a good mother is an intensive mother.

[3]Within the high-context culture in the Philippines, people are expected to read each other's nuanced sentiments through small talks and gestures over a period of time. Help should be readily extended and not asked for, especially when one is obviously burdened. Rosanna initially resisted asking for help to avoid hurting her relationship with her spouse, for doing so would be tantamount to depicting her husband as callous.

WORKS CITED

Baldassar, Loretta. "Transnational Families and the Provision of Moral and Emotional Support: The Relationship between Truth and Distance." *Identities: Global Studies in Culture and Power*, vol. 14, no. 4, 2007, pp. 385-409.

Baldassar, Loretta. *Visits Home: Migration Experiences between Italy and Australia*. Melbourne University Publishing, 2001.

Baxter, Janeen. "Patterns of Change and Stability in the Gender Division of Household Labour in Australia, 1986–1997." *Journal of Sociology*, vol. 38, no. 4, 2002, pp. 399-424. Print.

Bianchi, Suzanne M, et al. "Is Anyone Doing the Housework? Trends in the Gender Division of Household Labor." *Social Forces*, vol. 79, no. 1, 2000, pp. 191-228.

Bittman, Michael, et al. "When Does Gender Trump Money? Bargaining and Time in Household Work." *American Journal of Sociology*, vol. 109, no. 1, 2003), 186-214. Print.

Bottomley, Gillian. *After the Odyssey: A Study of Greek Australians*. University of Queensland Press St. Lucia, 1979..

Bottomley, Gillian. *From Another Place: Migration and the Politics of Culture*. Cambridge University Press, 1992.

Craig, Lyn. "Does Father Care Mean Fathers Share? A Comparison of How Mothers and Fathers in Intact Families Spend Time with Children." *Gender & Society*, vol. 20, no.2, 2006, pp. 259-81.

Craig, Lyn, and Killian Mullan. "Australian Fathers' Work and Family Time in Comparative and Temporal Perspective." *Journal of Family Studies*, vol. 18, no. 2, 2012, pp. 165-174.

Craig, Lyn, and Killian Mullan. "Lone and Partnered Mothers' Childcare Time within Context in Four Countries." *European Sociological Review*, vol. 28, no. 4, 2012, pp. 512-526.

Davis, Kathy. "Intersectionality as Buzzword: A Sociology of Science Perspective on What Makes a Feminist Theory Successful." *Feminist Theory*, vol. 9, no. 1, 2008), pp. 67-85.

Espiritu, Yen Le. "'We Don't Sleep around Like White Girls Do': Family, Culture, and Gender in Filipina American Lives." *Signs*, vol. 26, no. 2, 2001, pp. 415-440.

Hays, Sharon. *The Cultural Contradictions of Motherhood*. Yale University Press, 1996.

Hochschild, Arlie Russell. *The Commercialization of Intimate Life: Notes from Home and Work*. University of California Press, 2003.

Hochschild, Arlie Russell . "The Culture of Politics: Traditional, Postmodern, Cold-Modern, and Warm-Modern Ideals of Care." *Social Politics: International Studies in Gender, State & Society*, vol. 2, no. 3, 1995, pp. 331-346.

Hochschild, Arlie Russell . *The Second Shift: Working Couples and the Revolution at Home*. Viking, 1989.

Leahy, Mary, and James Doughney. "Women, Work and Preference Formation: A Critique of Catherine Hakim's Preference Theory."

Journal of Business Systems, Governance and Ethics, vol 1, no. 1, 2006, pp. 37-48.

Limpangog, Cirila P. "Gender Equality in Housework among Professional Filipinas in Melbourne: Painfully Slow and Illusory?" *Gender, Place & Culture*, vol. 23, no. 9, 2016), pp. 1240-1253.

Limpangog, Cirila P. "Racialised and Gendered Workplace Discrimination: The Case of Skilled Filipina Immigrants in Melbourne, Australia." *Journal of Workplace Rights*, vol. 17, no. 2, 2013-2014, pp. 191-218.

Mannino, Clelia Anna, and Francine M Deutsch. "Changing the Division of Household Labor: A Negotiated Process between Partners." *Sex Roles*, vol. 56, no. 5-6, pp. 309-24.

Medina, Belen Tan-Gatue. *The Filipino Family: A Text with Selected Readings*. University of the Philippines Press, 1991.

O'Brien, Margaret. "Shared Caring: Bringing Fathers into the Frame." Manchester: Equal Opportunities Commission, 2005.

O'Brien, Margaret, Berit Brandth, and Elin Kvande. "Fathers, Work and Family Life: Global Perspectives and New Insights." *Community, Work and Family*, vol. 10, no. 4, 2007, pp. 375-386.

Parreñas, Rhacel Salazar. *Children of Global Migration: Transnational Families and Gendered Woes*. Stanford University Press, 2005.

Roces, Mina. "Sisterhood Is Local: Filipino Women in Mount Isa." *Wife or Worker? Asian Women and Migration*, edited by Nicola Piper and Mina Roces, Rowman and Littlefield Publishers, Inc., 2003, pp. 73-100.

Rochlen, Aaron B, et al. "'I'm Just Providing for My Family': A Qualitative Study of Stay-at-Home Fathers." *Psychology of Men & Masculinity*, vol. 9, no. 4, 2008, pp. 193-206. Print.

Saroca, Cleonicki. "Filipino Women, Migration, and Violence in Australia: Lived Reality and Media Image." *Kasarinlan: Philippine Journal of Third World Studies*, vol. 21, no. 1, 2007, pp. 75-110.

Tibe-Bonifacio, Glenda Lynna Anne. "Filipino Women in Australia: Practising Citizenship at Work." *Asian and Pacific Migration Journal*, vol. 14, no. 3, 2005, pp. 293-326.

Wall, Glenda, and Stephanie Arnold. "How Involved Is Involved Fathering? An Exploration of the Contemporary Culture of Fatherhood." *Gender & Society*, vol. 21, no. 4, 2007, pp. 508-527.

Wilks, Antonietta Butler. "Brides and Grandmothers: Caregiving Challenges and Resources for Older Filipino Women in Australia." *Abstract and Proceedings of the 4th National Conference for Emerging Researchers in Ageing*, edited by M. Underwood and K. Suridge University of Queensland Press, 2005, pp 181-184.

12.
The Extraordinariness of Ordinary Immigrant Mothers in Jhumpa Lahiri's Writings

REHNUMA SAZZAD

VIJAY MISHRA PITHILY CONCLUDES his thoughtful book on cultural texts about Indian migration to various parts of the globe with the following: "All diasporas are unhappy, for if and when their subaltern absolute Other speaks she can only speak to herself" (255). As the writer explains in the book, living outside one's home culture involves a traumatic adjustment not only with losing a sense of community but also with learning the ways of an unknown society. Finding one's voice in such an unhinged condition can be really daunting, which adds to feelings of unhappiness. The writer stresses the fact that it is even harder for the immigrant "Other" to speak about the constraints of her position in the diasporic society because of her lack of agency. Especially as a female member of a marginalized group, the immigrant "Other" faces a dearth of socio-cultural tools with which to make her mark in the adopted environment. Nevertheless, Mishra emphasizes the importance of works of literature written about immigrant Indians that reflect both their powerlessness and their transcendence, which are part of their challenging life.

In this context, Mishra introduces Jhumpa Lahiri's Pulitzer Prize-winning collection of short stories, *Interpreter of Maladies* (1999), which is principally applauded "not for its examination of diasporic anxieties but for its exploration of human relations" (191). In accordance with Mishra, I read Lahiri as a successful chronicler of Indian immigrants, whose relationships reveal the extraordinary amount of courage and commitment underlying the continuity of the familial and social bonds in the diasporic context.

In fact, the immigrant mothers' adherence to their native culture and their acculturation suggest some of the biggest challenges of their uprooted life. Therefore, Lahiri's resounding success as a chronicler of displaced individuals, especially mothers, highlights "the question of whether diasporas provide enabling contexts in which previous gender norms can be challenged or whether they reproduce and possibly even harden existing gender ideologies and relations" (Al-Ali 119). Lahiri's second short-story collection, Unaccustomed Earth (2008), explores this question in a more dramatic way. I discuss both texts to highlight the cultural, familial, and personal challenges that the mother characters from West Bengal, India, encounter in the U.S., and the extraordinary conviction that marks their experiences in the alien country.

INTERPRETER OF MALADIES: TRIALS OF IMMIGRANT MOTHERHOOD

Interpreter of Maladies is a collection that has been acclaimed not only for the writer's art of storytelling but also for her "keen eye for observation and [her] admirable gift for details" (Noor 365). Notably, it is the ordinary details that signify Lahiri's remarkable portrayal of the Indian mothers' struggle against their estrangement and loneliness in the new country. "Mrs. Sen's" is a story in the collection that effectively echoes the pressure of isolation for an immigrant woman in an unnamed university town in the U.S. She acts as a caregiver for an eleven-year-boy called, Eliot, from whose point of view the story is narrated. Visiting Mrs. Sen's apartment on the first day, the youngster notices the oddities of the décor, indicating the influence of an unknown culture. For example, the commonly used drum-shaped lampshades still wear the manufacturer's wraps, whereas the TV and the telephone are covered by an embroidered fabric of bright colour. Mrs. Sen herself wears "a shimmering white sari patterned with orange paisleys, more suitable for an evening affair than for that quiet, faintly drizzling August afternoon" (Lahiri, *Interpreter* 112). Just as her coral gloss falls outside the borders of her lips, her superfluous sari announces her unsure existence in the New World, which resulted from her marriage with an Indian mathematician pursuing an academic career in the U.S. Paradoxically, Eliot finds that his primly dressed mother appears unusual in the apartment because her cuffs, shorts, and rope-soled shoes are "too lank and sensible" (113) compared to Mrs. Sen's lively presence and carefully arranged furnishings. The minimalist author, thus, suggests through her details that Mrs. Sen is more nurturing than usual in an American context.

It is no wonder that Eliot prefers staying at Mrs. Sen's after school to remaining in their beach house, which gets cold as soon as September arrives. The beach is as desolate as their home, and he becomes quickly bored gathering pieces of mussels or poking seaweed there. Compared to this, he enjoys watching Mrs. Sen chopping foodstuffs in her apartment: "Instead of a knife she used a blade that curved like the prow of a Viking ship.... She spilt things in half, then quarters, speedily producing florets, cubes, slices, and shreds" (114). It is not simply the novelty of Mrs. Sen's paraphernalia and procedures that entertains Eliot, though. Not only does she make sure that Eliot does not come near the blade during her hour-long preparation for cooking, but she also supplies him with peanut-butter spread crackers, carrot sticks carved by her blade, and Popsicles. Nevertheless, Eliot's mother does not like Mrs. Sen's hospitality in the form of Indian drinks and snacks, which are offered to her every evening when she goes to the apartment to pick up her son. Susan Koshy elaborates: "[Eliot's mother's] presence in Mrs. Sen's home creates unspoken tensions as the lines between kin and stranger, insider and outsider, work and home are redrawn through Mrs. Sen's position as surrogate parent and host-worker" ("Minority" 606-607). By being a surrogate mother for Eliot, Mrs. Sen unknowingly exerts her influence in changing the established disregard for her cultural practices, which is symbolized by Eliot's mother's terse appreciation of her delicacies. Mrs. Sen's mothering ability allows Lahiri to reveal the inefficacy of the "oversimplified definition of American culture . . . through the asymmetrical power relationships between white and non-white groups" (Bhatia 13). It is because the power relation is challenged by the social interactions of the citizens and the immigrants.

The porous nature of borders of belonging is evident from Mrs. Sen's cultural exchanges with Eliot, as well. He finds that she passes uneasy days waiting for letters from her home country. As she intently waits one day while Eliot shuffles through the mail box for her, he cannot fathom the reason behind her anxiety. However, weeks later when a nearly crumpled and heavily postmarked blue aerogram is discovered and Mrs. Sen hugs him by "clasping his face to her sari" (Lahiri, *Interpreter* 121), he realizes that this letter keeps her alive. In this way, her warmth brings him close to her, despite the remoteness of her culture, which is suggested by the "odor of mothballs and cumin" (121) that surrounds him during the cuddle. He is nonjudgmental when she eats clam cakes, which she imagines to be pakoras, some fried Indian snacks, with a lot of Tabasco sauce and black peppers. Despite being a child, he tries to empathize with her feelings of disconnection with her home culture. She pines for an event to put on her brocaded saris and to send pictures of her new life back home. Sadly, no invitation for such an event arrives. As a result, she regrets that people in India perceive her as being liberated.

Her unstoppable longing for fresh fish becomes a metaphor for keeping her Bengali-self alive. Fish is a staple food in her culture, and she makes every attempt to buy a whole fish and cook it fresh. Eliot notices how she treasures her raw collection procured from the market: "She stroked the tails, prodded the bellies, pried apart the gutted flesh" (127).

Eliot observes some of the passengers' complaints about the smell of the fish that they carry back to the apartment by bus. Therefore, her dramatic loss of interest in her regular fish store and in her hospitality towards his mother worries him. Nevertheless, her repeated listening of a recorded conversation reveals that she is missing her grandfather's voice, which she has recently lost. By being a witness to Mrs. Sen's struggle against cultural estrangement by sending letters home, adapting to untried food and lifestyle, and maintaining Bengali clothing and cuisine, Eliot also forms a significant bond with her.

This bond does not last long, however. Mrs. Sen's husband pressures her to learn how to drive as fast as possible so that she can become part of the new environment by achieving mobility, although she prefers to find her place in the U.S. in her own way. Her refusal of being suffocated by the expectation of speedy assimilation leads to a minor driving accident while Eliot and her husband are sitting in the car, which removes the boy from her life. He is to head back to his cold beach house from school and stay alone until his mother returns home. When his mother calls him from work to see if he is adjusting to the new arrangement, Eliot's reaction is sombre: "[He] looked out the kitchen window, at gray waves receding from the shore, and said that he was fine" (135). The short story ends by implying that the boy is anything but fine. Like the waves he looks at, his mind is indecisive after returning to his monotonous and frigid surroundings. Eliot, thus, comes to share Mrs. Sen's shoreless existence and longs for protection despite not being an immigrant.

Therefore, the title of the short story is significant for highlighting Mrs. Sen's mother-like warmth for the child. Laura Anh Williams elaborates that "the apostrophe 's' suggests what is present and elusive in the story; that is, an alternative knowledge and autonomy which, while not granted full fruition in the course of the narrative, at least hints at more productive and nurturing ways of creating relationships with others" (75). In other words, the thwarted interdependence of the Indian caregiver and the American youngster creates a space for imagining a fruitful coming together of vastly different cultures. Notwithstanding the severance of a mother-child-like bond, then, the truth remains that both Mrs. Sen and Eliot "have (criss)crossed the intercultural bridge while mourning the warm and colorful relationship they were able to have for a while" (Caspari 255).

In juxtaposition to this affectionate tie, Lahiri also depicts the distance between a mother and her children in another short story from the same collection. In fact, the reader gets to see how motherhood adds to the challenge of immigrant life through the unkind demand of fitting in with the unknown system of complete self-dependence. The short story "Interpreter of Maladies," after which the collection is named, presents this through Mrs. Das, "who is seeking a remedy for the responsibility of marriage and motherhood" (Brada-Williams 461-462). The story revolves around Mr. and Mrs. Das travelling to India with their children, where they play the part of American tourists on their way to the Sun Temple at Konarak. They hire Mr. Kapasi, a local tour guide, who knows English and also works as an interpreter for the general physician of his area as he also speaks Gujarati.[1] The reader is offered a picture of the young Das family through Mr. Kapasi's eyes.

The story opens with his first observation of the couple as a bickering pair, who cannot decide about accompanying their daughter, Tina, to the restroom. When Mrs. Das relents to do this and emerges from Mr. Kapasi's white Ambassador Car, he notes that the Americanized mother does not "hold the little girl's hand" (Lahiri, *Interpreter* 43) while walking by her side. Laura Karttunen's comment on this is trenchant, as she points out that "[n]egation is emphatically a feature of language: a camera-eye could not capture what is here expressed through negation" (430). What is unnarrated here is Mrs. Das's failure to be a caring mother according to Indian tradition. Performing as a good mother in Indian culture involves constantly keeping a watchful eye on and ensuring a warm presence around the child. What Shari L. Thurer describes as the prevalent norm of ideal motherhood in the Western world applies to an Indian setting as well: "Our current myth holds that the well-being of our children depends almost entirely on the quality of their upbringing (read mother, since it is she who usually has primary responsibility for raising children)" (xvi). The fundamentality of a mother's love is undeniable; however, by fixing the standard of good mothering to self-effacing duties, both Indian and Western cultures tend to obliterate a mother's voice, which Lahiri probes here. Therefore, the question remains whether Mrs. Das chooses not to support her child unnecessarily or whether she is really falling short of performing her motherly duties.

Notably, Mina's self-absorption, which is Mrs. Das's nickname, prevents her from realizing that Mr. Kapasi does not provide his patient-clients with remedies; he merely translates their statements into the main language of West Bengal for the benefit of the local doctor. The New Jersey woman still wants to confess to Mr. Kapasi her lack of self-control, which the pressure of motherhood created after Tina's arrival. Especially, the sight of the carved figures of lovers at the Sun Temple "and the processions of elephants, and the topless female musicians beating on two-sided drums" (Lahiri, Interpreter 57) on the Temple arouses the memory of her own sexual transgression with her husband's friend during his short stay with them. The neat positioning of the gods to greet the sun three times a day also assures her of the Indian power of precision. This makes her open her Pandora's Box after keeping it tight shut for eight long years. In order to convey her "malady" to Mr. Kapasi, she stays in the car when the rest of the family carries on exploring the area. Looking outside the car window, they both see her son Bobby in a stick fight with a monkey. As Mr. Kapasi compliments his courage, she bluntly states that the child is not her husband Raj's. The reader instantly realizes that Raj's bookishness does not match the boy's proactive presence. Nevertheless, she explains to Mr. Kapasi how the unexpected slip up happened.

Mina's and Raj's parents were close friends, and they arranged an early marriage for the pair. She had no close friends because she spent most of her time with Raj during her college days. Her parents had moved back to India after securing her future. Therefore, when motherhood bewildered her after the arrival of Tina, there was no one to share her worries with. She was left alone to bring up the baby, whereas Raj was busy with his day job teaching science to middle-school students. Despite being overwhelmed by "nursing, and warming up bottles of milk and testing their temperature against her wrist" (63), she readily conceived her second child Ronny. She had been homebound and exhausted by the constant childcare duties when one of Raj's Punjabi friends came to stay with them for a job interview. It all happened too quickly afterwards: "She made no protest when the friend touched the small of her back as she was about to make a pot of coffee, then pulled her against his crisp navy suit" (64). She becomes pregnant with Bobby after this. The confession forms the basis of Mr. Kapasi's criticism of Mina's "sexually liberal view that the affair demands expression as transgression" (Reddy 52). Her reiteration that she feels awful when she looks at her children and her husband confounds him because he cannot decide if the ground of transgression is pain or guilt.

By asking Mr. Kapasi to provide "a service that is beyond his paid labor as a tour guide," she also exposes the inseparable class difference between them, which is "produced through the uneven global expansion of and access to capital" (53). However, Mina's access to capital is gained through her migrant status in the U.S.

Ironically, this makes her share Mr. Kapasi's marginality in his own society. Whereas he stays on the threshold of the societal ladder as a self-employed person on a low income, her liminality is created by her double cultural loyalties. She is caught in the middle of two nullifying cultural aspirations: the Indian one leading to early motherhood and the American one requiring a remarkable self-reliance. The consequence of travelling simultaneously towards the opposite direction is Mina's indifferent demeanour, which leads to the disastrous liaison.

Mina's nonchalance also ushers in the chaos that ensues once she steps out of the car after finishing her tale. The puffed rice that she tries to eat while searching for her children causes a group of monkeys to follow her. She should have avoided eating the snack in order to protect her family members from being attacked by the primates. Therefore, the puffed rice symbolizes her "otherness" in India. She is unaware that a troop of monkeys is attacking Bobby and he is failing to win the fight against them. Her lack of proactive stance is further seen when she screams for Mr. Kapasi to do something about the monkeys without rushing forward to help her child. Having seen how scared Bobby is, Mr. Kapasi decides not to reveal anything to the young boy. And when he delivers the shivering child to his parents, both of them start to attend to him: "'Poor Bobby,' Mrs. Das said. 'Come here a second. Let Mommy fix your hair'" (Lahiri, Interpreter 68).This interaction again assures Mr. Kapasi of the family's integrity. As the five of them gather together, he learns that Mina will eventually transcend the challenges of immigrant motherhood, despite her obvious shortcomings.

The motherly attentiveness that Mina fails to show at the start of the story comes back to her. It rescues her from being drowned in lethargy. Thus, she transcends the trials of being born in a country yet rooted to another culturally, which makes the reader believe that the motherly qualities help "the female migrant to adapt better to the 'other land,' projecting the homely features of the motherland onto it" (Draga-Alexandru 125). Arguably, then, female migrants are able to veer from "the initial model of the cultures they come from, depending also on the extent to which they have emancipated themselves from the patriarchal system" (126).

The last story in the collection, "The Third and Final Continent," details one such migrant, who moves away from the commonly recognized Bengali model of submissiveness, although she fits into it right after her marriage. America turns the snivelling Mala into a strong pillar for her family, which allows them not only to establish themselves in the New World but also to ably raise their only son. Conversely, the first story of the collection, "A Temporary Matter," introduces us to another migrant mother, Shoba, whose stillborn child leads her to divorce her husband, which is an uncommon practice in her native culture.

By comparing Mala's initial helplessness with Shoba's "far more enabled" presence, Paulomi Chakraborty stresses that "the evaluation of the immigrant woman as a victim privileges, and comes from the privileged gaze of, the second-generation American woman" (238). In other words, Chakraborty believes that Lahiri's spotlight is on Shoba, since the writer shares her social background as a second-generation immigrant. I argue that despite the apparent contrast to Mala's and Shoba's situations, Lahiri depicts both as strong immigrant mothers, who experience dissimilar trajectories of adjustment in their diasporic homeland. In the end, both the mothers illustrate how the adopted culture sets them free from the burdens of subjection.

Mala is married to someone who left India in the 1960s "with a certificate in commerce and the equivalent, in those days, of ten dollars to [his] name" (Lahiri, *Interpreter* 173). Having survived the hardship in London with a degree from the London School of Economics and Political Science, he moved to MIT with a cataloguing job in its library. Before his marriage with Mala, the unnamed protagonist rented a single room in a house owned by an elderly lady called Mrs. Croft, whose only excitement in life at that point seemed to be the fact that an American flag had been transported to the moon. Compared to this spectacular achievement of the Americans, the two Bengali-Indians merely tied the knot in India with each other by repeating "endless Sanskrit verses after the priest" (180) without fully comprehending the word. The arranged marriage went ahead as Mala's husband "was told that she [Mala] could cook, knit, embroider, sketch landscapes, and recite poems by Tagore" (181), who was a Bengali Nobel Laureate. During the initial five days they spent together before he flew back to the U.S., she cried each night but helped his sister-in-law with the household chores during the day. Therefore, the vermillion mark on her parting representing her wedded status started to make sense to him only after the arrival of a brief letter, which warmed him up to her. More than the ritual of marriage and the outward appearance of the wedded status, the intimacy expressed in the letter started to unite the two souls separated by thousands of miles.

The real transformation from being complete strangers to committed partners started to happen once Mala migrated to America. The drape end of her sari was hung over her head as a mark of modesty, which her husband found old fashioned. However, when he introduced Mala to Mrs. Croft, the old woman declared her "'a perfect lady'" after a thorough scrutiny of her ethnic attire and polite presence "with the equal measures of disbelief and delight" (195). The reason for the old lady's skepticism is understandable, which Chakraborty explains above as the fragility of a first-time female migrant. Nevertheless, Chakraborty does not detect the positive attitude in Mala, which gives Mrs. Croft sheer joy in being introduced to her.

Years later, Mala's husband pays tribute to her positive outlook, adaptability, and careful planning with which she has created a secure nest for him and their only child. She still cries when she misses her son, who now studies at Harvard. However, her crying is no longer a sign of her helplessness in a new environment; it symbolizes her sincerity with which she has taken charge of her family in a foreign land. Despite being entrenched in tradition, she has broken the established mould of surrender to the husband's commands. Instead, she has become a fellow traveller with him in upholding their own flag of success on an unfamiliar part of the planet. This is why her husband cites her as an example of determination, despite being "alone and unprotected" during the initial days of migration, and reminds their son of his blessings of being supported by an encouraging father and "a mother who is happy and strong" (197). Thus, he asserts that the son of such a focused mother cannot be dispirited when he faces hurdles in achieving his own goals.

Like Mala, Shoba also transcends the boundary of her native

culture through decisiveness. Her challenge to the traditional norm of considering the marriage bond unshakable is forthright. Hence, Chakraborty finds her more powerful than Mala. Even so, Shoba's defiance appears to be "A Temporary Matter." Indeed, the story "records the process of restoration of faith after a long dividing" tussle between Shoba and her husband Shukumar by delineating a "gloomy conjugality" (Kamara 124) that arose out of the tragedy of losing their first child. Three weeks before Shoba's due date, Shukumar goes to attend a conference as a graduate student: "When the cab pulled away that morning for the airport, Shoba stood waving good-bye in her robe, with one arm resting on the mound of her belly as if it were a perfectly natural part of her body" (Lahiri, *Interpreter* 3). In other words, motherhood has been firmly woven into the fabric of her identity. Therefore, when an unexpected hospital call makes Shukumar come back to their home town, Boston, he encounters a stony Shoba, who is unwilling to accept the loss of her first child.

She regains her physical strength quickly but fails to survive the trauma that ensues. The shock that their baby will never have a rice ceremony at the age of six or seven months devastates her. Shoba struggles to accept the fact that the unborn child will never taste the first solid food in the loving presence of close relatives. Worse still, the sorrow starts to eat into Shoba and Shukumar's relationship. Shukumar hides himself behind his books and concentrates on finishing his PhD dissertation that he has been working on. Shoba becomes busy with her copyediting job. They stop going anywhere together and their conversations start to dwindle.

Nevertheless, the sudden power cuts in the city appear as a hidden blessing to the troubled couple. Shoba proposes a special play of sharing facts and feelings of the past in order to pass the time. The play progresses well for the first few days. Empowered by the curtain provided by darkness, Shoba eventually tells her husband that she has found an apartment to move into, which "sicken[s] Shukumar," as he knows that she has begun "preparing for a life without him" (21). Simultaneously, Shukumar realizes that blaming his inability to face the catastrophe together is one of Shoba's ways of dealing with the strain the stillbirth of their child has produced.

Therefore, Shukumar decides to let Shoba know that the reason why she regarded him uncaring was not true. He finds his way into the hospital just on time to be able to hold their child close to him. As a result, he knows that the baby was a boy with black hair, and his fingers were curled like hers. Her knowledge about his holding their son, "who had known life only within her, against his chest in a darkened room in an unknown wing of the hospital" (22), enabled her to unite with him in grief. This time he does not have to divulge this information only to protect her. This is why I believe that Shoba's real strength lies not only in deciding to live on her own by breaking her tradition but in making a conscious effort of connecting with Shukumar's pain, as well. The restoration of the emotional connection between Shoba and Shukumar creates the hope that their strained marriage will be repaired.

UNACCUSTOMED EARTH: IMMIGRANT MOTHER AS AN UNTENABLE MOORING

The fact that without emotional closeness marriages suffer is not taken into account in traditional Indian society. Therefore, frail marriages make immigrant mothers and their children's lives onerous most of the time. Lahiri's second collection of short stories, *Unaccustomed Earth*, examines the lives of the first- and second-generation Bengali expatriates in the U.S. from this perspective. The stories in the context of multiethnic America show that despite ensuring more favourable gender roles, the foreign land can thwart immigrant children's lives through the legacy of their mothers' struggle for diasporic adjustment, which makes the reader comprehend that the unsettled condition of immigrant motherhood may affect the progeny in unforeseen ways.

The collection ends with a three-part novella named after its protagonists, Hema and Kaushik. Despite being fervent lovers, they cannot unite in marriage because their paths have been irrevocably separated by the challenges of their parents' lives. Interestingly, the collection, which reveals the unfulfilled promises of the New World, starts and finishes with the absence of mothers with whom the children remain inextricably linked. The reader is reminded that the "ghosts of mothers who die suddenly and early appear in the opening and closing stories of the sequence" symbolize the continuation of the deficient life that the migrants endure through their continuous "struggle to come to terms with a legacy of loss" (Koshy, "Neoliberal" 375). The inheritance of loss is due to the lack of a secure identity. In Kaushik's case, his untimely and tragic death while imagining that his mother, who also left the world at a premature age, was swimming beside him in Thai waters represents his aborted search for a sustainable abode.

Kaushik's mother comes from an English-speaking, affluent, and elite educational milieu. His father, with his landlord lineage and an American-engineering background, must have been deemed a good match for her. After having built an affluent life in the U.S., they decide to move to Bombay, as Kaushik's mother wants to use her social privileges for assuming an upper-class American existence there. Their only child is unhappy about the topsy-turvy nature of the family, especially they move back to America a few years later. "'He was furious that we left, and now he's furious that we're here again'" (Lahiri, *Unaccustomed* 238), admits Kaushik's father to Hema's mother after having taken up temporary residence at their home. Hema's family is astonished that Kaushik's acquiescent father became "too solicitous of [his] mother, always asking if she needed a fresh drink, bringing down a cardigan if she was cold" (245). Kaushik, the reticent teenager, reveals to Hema the reason behind the dramatic change: his mother's days are numbered due to breast cancer. The son fails to face his grief with a straightforward resolve, whereas his mother "faced death with wry courage" (Sen 29).

The brief sketch of Kaushik's mother provided at the beginning of the story is significantly different from the more detailed picture of her as a nonchalant guest at the home of Hema's parents. During the early days of the parents' friendship, Hema and Kaushik's mothers "shopped together for groceries and complained about their husbands ... knitted together, switching projects when one of them got bored" (Lahiri, *Unaccustomed* 225). Those days in the U.S. marked a time when Kaushik's mother was clam, caring, and cooperative. As a returnee, however, she is seen to be self-absorbed, chick and self-indulgent. With her "short hair, her slacks, the Johnnie Walker" (235) that she and her husband drank after meals, Hema's parents find her changed demeanour stupefying. Nevertheless, their presence opens youngster Hema's eyes to the finesse and flair wealth can adorn one with, which suggests that creating splendour all around her gives Kaushik's mother's unsettled existence succour. The guest lady takes Hema under her tutelage and shows her what finery means. However, Hema has neither the means nor the support to develop an aptitude for refinement. Having grown up with a pragmatic, prudent, and patient mother, Hema becomes a successful career woman instead. She also learns how to be circumspect about her desires and wishes, which leads her to accept the totally unknown Navin as a groom—because her parents select him for her.

Hema's research work took her to Rome, where she has a chance to meet Kaushik, who has been roaming the globe as a photo-journalist for the last twenty years. If Kaushik's mother attempt to give her unstable life meaning was through elegance and poise, the son's calling is through an art form that captures moments by embracing the constant change of locales. Kaushik the photo storyteller and Hema the philological scholar do not even attempt to deny their mutual attraction and past bonding. It helps Kaushik a lot that Hema shares with him a clear memory of his mother. Nevertheless, their short-lived union obliterates the view that they were differently prepared for life through their mothers' legacies of confronting diaspora. Despite their unbounded passion, then, their uncompromising stance on their respective careers forces them apart.

Hema moves back to the U.S. to begin her new life with Navin, and Kaushik leaves for his stopover in Thailand, where he tragically killed by a tsunami. The narrator discloses that "his last thoughts are of his mother, how she would have loved Thailand's bright ocean, and how, unlike her, he could not build a home as a refuge" (Sen 30) from the debris of life. Her influence, however, is too strong to set him free. As a result, he fails to adapt to any situations not connected to the ethos of his mother. Obviously, the mooring that his mother provides in his unmoored life proves to be unviable. From this perspective, Kaushik's life represents an extended version of his mother's struggle as an immigrant. His absent mother maintains a profound presence in the story by reliving the tribulations of displacement through her son's pains to create meaning and purpose in his disjointed life.

Lahiri's tales of immigrant mothers, thus, show that surviving in an unknown continent may not be as glorious as conquering it. As Justine Dymond discusses in her chapter in this volume: "*Brother, I'm Dying* also enacts a counter-history to the exceptionalist narrative that has dominated the tradition of immigrant literature in the U.S. and that emphasizes full assimilation into the host country as the immigrant's ultimate goal." Reflecting on her own family's trials of settling in the adopted country, the writer of the memoir courageously presents the multitudinous aspects of the Haitian diaspora that defies the exceptionalism. Similarly, Lahiri's intimate recounting of the Bengali mothers' survival creates a counter-narrative to the immigrants' dream of easy assimilation into American life. Given the vast pressure that the process creates on mostly economically dependent immigrant mothers, readers should acknowledge the heroism involved in their seemingly unheroic acts. Lahiri shows the understated power of the mothers by presenting them as legends, "who manage to suffer through and survive extreme adversity" (Brada-Williams 460). Her mastery with details and day-to-day life shows that she "takes seriously her responsibility as an interpreter of maladies, of translating the pain of a whole group of Bengalis and Bengali-Americans into stories that all readers can understand" (Wilhelmus 137). The appeal of her writing is widely felt because it contains the wisdom of adjusting to reality and the celebration of positive thinking. Lahiri's writing is indeed a tribute to the Bengali mothers, whose courage and resolve dignify their painful adjustments to the uncharted norms and practices of America.

NOTE

[1]Gujarati is mostly spoken in the Indian state of Gurajat, where it is the official language.

WORKS CITED

Al-Ali, Nadje. "Diasporas and Gender." *Diasporas: Concepts, Intersections, Identities*, edited by Kim Knott and Seán McLoughlin,

Zed Books, 2010, pp. 118-122.

Bhatia, Sunil. *American Karma: Race, Culture, and Identity in the Indian Diaspora*. New York University Press, 2007.

Brada-Williams, Noelle. "Reading Jhumpa Lahiri's Interpreter of Maladies as a Short Story Cycle." *MELUS*, vol.29, no. 3/4, 2004, pp. 451-464.

Caspari, Martina. "Changing the Dominant Discourse and Culture, One Eater at a Time: Subversive Discourse and Productive Intervention in 'Mrs. Sen's' in Jhumpa Lahiri's Interpreter of Maladies." *Pacific Coast Philology*, vol.49, no. 2, 2014, pp. 245-261.

Chakraborty, Paulomi. "Refugee Women, Immigrant Women: The Partition as Universal Dislocation in Jhumpa Lahiri's Interpreter of Maladies." *Partitioned Lives: Narratives of Home, Displacement, and Resettlement*, edited by Gera A. Roy and Nandi Bhatia, Pearson Education India, 2008, pp. 227-239.

Draga-Alexandru, Maria-Sabina. "Constructing the Female Self in Migrant Postcolonial Fiction." *Crossing Boundaries: Thinking through Literature*, edited by Julie Scanlon and Amy Waste, Sheffield Academic Press, 2001, pp. 121-129.

Kamara, Madhoo. "Jhumpa Lahiri's Interpreter of Maladies: Interpreting Human Values." *Writers of the Indian Diaspora*, edited by R. K. Dhawan, Prestige Books, 2001, pp. 122-129.

Karttunen, Laura. "A Sociostylistic Perspective on Negatives and the Disnarrated: Lahiri, Roy, Rushdie." *Partial Answers: Journal of Literature and the History of Ideas*, vol. 6, no. 2, 2008, pp. 19-441.

Koshy, Susan. "Minority Cosmopolitanism." *PMLA*, vol. 126, no. 3, 2011, pp. 592-609.

Koshy, Susan. "Neoliberal Family Matters." *American Literary History*, vol. 25, no. 2, 2013, pp. 344-380.

Lahiri, Jhumpa. *Interpreter of Maladies*. Flamingo, 2000.

Lahiri, Jhumpa. *Unaccustomed Earth*. Bloomsbury, 2008.

Mishra, Vijay. *The Literature of the Indian Diaspora: Theorizing the Diasporic Imaginary*. Routledge, 2007.

Noor, Ronny. "Interpreter of Maladies by Jhumpa Lahiri." *World Literature Today*, vol. 74, no. 2, 2000, pp. 365-366.

Reddy, Vanita. "Jhumpa Lahiri's Feminist Cosmopolitics and the Transnational Beauty Assemblage." *Meridians*, vol. 11, no. 2,

2011, pp. 29-59.

Sen, Mandira. "The Immigrant Generations: Unaccustomed Earth by Jhumpa Lahiri." *The Women's Review of Books*, vol. 25, no. 6, 2008), pp. 29-30.

Thurer, Shari L. *The Myths of Motherhood: How Culture Reinvents the Good Mother*. New York: Penguin Books, 1995.

Wilhelmus, Tom. "Next." *The Hudson Review*, vol.57, no.1, 2004, pp. 133-140.

Williams, Laura Anh. "Foodways and Subjectivity in Jhumpa Lahiri's Interpreter of Maladies." *MELUS*, vol. 32, no. 4, 2007, pp. 69-79.

13.

Attaining a Balance between Showing Sensitivity to Local Norms and Upholding the Values of the Country of Origin

The Case of a Western Mother in Japan

MEREDITH STEPHENS

THIS IS AN EXPLORATION of my cross-cultural experiences as an immigrant mother from Australia, living on a sparsely populated island in Japan. My then-spouse and I were from mono-lingual English-speaking families; the only family contacts with other languages were our distant forebears, some of whom spoke Scottish Gaelic, and our parents who had studied Latin at school. We had not migrated to Japan for heritage reasons but rather for employment. Another motivation was linguistic: Japanese was and continues to be a popular foreign language in Australia, and I welcomed the opportunity for our daughters to be educated in Japanese schools.

I arrived in Japan when my first daughter was two months old and stayed until she was two and a half years old. My family relocated back to Japan when she was four and her sister was one. The two girls were educated in local Japanese schools from preschool until they turned sixteen (although I continue to remain in Japan). Attendance from preschool until the beginning of high school entailed spending long hours in the school environment. In addition to attending school from Monday to Friday, our elder daughter also attended kindergarten and her first years of primary school on alternate Saturday mornings, before Saturday schooling was phased out.

I had wanted my children to stay in Japan for as long as possible and only had them return to Australia, each at age sixteen, when the examination system became impossible for us as outsiders to navigate. As Elisabeth Bumiller explains, "even the best Japanese high school education is still an exercise in memorization, standardization and correctness" (152). Because their educational choices were becoming reduced at a time when I felt they needed to be expanded, I reluctantly decided to send them back to Australia while I continued to work in Japan.

The choice to educate my children from preschool to the first year of high school in an outlying area of Japan was unusual. In Australia, the Japanese language is an important subject in the curriculum, and as an applied linguist, I wanted my children to have two first languages, Japanese and English. The acquisition of Japanese by the elder daughter became the focus of a study on early childhood bilingualism, which was explored in studies conducted when she began her formal schooling (see Stephens and Blight "The Influence of Culture on the Development of Biliteracy"; "Positive Transfer of Literacy Skills from Japanese to English by a Bilingual Child"). I found myself as the sole mother of children from English-speaking countries in two of the schools that they attended. The purpose of this educational pathway choice was linguistic, and naively, I did not anticipate the enormous cultural challenges that would accompany this choice.

Having spent my teenage years in Australia in the 1970s made me particularly unsuited to motherhood in a traditional society. Books by prominent feminist thinkers— such as Germaine Greer, Simone de Beauvoir, and Betty Friedan—were strewn around the house and featured in informal discussions in the home. I remember discussions of other important social critics, such as Ivan Illich's *Deschooling Society*, and it was considered de rigeur to challenge traditional societal norms. In my final year of high school, the set text was Anne Summers' Damned Whores or God's Police, which critiques the extreme ways in which women were regarded in the beginning of the European settlement of Australia. Nevertheless, in my early thirties, I found myself as the mother of young children in a society in which many mothers conformed to traditional female roles. As Kyoko Mori explains:

> My friends and I, "nice" Japanese girls, had been taught that whatever we did for ourselves was "empty," while what we did to take care of other people, especially a hus-

band or children, was "fulfilling." We grew up watching our mothers work hard as housekeepers, silent hostesses, and errand-women for our fathers, who never thanked their wives except by a begrudging nod or barely audible grunt. (Mori 119)

I was unaware of this before I had the chance to witness it. Nevertheless, the decision to relocate to Japan was a choice. Foreign children were not subject to compulsory schooling, but I wished to have them attend local schools and show respect and sensitivity to Japanese cultural norms.

EXPATRIATE OR FOREIGN WORKER?

One factor that is not characteristic of the experience of many immigrant mothers around the world was that my native language was considered prestigious in the host culture. Unlike immigrants from non-Western countries, native English speakers are often exempted from the obligation to speak in Japanese. Although I was keenly interested in communicating in Japanese, there was a common expectation that I need not bother. When the obligations of Japanese mothers were onerous for me, I could always resort to the notion that as an English speaker, I could be exempt. The following discussion reports on how the cross-cultural differences resulted either in compromise or renegotiation of maternal duties in the host culture.

Andrea Simon-Maeda distinguishes between the terms "expatriate" and "foreign worker." She notes her "relatively advantageous social position in Japan" (32-33), which she attributes to her "white, western, English-speaking background" (32). She contrasts this with the disadvantaged position of foreign workers from the Philippines, South Korea, China, Southeast Asia and South America. African American Karen Hill Anton, another immigrant, reports being treated with more respect in Japan than in America and contrasts discrimination she experiences when shopping in America with the lack of it in Japan. She reports "being treated, if not with deference, with politeness and courtesy all the time" (Komisarof 53) in Japan. My status as an immigrant mother in

Japan conforms to those experiences described by Simon-Maeda and Hill Anton (Komisarof). I belonged to the category of "expatriate" rather than "foreign worker."

AN IMMIGRANT MOTHER AT SCHOOL

Although I was spared the normative demands of Japanese motherhood in the home, I was unable to completely escape these norms in my children's schools. The burden was not linguistic because I understood the demands being made of me but rather cross-cultural. Anne Allison states that "motherhood *is* state ideology" (205); for her, mothers in Japan are socialized into gender specific roles of providing elaborate boxed lunches and assuming responsibility for their children's education. She never witnessed a Japanese man who had made or had wanted to make a boxed lunch, and concludes that "a gendered division of labor is firmly set in place" (205).

Helen Vallianatos (this volume) describes "the customary and embodied knowledge shared through elders' teaching and enforcing traditions" that is given to mothers by the custodians of the traditional culture. Vallianatos describes the frustration experienced by one of the South Asian mothers in her study, who has a professional degree, with the unwanted advice. In my case, unwanted advice did not come from my culture of origin but rather the host culture. With the expression *kokoro o komete* ("Put your heart into it"), I was advised by kindergarten principals and other mothers to demonstrate my maternal affection by the physical effort that I made into producing food and goods for my children. This was an exhortation to demonstrate my affection for my kindergartener by conforming to the standard practices of providing a high-quality lunch box every day and equipping my child with items such as a homemade smock and a special flannel for wiping her hands. As I struggled to accept a new value system, I received a stream of criticism, advice, and help from well-meaning peers and teachers. As Merry White observes, "some teachers now say that they don't know who's being graded, the mother or the child" (125). The way in which I was socialized to express my maternal devotion is further explained by Lois Peak:

The very high expectations for maternal participation in Japanese preschools may be seen as an important influence in socializing Japanese mothers in their appropriate role in supporting their children's education. Preschools reinforce maternal compliance through frequent allusions to an assumed direct relationship between the strength of maternal love and the amount of maternal assistance. They also provide numerous subtle opportunities for mothers to compare each others' [sic] work. (62)

As a mother it was my duty to ensure that my daughter memorized her multiplication tables in Year Two, and the teacher exerted considerable pressure on me to achieve this end. Bumiller explains how "mothers are crucial to Japanese education" (151). The subject of Bumiller's study, Mariko, had to chair the PTA and organize school events and annual parties for her children's former teachers. My experience as a mother of a child in the Japanese education system was no different ten years after Bumiller's study. I was expected to participate in the PTA and school events, such as Sports Day and the School Fête. Mothers were assigned various duties, such as monitoring bicycle parking at school events and preparing items for sale at the School Fête (Stephens and Blight, "Cultural Expectations and Parental Involvement in Early Literacy"). As Anne Imamura reports:

What it means to be a good mother in Japan is measured by how much a mother does for the sake of the child. Society (the schools, in particular) demands that mothers work closely with their children, especially in the early years of primary school, preparing some of the supplies needed for attending school, monitoring the child's homework and preparations for school, and otherwise keeping a close eye on what the child is doing. Such close involvement by mothers has been a source of great success in assuring that small children acquire solid basic knowledge and skills (such as writing and arithmetic skills), and this involvement is not supposed to be given short shrift even if a mother is working. (138-139)

The expectations of mothers at the school were daunting. Each mother had to join one of the six class committees. One of them in particular intrigued me: the Bellmark Committee. Bellmarks are small symbols that are featured on commercial products, and mothers are encouraged to collect them in order to collect points and raise money for the school. The school gave the parents a chart displaying the commercial products that earnt Bellmark points. For nine years, I dutifully collected Bellmarks and sent them off to the school once a month in a specified envelope. Then mothers on the Bellmark committee would count them and use them to buy school equipment. It puzzled me that this could be considered a productive activity; the collection of marks on the wrappings of commercial products seemed to me inane and, therefore, a questionable use of mothers' time. Surely the public education system should not encourage parents to preferentially purchase brands or products. Indeed, Bumiller describes the conflict in a PTA between parents who are in favour of and opposed to the Bellmark method of school fundraising. I did not witness any conflict regarding the collection of Bellmarks myself, and not wishing to interfere with the customs of the host culture, I restrained myself from making comments.

The most anxiety-provoking obligation was the need to serve on the various committees. Mothers dreaded being appointed to a committee, and having a full-time job was not necessarily considered an excuse. Bumiller describes a similar process in a school in which none of the parents wanted to serve on the action committee and, therefore, decided to choose the committee members by drawing lots (313). I noticed that there was a particular expression for being assigned a role when one was unwilling to volunteer for it: *yaku ga ataru*. Mothers stoically performed their duties according to the roles that they were assigned. I once received a phone call congratulating me for having volunteered to fill one of these roles. I was unaware that I had "volunteered," so I used my outsider position as a foreigner as an excuse to avoid performing the associated duties. Furthermore, I was working at a prestigious local institution and acted on the assumption that I would be granted exemption from duties that conflicted with my professional responsibilities.

One of the roles I could not escape, however, was the park patrol and traffic monitor. Children usually go to and return from school unaccompanied by their parents, and groups of parents patrol the park when the children walk home. I was given a sash to wear that proclaimed "Primary school park control" and was told to meet a group of parents in front of the school gates on a Thursday afternoon once a month. This often conflicted with the faculty meeting at the university, and in all honesty, I was unable to decide whether my loyalty was owed to my employer or to the school. This pressure for mothers not to engage in even part-time employment has been described by Allison, who explains that mothers would either keep it secret or face a reprimand from the teacher "for insufficient devotion to their child" (203). Over twenty years after Allison's study, I noticed that when mothers were unavailable, a father or a grandmother would assume the mother's school-related duties. Thankfully, I was not subject to the extreme pressure described by Allison, but I was still expected to perform certain school-related duties. My name appeared on a list for park control, and I turned up accordingly and walked around the park adjoining the school for half an hour while the children walked home from school. I was later admonished by my colleagues for not attending the faculty meeting, and I then had to make my excuses to the primary school. I had no choice but to give my allegiance to my employer during working hours, so I resolved to attend faculty meetings and neglect the park patrol. Nevertheless, I was unable to find any excuses for early morning traffic monitoring. Once a month, I had to walk to the pedestrian crossing, retrieve the sash and flag from a special box, and monitor the children crossing the road on their way to school.

Mothers in Japan have an important role to play in directing their children's educational pathway (Simon-Maeda 139), although clearly this is not unique to Japan. Having spent most of my formative maternal years in Japan, I quickly adopted my Japanese peers' notion of maternal responsibility for my daughters' educational progress. Nevertheless, as a second-language speaker of Japanese, I became increasingly unable to assist my daughters with their homework the higher they progressed in the education system. Homework assignments were taxing, and as a mother, it was my duty to supervise them. Japanese children had lengthy holiday assignments. Math drills were particularly demanding. A math assignment consisted of six multiplication charts to be completed—each consisted of sixty-four sums, two hundred division problems, thirty-two addition problems, and thirty-four subtraction problems. Parents had to record the time it took to complete these sums. Furthermore, there were additional holiday assignments for literacy, music, and calligraphy (Stephens, "Expectations of Time Spent on Homework").

In order to maintain their English literacy, my daughters spent their spring and summer holidays in their native Australia, where homework was assigned from Monday to Thursday. This contrasted with their Japanese schools, in which homework was assigned five days a week and in the holidays. My younger daughter was assigned one hundred kanji characters to be copied daily, and on certain Fridays, she was assigned two hundred characters to copy. As a teacher from a foreign education system, I was unfamiliar with the practice of rote learning, but I realized that this particular writing system could not be mastered in the same way as the alphabet because of the sheer number of characters and the number of strokes in each character. I had to overcome my aversion to rote learning because of the advantages mastering the Japanese writing system would confer on my daughters.

Despite the extraordinary demands made of me as a mother of children in Japanese primary schools, I found the differences fascinating and appreciated the teachers' attention and commitment. Nonetheless, nine years of being a parent of children in Japanese primary schools inevitably came to an end, and I had to face the graduation ceremony of my younger daughter. I was bewildered as to why we needed to be seated thirty minutes before the ceremony started, so I arrived there twenty minutes early instead. Most of the other parents were already seated, listening to the solemn music. I was embarrassed to be the foreigner who was always out of step, but was greeted warmly and sincerely by the reception panel. Thankfully, another family of stragglers arrived even later than us. A poignant atmosphere was created by the long wait and the heart-wrenching music. Finally, the children appeared, and they walked onto the stage one by one to ceremoniously bow to the principal and collect their graduation certificates. The children performed songs, and finally the staff performed the well-known song by Yumi Matsutoya "Haruyo koi." This ceremony had been rehearsed extensively, was performed impeccably, and served to indelibly imprint the milestone of primary school graduation in my mind. I did my best to keep my tears silent during the ceremony yet could not help but feel the sadness of time passing whenever I passed the school for years afterwards.

IMMIGRANT MOTHER AS HOUSEWIFE

Maternal Attire

In Japan, one's roles and duties are often clearly expressed in one's personal attire. The Japanese language has an expression—*katachi kara hairimasu* ("It begins with one's form")—that explains how outward appearance can lead to specific behaviours. The attire of a mother or grandmother, whose duties are chiefly domestic, is a large apron in the form of a pinafore. For me, it was not a symbol of subservience but rather a convenient way to minimize the chore of washing. I unthinkingly donned the apron after observing other housewives in the university housing block wearing them. Women even wore them as they went to the supermarket on their shopping bicycles. It only occurred to me that the apron could be considered a sign of subservience after two separate occasions on which Western women dropped in to my apartment and burst into uproarious laughter on seeing me in my apron as I opened the front door. Their mock derision made me realize that they considered me to have been overzealous in my adoption of local customs.

Invisibility

Jane Condon explains the subservient role of the Japanese wife: "At home, a woman fills her own rice bowl last, after serving everyone else. She's last in the bath and last to bed and usually first up in the morning" (16). Kyoko Mori concurs and describes "the Japanese ideal that a woman should go through her life taking care of other people, leaving no trace of herself" (95). As an immigrant mother in a family of other Australians, I was spared the obligation to conform to these expectations in the home. My network of friends who were mothers consisted of two groups: one was a group of other expatriate mothers from the UK, Canada, America, Australia, and Russia, and the other a group of Japanese women who were the mothers of my daughters' friends. A Kenyan friend and I were the only mothers in my expatriate circles without Japanese spouses. Some of those with Japanese spouses would rebel against the expectations that they put themselves last, and they created more powerful roles for themselves within the family unit. They asserted that they had a right to activities for their own benefit, such as evening outings and travel, which were unrelated to their roles as wives and mothers. I looked on the attitudes of those with Japanese spouses with bemusement, because these mothers felt the need to assert themselves in ways in which I had always taken for granted in my own culture. In discussions with Japanese friends, they may have expected me to take advantage of what Simon-Maeda describes as the "gaijin card" (80)—the expectation that Westerners be exempt from traditional duties expected of Japanese. Accordingly, I was merely an observer of mothers performing the roles of putting their own needs last and only performed this role myself when it was self-imposed.

Many of the mothers with Japanese partners belonged to the Association of Foreign Wives of Japanese, an organization that has assisted foreign women with Japanese partners to adjust to Japanese society since 1969. A member of this group would recount to me stories of what wonderful support these women were to each other during their annual conference and local chapter meetings. I was secretly jealous that I would not be able to become a member of their association because my partner was Australian, not Japanese. Clearly, I was in a bubble within Japanese society and immune from the particular demands made of expatriate women enmeshed in local traditions.

IMMIGRANT MOTHER AS WORKER

Female Role Models

Diane Hawley Nagatomo describes the "gender isolation" (150) her female respondents experienced working at a Japanese university. Bumiller reports that it is "almost impossible" (81) to combine family and career in Japan. Nevertheless, she identifies some striking exceptions: those who were admitted to Tokyo University and who came from "the postwar ruling class of Japan" (83). Contrary to these previous studies, my most important role model at Tokushima University was Professor Megumi Kuwabara, who was also a mother of two. I first witnessed her providing input in meetings and then as a chairperson of a committee. Besuited and often bespectacled, the committee sat in a typical formal meeting room in which the chairperson sat at the front and the committee members sat in a U-shape around the room. Female committee members were a distinct minority, but the meeting was often both chaired and co-chaired by women professors. Thankfully and unexpectedly, my experience of witnessing women at work was unlike that described by Kyoko Mori in her classic exposition published in 1997. Mori describes the confined position of Japanese women's voices: "It doesn't matter who we are or what we are saying. A woman's voice is always the same: a childish squeak piped from the throat" (16). Although I was familiar with the voices in Mori's description, my most important female role model, Professor Kuwabara, in no way conformed to this image. Professor Kuwabara assured me that she was no exception in Japanese universities and provided me with examples of other leading women in Japanese academe. One example is Sachiko Takada, the former professor of ancient Japanese history at Osaka University of Foreign Studies, who later became vice president of Osaka University. My colleague also cited the case of the prolific Professor Haruko Wakita, who specialized in Japanese medieval history. Professor Wakita flourished in academe and, together with other researchers at Kyoto University, provided networking for women scholars in order to promote a society in which women in academe could thrive. She combined this career with being the mother of three sons, and was the recipient of the prestigious Order of Cultural Merit.

Nevertheless, these do appear to be outstanding cases, and current policy attempts to facilitate the employment of women researchers (Tokushima University). One of the important aims of the university Gender Equality Office is "to further improve the research capabilities and career prospects of female researchers" (27). Current government policy is devoted to increasing the number of women researchers and providing more favourable working conditions for women (Japan, Ministry of Education). These policy initiatives are resulting in greater participation of women in the workplace, in a move which is arguably beginning to free women from the constraints of the gender roles described by Allison, Condon, Bumiller and Mori approximately two to three decades ago. This change is suggested not only by the policy initiatives and the growing number of successful women in both management and academe but also by informal conversations with female Japanese academics. These conversations in no sense reveal the sense of gender isolation described by Nagatomo, the impossibility of combining family and career suggested by Bumiller, or the woman who devotes her life to others "leaving no trace of herself" described by Mori. Nevertheless, I currently find myself reading headlines about the government's Gender Equity Bureau having to revise downwards their overly ambitious targets for the participation of women executives in government and the private sector (Zarroli). Yet daily I witness powerful and visible women leaders in my workplace.

Length of the Work Day

Japanese workers are notorious for the long hours that they put in and their commitment to the workplace—the university is no exception. Because of the close physical proximity of people to each other in the workplace and the neighbourhood, Japanese people tend to be attuned to the comings and goings of others. Putting in long hours at the office is favourably regarded. Bumiller describes a couple who were career bureaucrats. The husband returned each night at midnight, whereas the wife left as early as she could, at around eight. This afforded the husband increased networking opportunities, which helped further his career.

In my case, I noticed that many male colleagues would remain working in their offices until late in the evenings. How was I to navigate this expectation with the conflicting demands of chil-drearing? When the children were in preschool, I was particularly anxious to pick them up early. Thankfully, there was respect for the role of the mother. One colleague even reassured me by saying, "Mothers are sacred." This was echoed by Bumiller: "motherhood is such a serious occupation in Japan," and it confers on her subject "a status unknown to most mothers in the United States" (329). Although I felt guilty for leaving the campus earlier than my male colleagues each day, my feeling of guilt for being away from my children was even stronger. I continued to leave the office earlier than my colleagues for the entire period that my children were in Japan. The Japanese have a special word for the returning of a favour, *okaeshi*. I felt the need to express *okaeshi* to my colleagues once my children left for Australia, and I tried, albeit unsuccessfully, to match their hours of devotion to the office.

Caring for Sick Children

Mothers experience conflict between the demands of the workplace and caring for sick or troubled children in any country, and Japan is no exception. At one university, I was berated by a member of the clerical staff when I had cancelled a day's classes in order to stay home to look after a sick child. Motherhood did not always attract the special status described above when it conflicted with the demands of the workplace. When I accepted a contract at the university in Japan where I continue to work, I voiced my concerns to the professor who hired me. To my great surprise and relief, he kindly advised me that my children were welcome at the university anytime. I purchased some sofas for the office with visions of bringing sick children to work and having them lie on the sofas while I worked. This experience again counters the stereotype of the efficient workplace in which professional concerns override personal ones. I took advantage of this freedom and had the children come in after school whenever they wanted to and let them decorate the blackboard in the office with their artwork. Although I had experienced discrimination both as a mother and an expatriate at previous Japanese universities, I had to acknowledge that the opposite sometimes occurred as well—acts of special treatment. This remarkable flexibility—which was accorded to me and allowed me to pursue my professional responsibilities and family obligations in one workspace—was indeed an example of this. If I had been an immigrant mother working in private enterprise, I might not have been offered this privileged treatment, and I attribute it to the liberal attitudes of the academic staff. Another factor may have been that there were no precedents. I was the only tenured female Westerner in a very large institution, and my treatment was due to individual decisions of my colleagues and administrators rather than a rulebook.

CONCLUSIONS

The expectations of me as an immigrant mother in Japan varied according to the context. In the community and in the schools, there was considerable pressure from teachers and other mothers to conform to the self-sacrificing norms of Japanese women. In the university, my role as mother was valued in addition to my professional role. There was recognition that I had important family obligations. I was completely free of having to conform to traditional Japanese female stereotypes in the workplace and was exhorted to voice my opinion. However, there was a concomitant respect for the demands of motherhood, and I was accorded freedom to fulfil this role.

I appreciated this respect, which enabled me to both work and devote myself to my children unapologetically. My Japanese peers appeared to take home duties associated with female roles much more seriously than I did myself. Apart from the insistence that I attend faculty meetings and fulfill other professional obligations, there was recognition from my colleagues of the reality that I had important duties other than those of the workplace. Nonetheless, it was understood that when my daughters reached adulthood, I would bring a renewed commitment to my professional life.

The most serious hardship was the unstable working conditions that I endured at other universities before attaining tenure. I had three successive nonrenewable contracts, which entailed considerable disruption to the children's schooling and irrevocable strain on my family life. In contrast to previous employers, my present employer offered me security on the day of the interview, and I was finally free from the pressure of constant job hunting.

My daughters sometimes tell me if they became mothers they would like to raise their children in Japan. They appreciate important aspects of the education system in Japan, such as the way that art and physical education are taught, and the opportunity to become bilingual and biliterate. The value that they place on having been educated in local Japanese schools is an important confirmation that the decision to raise them here was indeed a judicious one. Equally importantly, for me it has been an extraordinary cross-cultural adventure.

WORKS CITED

Allison, Anne. "Japanese Mothers and Obentos: The Lunch-Box as Ideological State Apparatus." *Anthropological Quarterly,* vol. 64, no. 4, 1991, pp. 195-208.

Bumiller, Elisabeth. *The Secrets of Mariko: A Year in the Life of a Japanese Woman and Her Family.* Vintage Books, 1995.

Condon, Jane. *A Half Step Behind: Japanese Women Today.* Charles E. Tuttle Company, 1985.

Illich, Ivan. *Deschooling Society.* Harper & Row, 1971.

Imamura, Anne. *Urban Japanese Housewives: At Home and in the Community.* University of Hawaii Press, 1987.

Iwao, Sumiko. *The Japanese Woman: Traditional Image and Changing Reality.* Harvard University Press, 1993.

Japan. Ministry of Education, Cultural, Sports, Science, and Technology. Josei kenkyuusha no katsuyaku suishin ni kansuru chuukan torimatome : Dai go ki kagaku gijutsu kihon keikaku e no teian ["Active Promotion of Female Researchers. Interim Report on the Proposal to the Fifth Science and Technology Basic Plan"]. Japan Science and Technology, Government of Japan, 2014, www.mext.go.jp/b_menu/shingi/.../1351755_02.pdf. 2014j.pdf. 2014. Accessed 24 Nov. 2015.

Komisarof, Adam. *At Home Abroad: The Contemporary Western Experience in Japan.* Reitaku University Press. 2012.

Mori, Kyoko. *Polite Lies: On being a Woman Caught between Cultures.* Fawcett Books, 1997.

Nagatomo, Diane Hawley. *Exploring Japanese University Teachers' Professional Identity.* Multilingual Matters, 2012.

Peak, Lois. *Learning to Go to School in Japan: The Transition from Home to Preschool Life.* University of California Press, 1991.

Simon-Maeda, Andrea. *Being and Becoming a Speaker of Japanese: An Autoethnographic Account.* Multilingual Matters, 2011.

Stephens, Meredith. "Expectations of Time Spent on Homework: A Comparative Study of Australian and Japanese Primary Schools." *Journal of Language and Literature,* vol. 15, pp. 173-190, 2007.

Stephens, Meredith, and Richard Blight. "The Influence of Culture on the Development of Biliteracy: A Comparison of Error Correction in Early Writing in Japanese and Australian Schools." *Japan Journal of Multilingualism and Multiculturalism,* vol. 8, no. 1, vol. 75-94, 2002.

Stephens, Meredith, and Richard Blight. "Cultural Expectations and Parental Involvement in Early Literacy." *Studies in Language and Literature,* vol. 22, no. 2, 2003, pp. 225-244.

Stephens, Meredith, and Richard Blight. "Positive Transfer of Literacy Skills from Japanese to English by a Bilingual Child." *Japan Journal of Multilingualism and Multiculturalism,* vol. 10, no. 1, 2004, pp. 47-81.

Summers, Anne. *Damned Whores and God's Police: The Colonization of Women in Australia.* Penguin Books, 1975.

Tokushima University. "Outline of Tokushima University 2015." Tokushima University, Tokushima University, 2015, www.tokushima-u.ac.jp/_files/00239165/gaiyou2015.pdf. Accessed 24 Nov. 2015

White, Merry. *The Japanese Educational Challenge: A Commitment to Children.* Free Press, 1987.

Zarroli, Jim. "Does Japan Need Some Binders Full of Women." *NPR: The Two-Way Breaking News,* NPR, 7 Dec. 2015, www.npr.org/sections/thetwo-way/2015/12/07/458770434/does-japan-need-some-binders-full-of-women?ft=nprml&f=1001,1003,1004,1090. Accessed 11 Dec. 2015.

14.
Intercultural Upbringing

The Benefits of Maintaining Home Language and Culture when Raising Migrant Children

AGATA STRZELECKA-MISONNE

THIS TEXT IS A PERSONAL REFLECTION on a mother's role in raising her children abroad (Strzelecka-Misonne).[1] In this case, an important part of the upbringing process is to kindle the children's interest and to broaden their knowledge of the language and culture of the country of origin. Building children's awareness of the cultural roots and the family's origin is also a way of providing children with additional tools for them to increase their self-esteem. Knowing the language—both in practical terms, that is being able to speak it fluently, as well as in terms of understanding culturally specific content— enables children to obtain full cultural competencies needed for moving with ease in the environment of the country of origin. Children must be able to communicate and be understood so to understand messages in the public space as well as those addressed directly to them.

Knowing the language and being able to move freely in a given culture enables children to obtain full independence and will make it possible for them to feel "at home;" it will provide them with emotional comfort and a sense of security. Therefore, the sooner this informal "education" of children starts, the easier it will be for them as adults to enjoy all the benefits of this type of upbringing.

One of the basic terms I am using in this text is "intercultural awareness." In my opinion, intercultural awareness has a chance of developing only when children's parents or guardians do their best to ensure that the culture of a child's origin has equal importance in a child's upbringing as the culture of the host country. Intercultural awareness is a unique chance for children to be not only *guests* but also *hosts* in both their place of origin and where they reside. It makes children even more open to the world, sparks their interest and enables them to enjoy all the benefits of living in a culturally diverse environment.

The observations and reflections discussed in this chapter stem from my parenting experiences and from the various activities that I engaged in with my daughters when they were outside of their school environment. I undertook the described actions in the first years of our stay in New York. My husband and I moved there from Warsaw, Poland, in 2013 with our daughters—Julia was four years old (she was born in 2009) and Sara was one year old (she was born in 2012). I still use many of the described techniques when playing with my children; some of them have, of course, been modified because the children have grown and their interests have changed. In the final part of this narrative, I discuss the results brought by the described techniques and the benefits of intercultural upbringing for children.

1. MULTILINGUALISM—THE KEY TO OBTAINING ADDITIONAL CULTURAL COMPETENCIES

My daughters spent the first years of their lives growing up in Poland, a homogeneous country in terms of language. However, during those years, before we migrated to the U.S., the girls were already growing up in a bilingual environment (Bhatia and Ritchie). My husband, a francophone Belgian, has spoken to the girls exclusively in French since the day that our first daughter was born. I do the same and speak to them in Polish. As a result, at the age of three, Julia and Sara spoke both languages fluently, and they are both their mother tongues.[2] Nevertheless, because of the place we were living in at the time—Poland—and the fact that I was spending more time with the children, they were growing up in an environment dominated by the Polish language. Our family language culture remains a mixed Polish-French one (my husband and I talk to each other in both languages, changing them spontaneously, regardless of the context). Nevertheless, while at the park, on the playground, on a street, or in other public places as well as during visits from grandparents, friends, and extended family members, the girls were living in a Polish environment. Therefore, Julia started to use compound sentences in Polish at the age of almost three and only later did she start to speak French. She systematically increased her level of French to match her Polish level, which has remained her dominant language.

When English came into our lives, the displacement of Polish as the dominant language started (Francis). In my opinion, children's emotional bond with the mother has a positive impact on the their attitude towards the language, as they have a permanent willingness to communicate in it with their mother; however, since Julia spent most of the day at an English-speaking school, it resulted in her having more and more difficulties speaking Polish.

Despite my efforts, we have not been able to create a group of Polish-speaking acquaintances in New York. Many Polish women I got to know say that their children, at different ages, do not want to speak Polish, do not speak it well, or only understand it; they treat it as only their mother's whim and a burden in their lives. This was not surprising to me considering that those families visit Poland far less often than we do, and from what I was able to find out and observe, I concluded that the issue of familiarizing their children with the Polish culture and language was not a priority for them. The language used in their homes was usually English (their husbands were American or were from countries other than Poland or the U.S.), and the children were not being motivated in a specific way to speak Polish.

Julia's above-mentioned language problems—particularly visible regarding all school-related topics because she knows the words used for describing events only from the English context—have been influencing the way that she feels. Repeatedly, my questions about what happened at school during art lessons, what classes were the most interesting and which were boring, or what they learned in writing lessons have been greeted with silence or irritation. Initially, I thought that her unwillingness to talk about school was a result of being tired and bored with her mother's repeated questions, but seeing how difficult it was for my child to build correct sentences in Polish, I understood that Julia's irritation stemmed from her lack of ability to express in Polish what "happened" in English.

Based on my experiences, the problem with speaking the dominant language arises usually when children start to attend kindergarten or school and their parents no longer accompany them. As Anna Kuroczycka Schultes writes in her chapter in this volume, children who start attending English-speaking schools find it increasingly challenging to engage in conversation with their parents about complex topics because the vocabulary range used with parents becomes smaller, whereas the vocabulary used in the new environment and in the new language expands. My daughter, who used Polish to communicate with me since the day she was born, has gradually found it more difficult to use Polish even though efforts had been made to consistently use Polish in conversations at home. Therefore, one should work with a child to eliminate vocabulary deficiencies not only to practise on a technical aspect of communication but also to ensure the child feels safe and comfortable in relations with the mother, the rest of the Polish-speaking family, other children in Poland, and in any other situation in a Polish-speaking environment. Moreover, I see what a source of pride it is for Julia to speak Polish in New York. I have heard her many times suggesting to school friends that she could teach them a given sentence in Polish.

In order to maintain her Polish proficiency during our stay in New York, it is helpful to have materials, such as CDs with recorded works of famous Polish specifically tailored for children. It is important for children not only to listen to the Polish spoken by their mother, grandmother, grandfather, or others within their inner circle, but also to have the ability to observe the "dynamics" of the language. Thus, they can experience different intonation, pronunciation of words, different idiomatic expressions, the creation and use of neologisms, and as many synonyms of already-known words as possible.

It is equally important to ensure that children have conditions for playing freely and undisturbed among family, friends and acquaintances during stays in Poland. It seems that "play" is the best and most effective tool when working with preschool age children. While children are playing, the same mechanism as in a kindergarten in New York is created whereby observing other children and the way they communicate as well as by needing to communicate, a child increases its language competencies. Play undisturbed by a lack of sufficient language competencies is good play, which is so important for children's development. Good command of a language—that is the ability to express one's material and emotional needs—translates into a sense of emotional safety and, at the same time, strengthens children's bonds with the culture of their origin.

Below, I present in more detail the ways in which I have been talking with my daughters about Poland and the role of the Polish culture in their lives as well as what role their cultural identities play in their lives and the process of forming those identities.

2. POLISH CULTURE—YES!

Working on the correct use of language and on making it possible for my children to communicate freely in Polish also became an opportunity for expanding our knowledge about Polish culture. The first long flight from Warsaw to New York enabled Julia to realize how far away from our previous home we were going to live. Initially, the notions of distance and time zones were quite abstract for her. However, when we sat down and took a closer look at a globe and a map together, Julia became interested in various topics related to geography and started to ask in which country it was currently night and in which day. It turned out that the notion of time differences helped my child understand the notion of distance. I explained, "When it is late afternoon here, Babcia [Grandma] and Dziadek [Grandpa] are sleeping. They both live far away, where the sun has already set." At that moment, Julia started to connect the word "Poland" with an actual place, a long distance away from the one we now live in. Poland became a spot on the map where her grandmother and grandfather, several of our close friends and other family members live. I started to hear Julia say that Poland is a place to which we will be returning regularly.

While observing my daughter trying to place the notion of "Poland" on the map of terms she already knows, I reflected on the way in which we would be talking about that country. Intuitively, I felt that my task was to be an attentive interlocutor for my child, asking open questions about what the term "Poland" actually meant. Those conversations would be a joint attempt at linking specific ideas with the idea of "Poland" Julia already knew and at creating a conceptual network behind that idea.

I intentionally mention the creation of children's bond with Polish culture and not with the country because it is not my intention to form in my children such feelings as, for example, Polish pride. I believe that the concept of "Polishness" may have strong political connotations and may also be interpreted as a concept closely linked to the notion of nationalism. There may be many pejorative connotations with nationalism—such as implicating a lack of acceptance of social diversity—therefore, I definitely excluded this notion from the upbringing of my children. Moreover, in my opinion, the feeling of pride from being Polish is also a concept too complex for a child of preschool or early-school age, as they do not have sufficient cognitive competencies to understand it. I reckon that it is also a mistake to say that it is important to form patriotic attitudes in children. I am not a supporter of raising children in a spirit of national or patriotic sentiments. My goal is to create in my children a relationship with the "space" of the Polish culture, of the culture circle and to make them aware of originating from a particular cultural area—defined by language, specific habits, landscapes, traditions, and even smells.

In this context, the role of the mother as an active participant in the process of establishing children's cultural identity becomes visible. A parent's attitude towards his or her mother tongue, country of origin and relatives in Poland will be reflected in the process of forming the cultural identity of his or her child being brought up abroad and away from the Polish diaspora. One should remember that the image of Poland a child forms—an image created to a large extent on the basis of the parent's words and the observation of his or her attitude toward the country—should not contain aspects of excessive idealization, which is so typical of people experiencing some symptoms of culture shock or difficulties in adapting in the first stage of migration to a new place.

That challenge has not been easy for me. At the beginning of my stay in the United States, I often experienced frustration when dealing with other residents of New York when I realized that I was, in effect, idealizing Poland. Luckily, I soon managed to cope with those feelings. To avoid both idealizing one's country of origin and depreciating the culture of the country in which one currently lives are the basic rules for raising children abroad. I realized from the time of our arrival in the U.S. that my children would grow up with American culture being the pillar of their education at school, and with popular culture, which, particularly in the U.S., enters into all aspects of life and has a strong impact on children. Separating children from what they find attractive and important or expressing negative opinions about those things may result in their losing the feeling of safety in the new place. Therefore, in order to find balance while living between two cultures, my husband and I link my daughters to Poland on a daily basis. Several times a week, the girls talk to their grandmother in Poland on the phone, and on weekends, we make video calls using Skype. In this way, everyday issues concerning our loved ones are a part of our lives. The actual distance to Poland seems not to play such a huge role as in the past when the traditional post office was used for international contact. Nevertheless, I encourage Julia to sometimes send her grandmother, grandfather, or great-grandfather a letter in an envelope containing some drawings that she made at school or at home. A trip to the post office is a great opportunity to talk about the letter's route crossing the ocean on a plane—another chance to talk about a topic relating to Poland.

Maintaining family bonds with loved ones in Poland is a perfect way to create positive attitudes towards the country and the cultural area from which our relatives come from. Because of the difference in age, the girl's attitudes towards Poland vary. Sara distinguishes between Polish, French and English, talks about her grandmother and grandfather, and reacts positively to meetings or conversations on Skype. For Julia, Poland is a place from where she remembers many things: she knows that she was born there, and she remembers her mom's and dad's workplaces as well as the route from her home in Warsaw to her grandparents' house.

Moreover, for some time I was considering the possibility of enrolling my older daughter in a Saturday school for children learning Polish as a second language (Gwóźdź). I started my search for a school by looking at the information available on the websites of

Polish supplementary schools in the U.S. I learned from them that much of what the children learn is based on educating them in the Catholic spirit, often in close cooperation with the local Catholic Church and the pastor. For example, in one of the charter Polish Saturday Schools, there is a provision stipulating that the school management body is composed of three elements: the school headmaster, the school council, and the pastor ("Szkoła Polska"). Another article of the charter stipulates that a teacher's duties include actively participating in "school events as well as those organized by the parish" ("Szkoła Polska"). I became concerned about this connection between the school and the church because of its exclusionary approach towards families and children growing up in environments based on principles and parenting models other than the Catholic tradition. A big concern for me was also the role of the pastor, who as a member of the de facto school management body has an impact on forming the worldview of school. Therefore, there is a threat that children not representing that worldview and, for example, not celebrating Catholic holidays will be excluded.

Thanks to a teacher I know who teaches in a Polish school in New York, I was able to see the supplementary materials for the teachers of one of the Polish schools. The introduction to that publication contained a detailed description of the newly created curriculum and how the school was established; the president of the Education Commission of the Polish American Congress says, among other things, "from those early days of Poles living on American soil [mid-nineteenth century] to the beginnings of the twenty-first century, the church and the school have been and will continue to head in the same direction" (Osysko). He also emphasizes that, "the curriculum used by the first Polish teachers in America as well as the current one in the twenty-first century are both based on the same principles: on promoting the idea of social integration as well as on preserving and protecting one's special heritage" (Osysko). There would be nothing wrong with that but for the fact that it has been almost two hundred years since the first Polish schools were established and their curriculum created. In addition, the concept of "social integration" as defined by the author of the introduction has changed—it has gained a new interpretation and now contains different concepts compared to those from the mid-nineteenth century.

In Osysko's text, there is a reference to raising children in the spirit of tolerance towards other religions; however, the word "tolerance" does not mean realizing the value of including children with other than Catholic backgrounds or being brought up in families with no religion and enabling them to freely form their attitudes toward the country. Although the Jan Twardowski Polish Supplementary School mentions on its website that, "The school does not discriminate on the basis of race, colour, national and ethnic origin and provides the students with equal rights regarding access to education, and athletic and other school-administered programs as well as during the school enrolment process and in the process of providing material help,"[6] it does not mention non-discrimination because of religion or a lack of it.

Therefore, when I was wondering what to do and how the process of my children building their own images of Poland should look like, I consciously decided not to have them attend any Polish supplementary school. Instead, creating the concept of Poland as a "safe haven" became most important for me. I thought that my daughters should view their grandparents' house in this way because this is where they have their room and their toys, and Poland could be for them a place that in the future they will be able to call "their place on earth," should they feel like it, regardless of where we will be living as a family. I believe that such an approach is particularly important for families such as ours who face the prospect of further migration experiences.

As I already mentioned, I see my role as being a partner for conversations about Poland and a guide on the path towards a better knowledge of Polish culture because I treat culture as a carrier of meanings, a set of concepts that will form conceptual networks known to my daughters, through which they will find it easier to move within Polish culture. At the same time, it is also important that the knowledge of Polish culture not be limited to only what happened in the past (for example, children's books and other works belonging to Polish literary culture that demonstrate the way in which Polish tradition and culture have formed) because it is important to create an image of Poland as a place that is attractive today and will be in the future. From this perspective, I have been trying to show Poland to my daughters as one of many places in the world where they can have interesting experiences, find inspiration and to where they might one day want to bring, for example, some of their friends from New York.

I attempt to build their interest in Poland with the help of their grandmother, their grandfather, and other family members and friends through using various activities. First of all, I try to offer my children attractive ways of spending time in Poland. As much as possible, I ensure that our visits are equally divided in terms of time spent with the family and friends, on rediscovering Warsaw, and on discovering unknown places in Poland. When planning our stay in Poland, I try to find new places, which they have not seen yet. When in Warsaw, we visit the Copernicus Science Centre, stroll in the Old Town, visit city parks, or go to a children's theatre. We usually eat lunch at home, made by their grandmother. We also talk about the fact that not only in New York but also in Poland there are people speaking different languages. I find it important to show my daughters that in Warsaw we can have experiences that are as exciting as ones in New York. (For example, this year we are going to see a ballet in Warsaw in order to compare it with one we saw in New York).

A trip to a public library in New York is a great opportunity to look for Polish books. Julia loves looking for books on shelves (I help her a bit); she recognizes them by the inscriptions on their covers. It helps that the words are written in Polish, so we look for Polish characters: ł, ą, ć, and so forth. In Julia's room, there is a map of the world on which we marked Poland, Belgium, and New York. A map is a valuable tool for working on forming a child's awareness of location and, in a broader context, in conversations about the country of origin. In the girl's room, I also put up a calendar on which I mark the day we are flying to Poland.

Meanwhile in New York, I pay a lot of attention to individual work with my children. Playing using attractive materials, both visually and substantially, is a basic tool helping me shape my daughters' notion of "Poland" and improving their linguistic competencies. Recordings of poems and fairy tales in Polish help a lot in this process. Every night, I read bedtime stories to my daughters, usually written and illustrated by Polish authors. I often use books I used to read as a child, which is a good incentive to have conversations about the fact that their mom went to kindergarten and to school in Warsaw.

Children of preschool age love talking about how it was and what their parents did when they were their age. I often tell my daughters what my childhood in Poland looked like. I tell them about the differences, about how, for example, I spoke only one language; I tell them about my first trip abroad. Julia often asks about the hospital in which she was born. She sometimes remembers events from kindergarten, which is also a good opportunity for us to talk about Warsaw. In this context, it is again very important not to treat topics about Poland as an occasion to bring back sad memories. I always try to speak in such a way for the image to be interesting, positive, or intriguing for my daughters.

I also make use of the possibilities offered by the multiculturalism of New York. A trip to Chinatown is a great opportunity to think about the habits of Chinese immigrants and how they differ from our habits at home. Together with the girls, we visit Chinese restaurants and compare the traditional Chinese dumplings with the Polish pierogi that we make at home. We look at Chinese characters and compare them with American letters of the alphabet, and later, at home, we take a Polish book and look for more differences.

Visits to places with different cultures are always a perfect opportunity to ask oneself, "Who am I?" We think then about how our life in America differs from that in Poland. The girls notice that Poland is culturally more homogeneous, and the social diversity in New York. All those conversations, reflections and experiences make it possible for them to feel that they belong to two worlds and that they can feel at home in both because they understand the language, can communicate in it and know how to interpret the world around them.

3. CHILDREN'S INTERCULTURAL AWARENESS

Migrating and adapting to life in a new place undoubtedly requires from parents or children's guardians much emotional care and attention. The process of adaptation for a child already starts in the first weeks. A child starts to absorb components of the new culture, resulting in fast progress regarding assimilating some of the culture's aspects. The situation of my children was similar. After arriving in New York, Julia was watching the new environment attentively. She realized that the people around her spoke a different language. I did not have the impression that that observation was a problem for her, although she herself admitted many times that she could not speak English. From the start, she has been curious about everything new around her: road signs, traffic lights, bigger trucks, different ambulances, fire trucks, but especially, different-looking people on the streets speaking different languages. When school started, she soon found her place in the new environment; she learned English quickly, and she was absorbing everything in American culture that for us, Poles, was new and intriguing.

I see the process of adaptation, which might result in partial acculturation, as enrichment and an opportunity for children to be able to fully experience growing up and living in an intercultural environment. Children from various cultural circles participate jointly in the life of the school community, along with neighbours from various countries, and use various languages and cultural codes to create the intercultural image of New York. All of them are building a space full of cultural diversity in which I am happy to find a place for me and my children. I see the multitude of different cultural models and the social diversity as tools for forming in children an open attitude towards "otherness," for accepting diversity and stimulating children's innate curiosity. However, I believe that in order to form children's intercultural identity, one should ensure that they have conditions to feel at ease in both cultures—the culture of the home and the family as well as the new culture or cultures acquired in the country in which the children are growing up.

The process of adapting to a new culture circle is not always easy or joyful for both children and adults, and the experiences that they have directly influence the children's everyday sense of wellbeing, their self-confidence, their self-esteem as well as the long-term process of forming their cultural identity. A collision of the two "worlds" can also have painful consequences in the form of a temporary feeling of being rejected, lost, or unsure. It is the mother whom I see as the one whose role it is to safely take her children through cultural structures, to show them the differences, and to emphasize the positive aspects of the experience of two cultures meeting. A mother's role is also to stimulate the children's innate curiosity about "otherness" and newness. Out of concern for the way in which the children will see themselves, for their sense of safety and emotional stability, I decided that my children while growing up in the U.S. would also have the possibility to feel safe and at ease in the Polish culture, whose cultural codes I use in interacting with my children.

4. FINAL REFLECTIONS

Every year I go back to Poland with the girls for the holidays. Visiting Poland is important because it lets us look back and once again think about what the experience of migration means for our family and for each of us individually. Each person experiences everyday life abroad in his or her own way, and this experience leaves different marks on everyone's psyche.

The process of adapting and finding one's place in a new reality takes time. Surely, one's age and previous experiences are of great importance regarding the place in which one feels safe and comfortable. For us adults, it took more time before we started to feel "at home" then for our children, and I think that it is still difficult for us to define our place here. This issue is related to our customs, the mentality formed within the family, in the home country and in the environment in which we grew up. However, we try to fight to not have those feeling at all costs. For those experiencing migration together, everyone should take time to experience all the changes at his or her own pace and listen patiently to one another. Keeping in touch with our friends and family in Poland has been of much help when dealing with these difficult but also positive experiences. Those contacts enable us to put our life here into perspective; they make it possible for us to share impressions and listen to opinions and comments from the outside. Constant and consistent contact with the culture of origin gives us, adults, support and makes it possible for our children to feel rooted in each of the two cultures. At the same time, it is worth trying to have an open mind towards residents of the new place and to be open to the enrichment resulting from meeting those who we can so easily classify as "others." One should remember that for both children and adults, intercultural identity may be a safe platform for understanding cultural codes and the messages hidden in those in each of the environments. Thus, intercultural identity is the most important element one can gain from the experience of migration, and it is worth preserving.

This text is dedicated to both my parents back in Poland and to the beloved memory of my grandfather, Henryk Trojanowski.

Translated by Anna Trojanowska.

NOTES

[1]This text is an expanded version of an earlier text, see Strzelecka-Misonne, Agata. "Wybrane zagadnienia związane z kształtowaniem się tożsamości kulturowej dzieci w warunkach migracji—perspektywa rodzica dzieci w wieku przedszkolnym."
[2]The model of upbringing children in bilingualism—that is, by providing children with conditions to grow up and develop in an environment in which they have equal access to the two mother tongues of its parents or guardians—was in our case a conscious decision. It also connected with believing in the role of a language as a tool for moving freely in a country and a method of acquiring cultural competencies, which the children will learn more easily by speaking both languages fluently. Moreover, it was important for us to teach our children respect for both their parents' cultures through languages as well as to ensure they can feel safe in a given culture and be able to interpret its culture codes. We both knew that in order to enable the girls to communicate easily in both languages, it would be necessary to create a cohesive and consistent system of each parent communicating in his or her mother tongue. Such an approach requires a lot of self-discipline

from parents or guardians, but is also a huge help for a child, who from its first attempts to communicate using words is, so to speak, "programmed" to communicate with each parent in his or her mother tongue (Baron-Hauwert).

WORKS CITED

Barron-Hauwaert, Suzanne. *Language Strategies for Bilingual Families: The One-Parent-One-Language Approach.* Multilingual Matters Ltd., 2004.

Bhatia, Tej K., William C., Ritchie, *The Handbook of Bilingualism and Multilingualism.* Wiley-Blackwell, 2012.

Gwóźdź, Barbara. Nauczanie języka polskiego dzieci cudzoziemskich—działalność wolontariuszy i wolontariuszek w projekcie "Teraz polski!" [Teaching Polish to Foreign Children—Volunteers Working within the Project "Polish Now!"]. Fundacja na rzecz Różnorodności Społecznej, 2010.

Francis, Norbert. Bilingual Competence and Bilingual Proficiency in Child Development. MIT Press, 2011.

"Polska Szkola Sobotnia Przy Parafii." Szkola Polska, Squarespace, www.szkolapolska.info/. Accessed 18 Aug. 2016.

Strzelecka-Misonne, Agata. "Wybrane zagadnienia związane z kształtowaniem się tożsamości kulturowej dzieci w warunkach migracji—perspektywa rodzica dzieci w wieku przedszkolnym" ["Selected Issues Regarding Creation of Cultural Identity Among Children in Migrant Conditions—View of a Parent of Pre-School Children"]. *Migracja, tożsamość, dojrzewanie. Adaptacja kulturowa dzieci i młodzieży z doświadczeniem migracyjnym [Migration, Identity, Maturation. Cultural Adaptation of Children and Adolescents with Migrant Experience]*, edited by Natalia Klorek and Katarzyna Kubin, Fundacja na rzecz Różnorodności Społecznej, 2015.

Osysko, Edmund, editor. *Program Nauczania dla Polonijnych Szkół Dokształcających w USA od Przedszkola po Klasy Maturalne [Curriculum for Polish Supplementary Schools in the U.S. from Kindergarten to Last High-school Year]*. Commission of Education of Polish American Congress, 2005.

"Witamy!" Śpieszmy się kochać ludzi, tak szybko odchodzą."

[Hello! "Let us love people now they leave us so fast"] *Jan Twardowski School*, Joomla, www.jantwardowskischool.org/. Accessed 18 Aug. 2016.

Conclusion

Mothering in Diverse Migratory Contexts

HELEN VALLIANATOS AND ANNA KUROCZYCKA SCHULTES

THIS VOLUME WAS ENVISIONED as a means to better understand the distinctive experiences of migrant mothers living in specific sociocultural milieus. To do so, we incorporated narrative and ethnographic research with literary analyses that delved into texts speaking to migration and motherhood. Whereas narrative and ethnographic research revealed details of women's lived realities and the challenges and joys migrant mothers experienced as they settled in new sociocultural contexts, literary analyses of texts related specific experiences of migration from places such as India and Haiti to the UK and U.S. and interrogated host countries as uniformly "better" than countries of origin. Thus, by purposefully uniting assorted ways of knowing (narratives, ethnographies, and literary analyses) in unexpected ways, we hope to bridge unique everyday experiences in diverse contexts by drawing commonalities between mothers living in diverse real and imagined places.

An examination of the migrant maternal necessitates an understanding of the role of motherhood in the construction of identities among migrant women as well as the pragmatics of performing this gendered role as migrants. Central to this role is the need for mothers to negotiate customary practices with new expectations. In many cultural contexts, motherhood continues to be a dominant element of women's identities, as evidenced by the studies in this volume that crosscut world regions and diverse cultures.[1] The challenge that we faced in this volume was to identify shared experiences among maternal migrants while simultaneously highlighting the unique communities, families, and individuals found in each contributor's chapter. This anxiety between addressing shared concerns and issues while privileging individual lived experiences echoes an ongoing challenge in feminist theorizing: commonalities among women are emphasized in women's (and gender) rights discussions while, simultaneously, the differences within the category of "woman" have long been recognized and continue to be explored (see, for example, classic works by Collins, hooks, Mohanty, as well as more recent research exploring womanhood and motherhood by George, Lan, Walks, and McPherson among many others). This tension has been labelled "the dilemma of difference" and applied to subjectivities of motherhood by scholars such as Patrice DiQuinzio.

Each author in this volume, implicitly or explicitly, recognizes the specific historical, sociocultural, political, and economic contexts that influence how motherhood is understood and practised. For instance, narratives shared by Lianidou, Stephens, and Strzelecka-Misonne illustrate specific cultural, classed, and racialized experiences of motherhood. Each explores how racialized, classed identities within specific sociocultural contexts shape maternal subjectivities in a very personal and evocative manner. The intersection of culture, social class, ethnicity, and racial categories demonstrated in these powerful narrative contributions are echoed in both ethnographic and literary analysis chapters, where cultural, classed, racialized identities influence what it means to be a mother and in turn, mothering practices. Some authors (Nichols; Limpangong) explicitly name intersectionality theory in their analyses, but arguably this approach underlines most, if not all, contributions. Intersectionality within feminist approaches was first articulated in the work of Kimberlé Crenshaw. Since then, it has widely been applied in analyses that attempt to address the various components that contribute to different identities, experiences, and relationships within specific sociocultural contexts, which contain implicit and explicit power relationships. Underlying most, if not all, of the contributions are histories of colonialism and neocolonialism that have influenced global economic, political and social relations. These histories underscore recent movements from the Global South to the Global North.

Of course, migrants are diverse. Whether they are forced to relocate (refugees) or choose to move (immigrants), this choice is itself constrained by economic, political, and social worlds. Although most of the participants in this collection faced some degree of dislocation and adjustment in the migratory process, an intersectional lens allows for an analysis that explores why "the migrant maternal" cannot be simplistically defined. Racialized maternal subjectivities are particularly evident in the chapters by Dymond, Sazzad, Hsiao, and the co-written chapter by Connor, Ayallo and Elliot. Conversely, the role of social class in shaping motherhood experiences and practices is explored in many chapters: Limpangong's work on mothers negotiating careers after migrating; Nichols's work focusing on unemployed immigrant mothers; and Baklacioglu's work with refugee mothers displaced by war. Many contributors— Bonfanti, Vallianatos, Schultes, and Kačkutė—identified cultural factors that influence maternal subjectivities and the identity work mothers performed to instill and propagate ethnocultural identities among their children.

To assist in the comparison of migrant mothers across diverse cultural, political, economic and social contexts, we have arranged the contributions into two main themes. Section one, titled "'Birthing' New Families Abroad," focuses on the reproductive work mothers perform in creating and recreating families, whereas section two, titled "Generational Dynamics in Settlement and Mothers' Responsibilities," hones in on the continuous work of building and maintaining family bonds that mothers perform while raising children. We purposively integrated various methodological approaches within each of these themes to illustrate how diverse ways of knowing and approaching an issue can provide unique insights that can lead to more holistic understandings about what "the migrant maternal" means and about her diverse experiences, perspectives, and attitudes. We contend that experiences grounded in lived realities are certainly crucial to understanding "the migrant maternal" but so are fictional realities, where authors can share common experiences of being a migrant mother and possibly address topics that are taboo or difficult to discuss openly.

In the first thematic section, the contributors explore what it means to reproduce in a new place, both physically and socioculturally.

All of these contributions focus on the maternal migrant with respect to how women cope with birthing and propagating their families in their host countries. These chapters are all grounded in mothers' embodied experiences and their efforts to negotiate what they understood motherhood entailed in their origin countries with new cultural norms and ways of performing motherhood after settling. The dislocations of migration in combination with gendered, classed, and racialized power relations are viscerally explicated by Lianidou's personal birthing narrative and Baklacioglu's account of refugee mothers residing in Turkey. The biological and cultural reproductive work that mothers perform is further advanced in contributions that examine mothers' procreative efforts through controlling family size (Bonfanti), food work (Vallianatos), linguistic work (Kačkutė), economic work or lack thereof (Nichols), and the work entailed in simply learning and adjusting to life in the host country, particularly in light of discriminatory practices and policies (Connor, Ayallo and Elliott). What underlies the chapters in this section is the centrality of motherhood as a key part of how women constructed their identities through reproducing and resisting natal and host-country cultural norms. It is through the unique ways that women negotiated hegemonic ideals with their own beliefs and lived experiences that the "dilemma of difference" is addressed; superficial similarities in experiences of racialized, classed, gendered power inequities are avoided when the specifics of participants' lives are investigated.

The second thematic section of the book explores reproducing families after settlement with respect to generational dynamics, particularly the work of mothering abroad and transmitting familial, communal identities across transnational spaces. Sazzad's analysis of fictional immigrant mothers highlights the everyday efforts to maintain and transmit ethnocultural identities and complements Dymond's interrogation of idealized representations of immigrant-receiving countries as places that support the achievement of "a good life" for migrants. Two of the contributions examine the work of raising bicultural children and what it means to teach the language of "home" (Strzelecka-Misonne; Schultes). Other contributions focus on the efforts mothers put forth to balance home-family commitments with employment (Stephens; Limpangong) and navigate school cultures (Hsiao). As in the first section, broad similarities in the experiences of "the migrant maternal" are evident, predominantly the challenges mothers in particular face in raising children that reflect the values and beliefs of origin countries and cultures while also fitting into host country normative cultures. Arguably, among the studies in this volume, it is mothers who bear much of the childrearing responsibility because of the salience of motherhood in constructing their identities as women. Mothering migrant families involves an ongoing interplay of teaching children ways of being based on "home" cultures while selectively incorporating and resisting hegemonic norms of the host society. Childrearing can be challenging regardless of whether one is a migrant or not, but arguably migrant mothering involves situations that make this experience particularly demanding, which is evident in teaching languages other than English, participating in school cultures, coping with financial stressors and balancing employment with family commitments. Again, although there are similarities in the mothering issues experienced postmigration, comparing the findings in these chapters allows for nuances to emerge, as one considers how social class, gender normative roles and responsibilities, ethnic-racial identities, and other cultural factors affect mothering experiences.

We hope that this framework shows the ongoing, gendered nature of (re)creating migrant families, from the processes of biological and social reproduction illustrated in part one through the mothering practices entailed in childrearing and transmitting ethnocultural and familial bonds across space (from countries of origin to settlement) and time (across generations) explored in part two. Just as mothering is an ongoing process, so too is the research examining the migrant maternal, as it needs to continue to investigate specific experiences that are contextualized in particular moments in time. We began this volume by referring to Thomas Nail's contention that the twenty-first century is the "century of the migrant" (1) and by alluding to current crises in the Middle East. Unfortunately, there is no world region that is not affected by issues of migration, whether that includes internally displaced persons, refugees fleeing home countries, or host countries attempting to control and regulate which migrants (both refugees and immigrants) are acceptable for resettlement. Building on the findings reported in this volume, more work is needed in exploring how migrants navigate processes of admission and settlement, how mothers reframe their identities as women and mothers in light of specific family structures and cultural contexts, and how they cope with the various challenges they face after settlement. Although racialized, classed and cultural factors are important in most contributions in this volume, further research needs to take into account other categories of analysis (women who are differently abled, religious affiliations, etc.) as well as the nuances of how the aforementioned factors intersect. It is equally important to document how women have successfully adjusted to the trials that accompany migration. Part of this future research would need to further develop work conducted within the Global South and between regions within the Global South, as the authors featured in this collection work primarily in high-income immigrant-receiving nations within the Global North.

In sum, we hope to leave the reader with a newfound appreciation for all mothers who endeavour to not only protect and provide for their children but strive to propagate their families' and communities' cultural values in both familiar and new environs.

NOTE

[1]We recognize the lack of contributions from South America and that only one chapter examines migrant mothers from Africa, in this case from Southern Africa (see Figure 1 in Introduction).

WORKS CITED

Collins, Patricia Hill. *Black Feminist Thought: Knowledge, Consciousness, and the Politics of Empowerment*. 3rd ed., Routledge, 2000.

Crenshaw, Kimberlé. "Demarginalizing the Intersection of Race and Sex: A Black Feminist Critique of Antidiscrimination Doctrine, Feminist Theory and Antiracist Politics." *University of Chicago Legal Forum*, vol. 1, 1989, pp. 138-167.

DiQuinzio, Patrice. *The Impossibility of Motherhood: Feminism, Individualism and the Problem of Mothering*. Routledge, 1999.

George, Sheba. *When Women Come First: Gender and Class in Transnational Migration*. University of California Press, 2005.

hooks, bell. *Ain't I A Woman? Black Women and Feminism*. South End Press, 1981.

Lan, Pei-Chia. *Global Cinderellas: Migrant Domestics and Newly Rich Employers in Taiwan*. Duke University Press, 2006.

Mohanty, Chandra Talpade. "Under Western Eyes: Feminist Scholarship and Colonial Discourses." *Boundary*, vol. 2, no. 12.3, 1986, pp. 333-358.

Nail, Thomas. "Introduction." *The Figure of the Migrant*, Stanford University Press, 2015, pp. 1-10.

Walks, Michelle and Naomi McPherson, editors. *An Anthropology of Mothering*. Demeter Press, 2011.

About the Contributors

Irene Ayallo (PhD, MTh, PGDip Theology, CoP Social Justice, BDiv) is of Luo (Kenya) descent. She has been living in Auckland, New Zealand, for nine years. Irene's research interests include gender (empowerment of young women), politics (political theories, political participation, social justice, and human rights), HIV/AIDS prevention, spirituality, political theology and research with marginalized groups. Irene is a lecturer in the Department of Social Practice, Unitec Institute of Technology, New Zealand.

Sara Bonfanti is a cultural anthropologist, a PhD candidate in migration studies at Bergamo University (IT) and a visiting fellow at Max Planck Institute for the Study of Religious and Ethnic Diversity. She has done extensive research on immigrant women's access to public healthcare and has recently carried out a multisite ethnography between Italy and India to investigate gender and generational change in Punjabi diasporic families.

Helene Connor, (PhD, MEd 1st class honours, PGDip women's studies; DipTchng, BA, RPN) is of Māori, English, and Irish descent. She has *whakapapa* (genealogy) links to *Te Atiawa* and *Ngati Ruanui iwi* (tribes) and *Ngati Rahiri* and *Ngati Te Whiti hapu* (sub-tribes). Helene's research interests include gender, ethnicity and cultural representation; narrative and (auto)biographical research; and research on aspects of mothering. Helene is a senior lecturer and program leader in the Department of Social Practice, Unitec Institute of Technology, New Zealand. Helene's chapter on "Maori Mothering: Repression, Resistance and Renaissance" was published in 2014, by Demeter Press in the volume, *Mothers of the Nations: Indigenous Mothering as Global Resistance, Reclaiming and Recovery*, K. Anderson and D. Lavell-Harvard (Eds.).

Justine Dymond is associate professor of English at Springfield College and co-editor of *Motherhood Memoirs: Mothers Creating/ Writing Lives* (Demeter Press, 2013). She has published articles on Linda Hogan, Mourning Dove, Gertrude Stein, and Virginia Woolf. Her creative work includes the story "Cherubs," selected for *The O. Henry Prize Stories* 2007.

Sue Elliott (M.Sc 1st class hons with distinction in development practices, B.Ed, DipTchng, advanced certificate in adult education) is a third-generation Pakeha (of European descent) New Zealander and has worked in the refugee sector for more than thirty-five years as a teacher, researcher, consultant, facilitator, mentor, volunteer, and ally. She has worked in New Zealand and the United Kingdom as a teacher and internationally as a consultant for UNHCR. Currently, she works most of the time as a lecturer in Social Practice at Unitec Institute of Technology, New Zealand, where she teaches community development and human rights, including refugee issues.

Yu-Ling Hsiao is from Taiwan and an active qualitative researcher in the topic of understanding and empowering Chinese-immigrant parents in the U.S. She is a doctoral candidate in the Social Foundations and Qualitative Research Department at Oklahoma State University.

Eglė Kačkutė is currently a lecturer in French at Vilnius University. Her monograph on contemporary British and French women's writing was published in 2012 by Vilnius University Press. Her postdoctoral research project was entitled "Motherhood and Migration," and she continues working on fictional narratives of migrant, refugee, and expatriate mothers.

Anna Kuroczycka Schultes holds a PhD in English-Modern

studies and a women's studies certificate from the University of Wisconsin, Milwaukee (UWM). A former Advanced Opportunity Program Fellow at UWM, Anna's research focuses on migrant female domestic workers, immigration, mothering and care work. Her publications have appeared, among others, in *The Journal of Research on Women and Gender* (2010), *An Anthropology of Mothering* (Demeter Press 2011), and in *Anti-Immigration in the United States: A Historical Encyclopedia* (2011). Anna's interest in migration is fueled by feminist research theories. Over the past several years, she has been conducting research on Polish mothers in the Chicagoland area.

Theano Lianidou wrote her article in the course of her recent studies in public affairs at Columbia University. Before her studies, Theano was a corporate executive in Greece, Netherlands, Poland, and Italy. Through her experiences with different cultures, she has developed a strong interest in issues of diversity.

Cirila P. Limpangog teaches in the RMIT School of Global, Urban, and Social Studies, and in the Victoria University College of Arts, both located in Melbourne, Australia. She has worked in social development for twenty years, mainly in the Philippines and Australia in the specialist areas of gender equality, women's rights, sustainable development, and good governance.

Leslie Nichols is currently a visiting researcher at Osgoode Hall Law School. She has a PhD from the Policy Studies Program at Ryerson University. Dr. Nichols's research focuses on the social conditions of women in Canadian society through feminist theory and methods, with a focus on women workers in Canada.

Nurcan Ozgur Baklacioglu is an associate professor at Istanbul University, Department of International Relations, Faculty of Political Sciences. Nurcan's research interests include critical migration and asylum studies, critical border studies, Balkan politics, and society.

Rehnuma Sazzad is a research associate at the School of African and Oriental Studies (SOAS), and an associate fellow at the Institute of Commonwealth Studies, University of London. Her monograph, *Edward Said's Concept of Exile: Identity and Cultural Migration in the Middle East*, will be published soon. Her current research focuses on South Asian nationalism and diaspora.

Meredith Stephens is an applied linguist in the Department of Comparative Cultures at the Institute of Socio-Arts and Sciences, Tokushima University. Her research interests concern the teaching methodology of English in Japan, the development of childhood bilingualism and biliteracy in Japanese and English, and the experiences of English-speaking expatriates in Japan.

Agata Strzelecka-Misonne is a graduate of intercultural relations at the Institute of Oriental Studies of Warsaw University (Poland). Agata is affiliated with the Foundation for Social Diversity and has authored analyses and essays concerning various phenomena related to multiculturalism and counteracting social exclusion. She lives in New York and works in the Middle East cultural center Alwan for the Arts.

Helen Vallianatos is an associate professor in anthropology and associate dean in the Office of the Dean of Students, University of Alberta. Her research and teaching interests focus on food, gender, body, and health issues, and the majority of her research involves collaborative, interdisciplinary work with various community organizations. Much of her recent research has focused on migrant mothers' health and wellbeing.